Collaborative Home/School Interventions

The Guilford Practical Intervention in the Schools Series

Kenneth W. Merrell, Founding Editor
Sandra M. Chafouleas, Series Editor

Books in this series address the complex academic, behavioral, and social–emotional needs of children and youth at risk. School-based practitioners are provided with practical, research-based, and readily applicable tools to support students and team successfully with teachers, families, and administrators. Each volume is designed to be used directly and frequently in planning and delivering educational and mental health services. Features include step-by-step instructions for assessment and intervention and helpful, timesaving reproducibles.

Recent Volumes

Helping Students Overcome Substance Abuse: Effective Practices for Prevention and Intervention
Jason J. Burrow-Sanchez and Leanne S. Hawken

School-Based Behavioral Assessment: Informing Intervention and Instruction
Sandra Chafouleas, T. Chris Riley-Tillman, and George Sugai

Collaborating with Parents for Early School Success: The Achieving–Behaving–Caring Program
Stephanie H. McConaughy, Pam Kay, Julie A. Welkowitz, Kim Hewitt, and Martha D. Fitzgerald

Helping Students Overcome Depression and Anxiety, Second Edition: A Practical Guide
Kenneth W. Merrell

Inclusive Assessment and Accountability: A Guide to Accommodations
for Students with Diverse Needs
Sara E. Bolt and Andrew T. Roach

Bullying Prevention and Intervention: Realistic Strategies for Schools
Susan M. Swearer, Dorothy L. Espelage, and Scott A. Napolitano

Conducting School-Based Functional Behavioral Assessments, Second Edition: A Practitioner's Guide
Mark W. Steege and T. Steuart Watson

Evaluating Educational Interventions: Single-Case Design for Measuring Response to Intervention
T. Chris Riley-Tillman and Matthew K. Burns

Collaborative Home/School Interventions: Evidence-Based Solutions for Emotional, Behavioral,
and Academic Problems
Gretchen Gimpel Peacock and Brent R. Collett

Collaborative Home/School Interventions

Evidence-Based Solutions for Emotional, Behavioral, and Academic Problems

GRETCHEN GIMPEL PEACOCK
BRENT R. COLLETT

THE GUILFORD PRESS
New York   London

© 2010 The Guilford Press
A Division of Guilford Publications, Inc.
370 Seventh Avenue, Suite 1200, New York, NY 10001
www.guilford.com

Printed in the United States of America

This book is printed on acid-free paper.

Last digit is print number: 9 8 7 6 5 4 3

Library of Congress Cataloging-in-Publication Data

Gimpel Peacock, Gretchen.
   Collaborative home/school interventions: evidence-based solutions for emotional, behavioral,
and academic problems / Gretchen Gimpel Peacock, Brent R. Collett.
       p. cm. — (The Guilford practical intervention in the schools series)
   Includes bibliographical references and index.
   ISBN 978-1-60623-345-0 (pbk.: alk. paper)
     1. Children with disabilities—Education—United States.   2. Home and school—United
States.   3. Parent–teacher relationships—United States.   I. Collett, Brent R.   II. Title.
   LC4031.G536 2010
   371.19′2—dc22
                                                                                        2009026716

About the Authors

Gretchen Gimpel Peacock, PhD, is Professor of Psychology at Utah State University, where she has coordinated the specialist-level program in school psychology approved by the National Association of School Psychologists and served on the program faculty of the Combined Psychology (School/Clinical/Counseling) American Psychological Association-accredited PhD program. Dr. Gimpel Peacock is both a licensed psychologist and educator licensed school psychologist. She has been the faculty internship supervisor for the school psychology students and also supervises students' practicum experiences in the department's community clinic. Dr. Gimpel Peacock's publications and professional presentations focus on child behavior problems and family issues as related to child behaviors, as well as professional issues in school psychology. She currently serves on the editorial advisory boards of several school psychology and related journals.

Brent R. Collett, PhD, is Assistant Professor of Psychiatry and Behavioral Sciences at the University of Washington in Seattle and Attending Psychologist at Seattle Children's Hospital. Dr. Collett's clinical interests include early childhood mental health and pediatric psychology. He supervises child psychiatry and psychology trainees and teaches didactics on normative early childhood development, developmental psychopathology, and the assessment and treatment of early-onset conduct problems. Dr. Collett's research focuses on infant mental health, disruptive behavior disorders, and the developmental and psychosocial sequelae of pediatric illnesses (e.g., craniofacial anomalies, pediatric cancer).

Preface

As anyone who works with children can attest, parents are typically the most important adults in a child's life. Parents spend more time with their children than any other adult and have a tremendous influence on their children's social, emotional, and academic development. In addition, parents usually *know* their children better than anyone else, including their strengths; the home, community, and cultural context in which they reside; their histories; and their quirks. Even when their specific strategies are not effective, parents are almost universally invested in seeing their children succeed in school and in life in general. These notions are not particularly controversial, and most would acknowledge that it is important to "involve parents." Nonetheless, there continues to be a significant gap between what happens in the schools and what happens in the home, with parents often left out of their child's education or even viewed as a barrier to be overcome. Our firm belief is that this is not due to a lack of interest on the part of school personnel or the parents. Rather, inadequate attention has been given to the translation of evidence-based interventions for use in the schools and limited information on the "nuts and bolts" of home/school collaboration. In this book we have outlined specific strategies that school-based mental health professionals can use in collaboration with parents when they are developing interventions to address emotional, behavioral, and academic problems. The goal of this book is to help school-based professionals move from simple lip service of parent involvement to actually involving parents as full partners in the assessment and intervention process.

This book begins, in Chapter 1, with a discussion of the importance of home/school collaboration, including ways to facilitate this as well as barriers that may arise when addressing problems in a partnership. In Chapter 2 we provide a brief overview of some of the common emotional, behavioral, and academic problems seen in school-age children. We also discuss prevention, the evidence-based practice model, and the importance of delivering services in a school-based setting. In Chapter 3 we cover assessment and use the problem-solving model to frame this discussion. We discuss how to involve parents in the assessment process to ensure that feedback from all key individuals in a child's life provide input into identifying and solving the presenting problems. In Chapters 4 to 6 we present intervention strategies that can be used in collaboration with parents to address externalizing (Chapter 4), internalizing (Chapter 5), and academic (Chapter 6) problems. Each chapter begins with an overview of the empirical literature to support the interventions discussed. We have emphasized evidence-based collaborative home/school interventions. However, in a few cases we present interventions that show promise or are supported by emerging research but not yet considered "empirically supported." We have also included suggestions for increasing home/school collaboration for interventions that do not typically include parents (e.g., child-focused or classroom-based interventions), with the belief that such collaboration is likely to enhance outcomes and facilitate ongoing parent involvement. In addition to collaboration with parents, we recognize that it can be important for school-based professionals to consult with community-based professionals in many cases (e.g., pediatricians), and school-based professionals may help parents navigate the complex system of health and mental health services. Thus, collaboration with other professionals is discussed briefly in several chapters in the interest of providing the most appropriate and comprehensive services to children and their families.

We hope that this book will be a useful resource to school psychologists and other school-based mental health professionals who are interested in increasing their connections with families and working with parents in a collaborative manner. Although this book is written from a school-based view, it may also appeal to mental health professionals who work with children outside of the schools who are also interested in being more collaborative in their approach to child assessment and treatment.

ACKNOWLEDGMENTS

We are grateful to the many families with whom we have worked, who have helped to shape our views on the importance of working collaboratively and maximizing parent involvement. We thank these families for sharing their experiences and for helping us become better professionals.

Contents

List of Figures, Tables, and Forms

FIGURES

TABLES

FORMS

Collaborative Home/School Interventions

1

Working Collaboratively
with Parents

Parents play an integral role in the lives of their children and can be key components in effective intervention and prevention programs. As such, working collaboratively with parents to develop interventions to target emotional, behavioral, and academic problems is an important role for school-based clinicians. Such collaborative work can increase the impact of the intervention as well as increase positive relationships between parents and school personnel. Of course, collaborative home/school interventions frequently require a significant amount of up-front work. Therapeutic alliances need to be formed with those who will be involved in the intervention process. This obviously includes parents but may also include teachers, students, community mental health providers, pediatricians, and others. The development of these collaborative relationships will be familiar territory for some school-based mental health professionals. For others, working with multiple individuals outside of the school system will be a new endeavor. To set the stage for the remainder of this book, in this introductory chapter we review strategies for engaging parents in collaborative interventions. Common barriers are discussed, along with strategies for establishing and maintaining communication. We briefly discuss consultation with other community providers and the important role that school-based professionals can play in helping families get the most from community resources. Finally, we close with a discussion of ethical and legal issues that are important to consider in this type of service provision.

DEVELOPING A WORKING RELATIONSHIP WITH FAMILIES

Many parents are eager to solicit help and learn of available services in the schools for their children who may be experiencing emotional, behavioral, or academic problems. However, teachers and school administrators often express the sentiment that the parents who should be the *most* involved in their child's education are the *least* available and most difficult to engage. Often this refers to the parents of children with behavior problems that interfere

1

with their education or the education of other students. School-based mental health professionals may be in a good position to form an alliance with these families and help them access and develop interventions that will remediate these problems. At the outset, it is important to emphasize that we use the terms "families" and "parents" broadly. Collaboration will most often be with a child's mother, because mothers continue to be the primary caregivers for children in this country. However, this is not the case in all families, and it is important to look at the whole family (including extended family such as grandparents, aunts, and uncles) and attempt to involve all key adults in a child's life. As discussed later in this chapter, we have found that fathers are often willing and eager to be involved in the intervention process. Even if they are not able to regularly attend intervention related meetings, a father's awareness of his child's academic and mental health needs may provide additional support for a mother participating in an intervention. Similarly, a child's aunt, grandfather, or other family member may have a primary caregiving role and offer important information if involved in the intervention process.

Although teachers and school administrators will be in contact with parents of children with academic and behavior problems, often to inform them of problems that their child is having at school, school psychologists and other school-based mental health professionals can approach families with assistance and a tangible service. This flows nicely from a problem-solving model (discussed more in Chapter 3) in which we are less interested in labeling a child with a psychiatric diagnosis or educational classification and more interested in determining what will allow the child to be successful. With their background and education in mental health, school psychologists are also very aware that behavior problems are almost never entirely environmental but rather reflect the interplay between disposition and environment. (One only has to spend a few hours with a child who is highly disruptive and irritable to realize that such children do not bring out the most nurturing responses!) Thus, mental health providers can reassure parents that the purpose of their collaboration and any resulting assessment and intervention is not to determine who is at fault but instead to focus on what can be done to help the child make the most of his or her educational experiences.

When working to form home/school collaborations, it may be useful for clinicians to review some of the theoretical work and empirical research devoted to this topic. Both Sandra Christenson and Susan Sheridan have written extensively about home/school collaboration (e.g., Christenson, 2004; Esler, Godber, & Christenson, 2008; Christenson & Sheridan, 2001; Sheridan & Kratochwill, 2008), including basic considerations in developing collaborative relationships, methods for promoting effective partnerships with parents, and the conjoint behavior consultation model. Interested readers are encouraged to review this work for further information on the foundations of home/school collaboration. Christenson and Sheridan are both strong supporters of collaborative partnerships and provide some excellent resources for developing these relationships. For example, Christenson and colleagues (e.g., Esler et al., 2008, p. 925) outline what they refer to as the "eight-p philosophy" for effective home/school collaboration:

- **P**artnership as a priority
- **P**lanned effort

- Proactive and persistent communication
- Positive
- Personalized
- Practical suggestions
- Program monitoring
- Attend to the Process for building relationships with families

These building blocks form the basis for a positive, ongoing home/school collaborative relationship. In schools where this philosophy is the norm, school-based mental health providers and parents are likely to be comfortable with this approach and additional collaboration (e.g., targeting child behavior problems) will likely flow smoothly. School psychologists working in schools where adherence to this philosophy is less then optimal, however, may face some challenges in attempting to engage parents in collaborative interventions. This is not to say that collaborative interventions are impossible in such settings, only that they may take more effort to establish.

Susan Sheridan and her colleagues (e.g., Sheridan & Kratochwill, 2008; Sheridan, Clarke, Marti, Burt, & Rohlk, 2005) have developed and evaluated a specific model of home/school collaboration: conjoint behavioral consultation (CBC). In the CBC model, school personnel, families, and service providers within the community work together in a problem-solving framework to evaluate and address the needs of the child. The CBC model follows the traditional behavioral consultation model (and problem-solving model, discussed more extensively in Chapter 3) involving the following four steps: need/problem identification, need/problem analysis, plan development/implementation, and plan evaluation. At each of these stages, all key individuals are involved in a collaborative manner. Results of studies evaluating CBC have generally been positive, with CBC leading to increases in prosocial behaviors, decreases in problem behaviors, and increases in academic performance. In addition, those participating in the CBC intervention model have rated this intervention positively in terms of acceptability and satisfaction (e.g., Sheridan et al., 2005; Sheridan, Eagle, Cowan, & Mickelson, 2001).

Christenson's and Sheridan's models provide a solid, research-based foundation for models of home/school collaboration. In the remainder of this chapter we focus more specifically on what school psychologists can do with families currently presenting with child concerns, whether this occurs in the context of a system that prioritizes collaborative efforts or in a system that has not yet made this an institutional priority.

Parent Engagement and Motivation

As noted, some parents will be eager to work collaboratively with school-based mental health professionals, whereas others will be more reluctant. This reluctance might be due to several factors, including parents' lack of awareness of the important role that they can play in helping remediate their child's academic and behavioral problems. Because collaborative interventions make active use of parents in the treatment process, it is important to obtain parent buy-in for the treatment plan. Developing strategies to help engage these more reluctant parents is an important part of the collaboration process.

Recently, researchers have begun to examine the use of motivational interviewing (MI) and other motivational enhancement strategies to assist with the engagement of parents. MI was initially developed for use with problem drinkers as a strategy for helping them prepare for intervention (e.g., Miller & Rollnick, 2002). However, since its original development, it has been applied to a wide variety of problems and populations. Based on a *stages of change* model (Prochaska & DiClemente, 1982, 2005), MI recognizes that people at different stages of readiness are likely to require different types of intervention.

In Table 1.1 we provide descriptions of the different stages of change as well as examples of techniques clinicians can use when working with parents at each of these stages. Figure 1.1 provides example questions that clinicians might use at each stage of change. For example, parents in the *precontemplation* or *contemplation* stages may not be aware that their child has a problem and might not have considered seeking help for their child. Parents at these stages may not be ready to make changes in their parenting or home routines to incorporate intervention methods or may feel ambivalent about such change. Efforts at this level are, therefore, most likely to be successful if they involve providing feedback, recognizing that the parent is not ready to engage in the change process and emphasizing that the decision to change is theirs to make. Additionally, focusing on encouraging self-exploration and consideration of pros and cons of behavior change can be helpful at this stage. If the clinician believes that intervention is imperative when a parent is at this stage, then interventions based in the school setting rather than those provided in collaboration with parents may need to be the first step.

Parents in the *preparation* or *action* stages have realized that there is a problem and have either made changes recently or plan to do so soon. At this point, interventions may focus on removing barriers to treatment and encouraging parents to think about small changes to which they can commit.

Finally, parents in the *maintenance* or *relapse* phases have implemented a few changes and need assistance to continue with those new behaviors or help returning to those new behaviors after a relapse. At this point, interventions focus on helping to identify rewards for continued behavior change, anticipating the possibility of relapse, coping, and identifying triggers for relapse (i.e., what went wrong).

It is important to note that movement through these stages may not be a continuous or linear process. For example, a parent who seems to be in the action stage one week may be in the contemplation stage the following week. The clinician, therefore, assesses motivation on an ongoing basis and meets the parent where he or she is on a given day.

The MI approach has broad application in working with parents, particularly in the schools. Many families who have received the dreaded phone call from teachers and principals informing them that their children are exhibiting behavior problems or are struggling academically will have a degree of defensiveness that may obstruct their engagement in the intervention process. Views of child behavior can vary greatly, and a parent whose child has been referred for intervention may disagree with the need for services altogether, let alone services that require them to be active participants. Other parents may be eager to participate and actively seek help but need assistance identifying concrete "next steps" in intervention or encouragement to maintain changes that they have already made.

TABLE 1.1. Prochaska's Stages of Change as Applied to Families

Stage of change	Description	Application with families
Precontemplation	Parent is not yet considering a change in behavior. He or she may not be aware that there is a problem or that his or her behavior is linked with the child's behavior.	• Provide evaluative feedback (e.g., how child's behavior compares with peers, prognosis with no intervention) and information regarding the link between parent's behavior and child's behavior. • Validate the parent's lack of readiness for change and emphasize that the ultimate decision to change is the parent's to make. • Encourage the parent to reevaluate his or her behavior and engage in self-exploration (e.g., "Is this the kind of relationship that you hoped to have with your child?").
Contemplation	Increasing awareness of the need for behavior change in the abstract, but feelings about change are mixed and action is not considered imminent.	• Validate the parent's lack of readiness and ambivalence about change and emphasize that the decision is his or hers to make. • Have a realistic discussion of the pros and cons of behavior change. • Discuss outcome expectations (e.g., "If you decide to make a change, here's how it might benefit you and your child …").
Preparation	Parent is ready to make a change and may be experimenting with changes in his or her behavior.	• Verify that the parent has the necessary skills to make a change (e.g., observe a parent–child interaction to assess skills for engagement, limit setting, giving effective directions, social reinforcement). • Help problem solve likely obstacles to change. • Help the parent identify next steps (e.g., "If you're interested, I'd recommend watching this video about limit setting" or "If you'd like, we can plan to meet for two to three appointments to talk about a behavior plan"). • Encourage the parent to think small (e.g., "We know that you want to spend more positive time with your child, but it might be too much to try to go to the park every day. How about just setting aside a few minutes each day for uninterrupted play at home?").
Action	Parent has made changes and has begun practicing his or her new behaviors for a brief period of time (e.g., 3–6 months).	• Help parent to identify and engage social supports that will facilitate continued progress (e.g., outreach to friends/family or parent support groups, scheduling respite/time for him- or herself). • Assist parent to deal with obstacles and challenges increasingly independently (e.g., applying acquired skills for new child behavior problems).
Maintenance	Parent has integrated behavior change into his or her daily life for a long period of time (e.g., ≥ 6 months) and has an ongoing commitment to continue with his or her new repertoire of skills.	• Discuss potential ongoing supports (e.g., a booster session/check-in, other sources of information or support). • Emphasize internal rewards and self-reinforcement for continued progress. • Anticipate relapse and decatastrophize (e.g., "It's great that you've made all of these changes, and that your child has been so responsive. It would not be at all unusual for new problems to come up in the future or for you to have trouble using these new parenting skills during times of particular stress. Let's talk about what you might do if that happens").
Relapse	After a period of change, parent returns to his or her old behavior, potentially after a time of particular stress or when faced with a new set of child behavior problems.	• Discuss what went wrong and what the precipitants were. • Reassess motivation and barriers. • Bolster coping strategies for the future.

Assess and Personalize Child's Behavioral Concerns

"Based on the information from you and your child's teachers and my observations of him in the classroom, I am worried about _____. I think that these problems are likely to make it hard for him to be successful in school and get along with other kids."

↓

Stages-of-Change Assessment

"What concerns do you have about your child's behavior and how this might affect him later?"

"Have you thought about things that you might be able to do to help him with this?"

"What are some of the pros and cons of trying to do some things different at home? Do you think that the pros outweigh the cons?"

↓

Provide Education about Risks, and Advise Concrete Next Steps

"Research suggests that without intervention, behavior problems like these get better for ____% and continue or get worse for ____%."

"Kids with similar problems are 'at risk' for other things, like …."
"I recommend ____ sessions of consultation to focus on …."

↓

Assess Parents' Understanding and Concerns

"I've given you a lot of information today. What do you think about what I've said? Does this make sense and fit with what you know about your child?"

"On a scale of 1–10, with 1 being not at all ready to take action and 10 being 100% ready, how ready are you to try an intervention at home?"

↓

Facilitate Motivation

Precontemplators

Goal: Move from "no" to "maybe"

"I do think that behavioral intervention is likely to be helpful, but I understand that you're not ready for treatment at this point. Do you mind telling me a little bit about what your concerns are?"

"Obviously, this will be your choice to make, and there is no pressure to decide today. If you change your mind or would like more information, you are welcome to give me a call."

Contemplators

Goal: Move from "maybe" to "what next"

"It sounds like you're thinking about treatment. What are some of the potential benefits in your mind?"

"I do understand that you're a little 'on the fence' about treatment, and that decision will, of course, be completely up to you. Is there any more information that I can offer that might help?"

Preparation

Goal: Move from "what next" to "let's get started"

"I think you've made a good decision. I really do think that behavioral treatment is likely to help. As we've discussed, I think that our first step should be _____."

"Just thinking ahead a bit, is there anything that we'll need to do to make it easier to follow up with treatment?"

"It can be helpful to have Dad involved as well. Is there anything that I could do to make it easier for him to join us for at least some of our appointments?"

FIGURE 1.1. Motivational enhancement algorithm: Engaging parents in precontemplation through preparation. (Based on Motivational Interviewing Algorithm: *www.cellinteractive.com/ ucla/physcian_ed/interview_alg.html*)

Dishion and colleagues (Dishion & Kavanagh, 2003; Dishion, Kavanagh, Schneiger, Nelson, & Kaufman, 2002; Shaw, Dishion, Supplee, Gardner, & Arnds, 2006) have used MI techniques in their family check-up (FCU) model. This program is intended to provide parents with information about their child's behavior, areas of vulnerability and strength, and intervention options. The FCU includes an initial interview, an assessment session, and a motivational feedback session. During the motivational feedback session, the clinician works with the parents to identify one or more intervention options that are a good fit for their child's needs and the parents' readiness for change. Promising results for this model have been shown with the mothers of very young children in a low-socioeconomic-status population (Shaw et al., 2006) and when implemented as part of a multilevel school-based intervention for adolescents making the transition to middle school (Dishion et al., 2002). Specifically, in a randomized controlled study with a sample of mothers and children receiving assistance through the Women, Infants, and Children Nutritional Supplement Program, Shaw et al. (2006) found that the FCU model resulted in reduced child behavior problems and increased maternal engagement, particularly for high-risk families. In a series of recently published studies, Dishion and colleagues (Connell, Dishion, Yasui, & Kavanagh, 2007; Dishion et al., 2002; Dishion, Nelson, & Kavanagh, 2003) examined the efficacy of the Adolescent Transitions Program, a middle school-based program that includes the FCU among other prevention/intervention components. They found that only about a quarter of parents engaged in the FCU. However, those who did participate were at higher risk than nonparticipants, suggesting that this model was effective in reaching youth who were in the most need of service. Further, there was evidence that involvement in the FCU reduced substance use and problem behaviors among participating teens.

In a comparable line of research, Nock and Kazdin (2005) have shown that the addition of motivational enhancement significantly improved outcomes in their clinic-based parent training program (see Chapter 4 for a discussion of parent training). The Participation Enhancement Intervention (PEI) included brief discussions (i.e., 5–15 minutes per session) with parents dispersed throughout the parent training intervention in which therapists elicited self-motivational statements from parents regarding their plans to change their parenting behavior, continued participation in treatment, and problem solving. After each PEI session, parents received a written copy of a treatment plan and brochures discussing the importance of treatment participation. Participants were randomized to receive either parent training alone or parent training plus PEI. Results suggest that this relatively simple treatment addition resulted in significantly higher parent motivation, treatment attendance, and parent and therapist ratings of quality and quantity of treatment adherence. The influence of PEI on the magnitude of change in child behavior problems was not reported.

Practical Issues for Increasing Participation

In addition to the efforts that may be needed to engage and prepare parents for change, collaborative interventions are likely to require more accommodation on the part of the clinician than interventions delivered only within the school setting. Although many parents are willing and able to miss work or make child care accommodations for a one-time appointment, this becomes less practical in ongoing intervention over several weeks. Thus, accommodations might include things like meeting in the late afternoon or early evening hours for parents who work traditional 8:00-to-5:00 jobs to minimize the time that parents have to miss from work, helping to arrange for transportation, or helping parents find care for other children in the family. Acknowledging these realities and problem solving with parents, including informing them of community resources (e.g., transportation assistance through community agencies), are often helpful and send the message that the clinician understands these are real barriers and that parents' participation is valued. Of course, it may not be feasible (or desirable) for a school-based clinician to add late afternoon or early evening appointments onto an already busy day. In some settings, it has been possible for school-based clinicians to receive additional compensation for work done outside of the typical work day, to utilize flexible scheduling (e.g., starting some work days later), or to receive compensatory time. Clearly, this may not be possible in all settings, although we are aware of school districts that have made this level of commitment to family-focused intervention services. We encourage school psychologists to be creative in developing solutions to some of these logistical problems.

Inclusion of fathers and other nonprimary caregivers may require additional effort on the part of the clinician. We have found that fathers often do participate in interventions when invited, when the accommodations noted previously are made, and when the importance of their role is emphasized. Often mothers are the individuals with whom the school-based mental health professional first connects; thus, it is important to communicate with them that participation by the child's father is desired. Of course, if a child's mother does not wish to have other caregivers involved, this should be discussed and respected. It may be that with further explanation the mother is more amenable to the idea or that additional discussion reveals clinically important information (e.g., concerns regarding parents' marital relationship, safety issues). A clinician may also choose to make phone contact directly with a child's father to request his participation or, at a minimum, elicit his perspective on the child's behavior. Even when unsuccessful, efforts to actively involve and communicate with both parents help convey to families that their needs are being taken into consideration and that their participation is genuinely valued. Although outcome data related to father involvement are limited, at least a few studies show that fathers' participation facilitates long-term maintenance of treatment gains (e.g., Bagner & Eyberg, 2003; Webster-Stratton, 1985).

Prevention and Home/School Collaboration

As we discuss more in Chapter 2, prevention is increasingly being emphasized in the mental health field. We view school systems as an ideal setting for prevention efforts, particularly those with a parent involvement component. The vast majority of children in this country attend school, and schools have traditionally been considered a hub for other community activities. When asked, most parents, teachers, and other community members support an educational system that addresses social–emotional well-being, health, and civic engagement along with traditional academic outcomes (Greenberg et al., 2003). Cynical readers will correctly note that the endorsement of these nonacademic outcomes often does not translate into financial support. Preventive mental health interventions are among the first things to go when finances are restricted. Nonetheless, we believe that school-based mental health practitioners are in a position to advocate for these services. This advocacy is likely to include education for school staff as well as parents. For example, parents may initially resist having their child participate in a prevention program, arguing that he or she does not have a mental health problem, or teachers may resist having their students spend time on social–emotional health when they are required to get through an entire curriculum in a short period of time. School-based clinicians can advocate for prevention with both parents and teachers by noting the potential benefits for learning, reduction in teacher time spent on classroom behavior management, improved coping with future stressors, and reductions in the financial burden for the community. Perhaps more importantly, school-based mental health providers can advance this cause by using strategies that are evidence based and collecting their own outcome data. For example, a school psychologist who is able to show that a parenting program substantially reduces teacher-reported behavior problems and principal referrals is likely to be persuasive to school administrators. This type of program may also be viewed favorably by parents who desire that their children be able to attend a safe, problem-free school with a positive, supportive learning environment. In fact, parent participation rates and ratings of treatment satisfaction can help to show the need for services with administrators and desirability among families. Several commonly used measures of satisfaction (e.g., Consumer Satisfaction Questionnaire [McMahon & Forehand, 2005]; Therapy Attitude Inventory [Eyberg, 1993]) can be adapted for use with a specific program. Parents as well as teachers may also be consulted regarding the type of prevention programs they believe are needed in their children's schools. For example, a brief needs assessment may be conducted with parents to gauge their priorities (e.g., are they most interested in a bullying prevention program or a drug and alcohol prevention program?) for the implementation of prevention programs.

Barriers to Effective Collaboration

Although we believe home/school collaboration can lead to the development of many effective intervention and prevention efforts, we realize that there are barriers to making this collaboration work, many of which we have already alluded to. The timing of visits, pragmatic issues with transportation and child care, stigma associated with mental health, or a real or perceived adversarial stance by school personnel are all potential deterrents. A few others warrant consideration. We discuss these next and summarize some common barriers to home/school collaboration and potential solutions in Table 1.2.

Given the heritability of learning and behavior problems and some of the known psychosocial risk factors for these concerns, one can anticipate that some of the parents of children with behavior problems will not have pleasant memories of their own education. Such memories might include feeling inadequate, being belittled by their teachers, or being ostracized by peers because they spent their day in the resource room. Similarly, for some ethnic/racial minority families, the school system may be viewed with skepticism because of a history of bias in education (e.g., the overidentification of certain ethnic minorities for special education). Some parents may have ongoing mental health concerns that interfere with their ability to be actively involved in collaborative interventions. All of these issues can

TABLE 1.2. Common Barriers and Potential Solutions to Home/School Collaboration

Common barriers to collaboration	Potential solutions
Systems-level barriers (e.g., limited support from administrators, competing demands on the school-based mental health provider's time)	• *Think small.* A schoolwide family resource center might be the long-term objective, but in the short term offering a three-session parenting group might be more manageable and acceptable to colleagues and administrators. • *Collect data.* In addition to being good clinical practice, having data to support the efficacy of interventions is likely to be compelling to administrators. Also think about collecting data on the outcomes most relevant to key decision makers (e.g., parent satisfaction and session attendance, teacher satisfaction, child's school attendance, classroom behavior problems). • *What works elsewhere?* Talk to colleagues in other districts about alternative models and how they have been able to integrate home/school collaboration into their jobs. Sharing information about these models with administrators may be helpful, particularly if supported with data. • *Be patient.* Systems are notoriously slow to change. Providing good-quality services, even if on a very small scale, will help to develop a reputation and demonstrate the value of collaborative intervention.
Low parent involvement/attendance	• *Think practical.* Beneficial as it might be, parents may be less likely to attend a long-term intervention vs. a more focused short-term program. For many families, accommodations will be needed to facilitate attendance (e.g., flexible scheduling). • *Find out what's needed/desired.* Survey families, teachers, and administrators about the services they view as most important. A survey of parents, in particular, might also provide information about what accommodations are needed to facilitate participation. • *Advertise.* Offering collaborative interventions will be new in many settings, and teachers and parents may simply not know what's available, who's eligible, or how to go about accessing services. Look for ways to disseminate information through mailings, posters, and announcements.
Resistance among families	• *Normalize participation.* Having programs for a broad range of families as well as targeted interventions for those with clinically significant behavior problems may help to reduce stigmatization. • *Assess reasons.* Consider potential reasons for resistance, such as prior experience, concerns about privacy, and misinformation. • *Motivational enhancement.* Assess parents' level of motivation and integrate motivational enhancement strategies.

affect parents' perception of the school system and their willingness to participate in their child's education. When approached sensitively, discussing parents' own experience can shed light on their view of their child's difficulties and help to engage them in a proactive way. A school-based practitioner can acknowledge that the system has not always served individuals with special needs particularly well but that direct collaboration with parents is an important step in the right direction. A motivational enhancement approach may help to overcome some of these barriers by identifying small, tangible steps that parents can take to achieve their goals (e.g., acknowledging the parents' discomfort with the school system while also pointing out steps that they might take to improve their child's experience). Although it takes time, establishing a norm of home/school collaboration is likely to be helpful in overcoming these barriers with parents.

Unfortunately, perhaps because of the perception that collaborative interventions take more time and effort to develop, we have found that some parents who are interested in working with school professionals to help their children meet resistance from school staff who are used to handling problems internally. For parents to be full partners in any intervention program, it is imperative that school personnel take the time to actively involve parents in identifying the problems and developing potential solutions. School personnel should explain the difficulties seen in the school setting and obtain parents' perceptions of their child's difficulties and strengths in the home setting. When developing an intervention plan, the rationale for the proposed intervention, including everyone's role in it, should be explained, and parents' input regarding the feasibility of the intervention in their home should always be obtained and respected. Parents and school personnel should also be on "the same page" in terms of expected outcomes and progress assessment.

Additional school-based barriers may involve resistance on the part of administrators who may argue that school-based professionals do not have the time and resources to be developing intervention programs that target home behavior and may not directly impact the child's performance in school. Clearly, there will need to be some limits on the intervention services provided, and, as discussed later, not all needs can be met within the school system. Sometimes the most appropriate collaboration with parents will be to provide a referral and help them establish a connection with a provider in the community. However, it may also be important for school-based clinicians to "sell" the benefits of collaborative interventions to administrators and to collect data to demonstrate how interventions involving parents can have a positive impact on school-specific outcome criteria (e.g., decreased office referrals, increased academic performance). Another source of resistance may be the view (by those both within and outside of the school) that school psychologists' role is to conduct testing, not intervention. Although this view seems to be shifting, in part because of the recent emphasis on the response to intervention model, in many settings time for anything other than assessment-related activities still remains limited. We believe this greatly underutilizes the skills and abilities of school-based practitioners. It makes little sense to focus all of one's resources on identifying children for services without also taking preventive steps to reduce the number of children who need intervention in the first place and ensuring that there are quality interventions to offer those who do require special services.

There are no easy solutions to these challenges, because systems are difficult and slow to change. However, as noted previously, data can be compelling for administrators and colleagues alike. In addition to being good clinical practice, collecting objective data before, during, and after an intervention helps to support the need for and potential benefits of intervention. It would be unreasonable to expect teachers to devote their time and school administrators to devote money and other resources without also being prepared to demonstrate meaningful results. Benchmarks of success should include those valued by these relevant stakeholders. For example, time missed from school, schoolwork completion, and office discipline referrals might all be outcomes valued by school staff that would be expected to improve with intervention. Further, it may be argued that an important role of the school system is to prepare children to be successful members of their community and society. Thus, even for behavior problems that manifest primarily at home, an argument can be made that intervention should be considered within the scope of practice for school-based mental health providers. Again, data can be compelling, and administrators may be persuaded by interventions that result in meaningful differences in community involvement with a more indirect effect on school-related issues (e.g., reduced rate of juvenile justice involvement and, by association, increased school involvement and higher graduation rates).

It is also helpful for clinicians to take a consumer satisfaction approach. When interventions fail, or when attendance or engagement is limited, it is tempting to blame the consumer (in this case, parents, teachers, students, administrators) for being unmotivated, unappreciative, and so on. This would be akin to an unsuccessful restaurant blaming the public for not eating out more, failing to appreciate their fine cuisine, or being unaware of their existence altogether. The bottom line is that if the service/product is not desired and is not offered in a consumer-friendly way, the business will fail. The same applies for intervention services offered in the schools. Practitioners can help their cause by seeking input about the services most needed, marketing their services to potential consumers, and collecting customer satisfaction data (e.g., parent/teacher feedback about the acceptability of an intervention). Unfortunately, these business skills are often unfamiliar for clinicians and are generally not well integrated into training programs. Marketing efforts might include direct contact with families via mailings, flyers, and posters or announcements in parent-directed newsletters. Often building awareness among teachers and other school staff can also be helpful. Because teachers typically have more ongoing contact with parents than do mental health professionals, they can be excellent allies in promoting home/school collaborative interventions. Unfortunately, some teachers may not realize the range of services school psychologists can provide. Thus, informing teachers about the range of available services and developing an identification and referral system to target high-risk children can be particularly helpful. School-based professionals can do this through ongoing individual contacts with teachers and through formal presentations at school staff meetings. We have generally found that once teachers become aware of the broad array of services school psychologists can provide, they are eager to take advantage of them.

Finally, as might be anticipated from the prior discussion, engaging families is likely to require a great deal of communication both to establish a working alliance and to keep families involved in the process. When talking with families, it is striking how often parents report that they never received evaluation feedback, are unsure of what services their child is receiving, or were not aware their child was struggling. Of course, in some cases, efforts were likely made to communicate and more information would have likely been accessible if requested. Nonetheless, it is apparent that home/school communication often falters and is likely to require ongoing efforts on the part of school-based providers. For some of the reasons listed earlier (e.g., feelings of inadequacy during their own schooling, skepticism regarding the school system), parents may be reluctant to ask questions when they do not understand their child's evaluation results or what is being said during a meeting. Additional effort is often needed to check for understanding. For example, after verbally providing feedback, a clinician might ask the parent, "How does this fit with what you know about your child?" or "Were there other questions or concerns that you had that we haven't addressed yet?" Or, after providing a written report and allowing some time for the parent to review it, a clinician might call to check in and solicit questions. It is also helpful to provide information in multiple formats. For example, in addition to providing information verbally at an evaluation feedback session, we often use a whiteboard to visually illustrate concepts, provide a handout highlighting key points (e.g., key assessment results, next steps, recommendations), and offer other resources such as parent-oriented publications or videotapes, or useful web sites. Similarly, when ongoing services are being provided, parents need and deserve feedback about the implementation of interventions and progress. Such feedback communicates an interest in making sure the intervention is working and can instill hope as they see their child making gains. This might be done in multiple ways, ranging from brief check-ins by phone, to home/school notes, to tracking and visually charting a child's behavior over time. To extend the prior consumer analogy, failing to put forth these efforts to increase and improve communication with parents is simply bad customer service.

CONSULTATION WITH NON-SCHOOL-BASED PROVIDERS

Although we are strong advocates for school psychologists as comprehensive educational and mental health providers, we do realize that there may be issues that cannot be dealt with in the school settings. In fact, at times, the most effective service that a school-based provider can offer parents is a referral to a professional in the community with expertise in a given condition. Examples might be a referral to a child psychiatrist for a medication evaluation or to a pediatrician to rule out a medical condition as a contributor to a child's behavioral problems. In other cases, it will be evident that a child's needs are beyond the scope of what can be provided in most school settings, such as a child needing comprehensive wrap-around services that would be offered in a community mental health setting. These services may include behavioral intervention, medication management, and case management to help families access other available resources. School-based clinicians may also be in a position to provide a referral for parents needing mental health services for themselves. For example, it may become clear that a mother's ability to care for her child and participate in her child's education is impaired by her own substance use, depression, anxiety, and so on. Addressing those concerns may be a necessary first step, without which the mother would not be able to fully participate in intervention on behalf of her child.

Despite all of the barriers described previously, most parents and children view the school as a safe place and value the opinions of teachers and other school personnel. School-based mental health professionals can use this credibility to advocate for children receiving needed services in the community, be it a well-child visit to their pediatrician or consultation with a specialist. This will often involve providing some education, such as talking with families about what to look for in a child psychologist, talking about how to access social services, or addressing common misconceptions about mental health services. Once a referral is made, school-based mental health providers can continue to provide an important function, the nature of which will depend somewhat on the discipline of the other providers and their knowledge base. As discussed later in the chapter, if school-based providers plan to collaborate with outside providers in an ongoing manner, they must ensure that parents have provided consent for communication with other providers. In addition, school-based professionals should ensure they are in compliance with relevant state laws as well as school district policies when making referrals.

In the following sections, we provide an overview of some of the common community professionals with whom school-based mental health professionals may consult. We discuss the training of these individuals and how school-based professionals can consult with them in targeting the needs of families and children in a collaborative manner. In the three intervention-focused chapters, we provide more details on collaborating with outside professionals related to specific issues.

Mental Health Providers in the Community

Mental health providers in the community include child clinical or pediatric psychologists, social workers, and counselors. School-based professionals may make referrals or consult with community mental health professionals when a child needs more specialized or intense services than those that can be offered in the schools or when a parent needs mental health services. Additionally, community-based mental health providers who are already providing services to a child may consult with school-based professionals to more directly address the school-based manifestations of a child's problems.

Most child mental health providers will have a good understanding of developmental issues and learning and behavioral problems of childhood and at least a rudimentary knowledge of the school system. However, more specific understanding of special education law and educational resources available to children and families will be highly varied depending on background and experience. Even high-quality training programs in child clinical psychology and social work often do not include specific training and course work in these areas. Thus, among colleagues, the school-based mental health professional is the expert regarding children's educational rights and options. Clinicians in the schools are also likely to have special expertise in some areas (e.g., learning disabilities, classroom interventions) and may provide consultation to other providers on best practices for assessment and treatment. A community mental health provider may also turn to school psychologists and others within the school system to gather information about the child's functioning at school or manifestation of symptoms, providing additional data for a comprehensive evaluation. There may be opportunities to join efforts in treatment, with the school-based provider offering intervention to target an issue in school (e.g., classroom-based intervention, participation in a social skills group) and the community provider offering more in-depth individual interventions. In turn, community-based providers may have particular expertise to offer on a specific condition or knowledge of community resources and agencies not commonly dealt with by a clinician working in the schools. Through each of these types of collaboration, a school-based provider can serve as a liaison for families, relaying information and helping to coordinate comprehensive treatment. There can and should also be an advocacy role, helping parents to learn questions to ask, where to turn for services, and how to best participate in their child's care.

Child and Adolescent Psychiatrists

Psychiatrists are commonly a part of the intervention picture when children are receiving psychotropic medications, particularly those youth taking multiple medications or who have complicated presentations of disorders. Child psychiatrists receive clinical training with children and adolescents as well as adults. Most will also have background knowledge in pediatrics and neurology. General psychiatrists, who do not receive extensive training in working with children/adolescents and who have varying levels of training and experience with this population, may also see child patients. Because of the short supply of child and adolescent psychiatrists, particularly in rural areas, access to a general psychiatrist will often be the only option beyond a child's primary care provider. Psychiatrists will typically have the most current knowledge regarding medications and the impact they may have on behavior, including side effects. In addition, most psychiatrists will have a good understanding of mental health problems, including severe forms of psychopathology. Training and clinical practice in behavioral intervention (vs. pharmacology) vary significantly among providers: most receive at least some training, although experience during and beyond residency may be limited. As with other child mental health providers, knowledge of the school system will also be highly varied. Again, school-based clinicians can offer consultation regarding disorders that they are likely to have particular expertise with and applicable educational rights and laws. Another important function relates to medication trials. During their assessments, psychiatrists may turn to school staff for information regarding specific behavioral targets for intervention (i.e., symptoms or symptom clusters likely amenable to medication). School-based providers can also be very helpful with developing a system for monitoring medication response and behavioral side effects. For example, once targets for medication are identified, the school-based clinician may serve as a liaison between the prescribing psychiatrist, parents, and teachers and other staff to monitor change at baseline and after intervention. In the process, parents will become increasingly educated about monitoring their child's progress across settings so that they might ultimately take a more active role and rely less on the school-based mental health provider. There may also be times when a child is participating in behavioral interventions at school along with a medication trial. Psychiatrists often have particular interest in collaborating with school staff, because they may be prescribing medications for symptoms that manifest primarily at school (e.g., attention problems) and they rely on good information about the effects of their treatment. Consultation from child and adolescent psychiatrists will often be helpful for school-based staff, particularly when confronted with relatively rare forms of psychopathology (e.g., psychosis) and when questions arise regarding the appropriateness of medication.

Pediatricians and Family Physicians

Most (but not all) children will have a primary care medical provider who is a pediatrician or family physician. Pediatricians have a unique perspective on the patients and families under their care, often having known them since the child was born. This gives them a long-term view of the child's development and, for most, a high level of investment in the child's care. A child's pediatrician is viewed as a respected authority by both the child and his or her parents and is often the first person they turn to with concerns related to behavioral issues. Pediatricians have very good knowledge of developmental issues, and most have at least some understanding of the school system. In addition, because of the shortage of child and adolescent psychiatrists, pediatricians are increasingly called upon to provide psychiatric medication, with varying levels of comfort and expertise in this area.

Many children receive their primary medical care from a family physician rather than a pediatrician. Family physicians receive broad training, preparing them to care for the continuum of patients from newborns to older adults. Like pediatricians, family physicians will generally have an ongoing relationship with patients and their families and are viewed as a respected authority. Family physicians are increasingly called upon to prescribe and manage psychiatric medications, although their training and experience will be highly varied.

School-based clinicians can offer several functions in collaboration with pediatricians and family practice physicians. This may include consultation regarding a child's learning and behavior problems or educational rights and services available. Those working in the schools can offer primary care physicians information about the impact of a child's medical condition on his or her education, such as days missed from school, interference with peer relationships, or diminished participation in age-appropriate activities. As discussed previously, in concert with a pediatrician or other physician providing medication, a school-based professional can assist with initial and ongoing assessment of a child's symptoms and behavioral side effects. In the context of home/school collaboration, parents can and should be involved in this process so that communication among providers is transparent (i.e., the parent is aware that providers are in communication and working as a team).

Of course, consultation with a child's primary care provider is important for understanding the child's medical status as it might relate to school functioning. Further, as noted previously, primary care physicians provide a long-term view of a child's development and can use their credibility with families to reinforce efforts to intervene on the child's behalf. Often mental health providers, including those working in the schools, fail to adequately communicate with a child's physician. Potential barriers might include intimidation or the perception that the physician is too busy to discuss the child's care with mental health providers. Pediatricians and family physicians are busy, but we have found that most are quite good about returning phone calls to discuss one of their patients and desirous of information about how their patients are doing. In fact, one of the complaints that we hear from physicians is that they want such contact and do not receive it. Within a medical model, doctors assume that when their patients see a specialist in the community, they will receive a phone call or note summarizing the visit, and they generally assume that the same might apply when the child receives mental health or educational services. To build effective ongoing relationships with medical professionals, school-based practitioners would be wise to follow the medical model in terms of communication and feedback.

However, it is worth noting that school personnel and medical personnel may have a different style of communication, and these may need to be adapted for effective collaboration to occur. In a survey of pediatricians regarding information they receive from schools when conducting assessments for attention-deficit/hyperactivity disorder (ADHD) and monitoring treatment effects (HaileMariam, Bradley-Johnson, & Johnson, 2002), most physicians reported not receiving the type of information they would prefer. For example, when evaluating treatments, more than 60% of physicians reported wanting rating scales, informal observational data, one- to three-paragraph summaries, and achievement data. However, fewer than 40% of the physicians received this information. Based on the results of this survey, it seems clear that school personnel and physicians could do a better job communicating with each other. Physicians may need more information on the type of data that are available in the schools and may need to specifically request additional data. In addition, school personnel may need to be more attuned to the time constraints physicians face and provide data that are clear and concise. An ongoing collaborative relationship is likely the best avenue to facilitate the communication process so that it is helpful to all involved and ultimately results in the most effective services for the targeted child.

A collaborative model that has received a significant amount of attention from primary care providers, in particular pediatricians who work with children with special health care needs, is the medical home model. The medical home, as described by the American Academy of Pediatrics on their medical home web site, is "a model of delivering primary care that is accessible, continuous, comprehensive, family-centered, coordinated, compassionate, and culturally effective." Essentially, a child's medical home is the coordination center for his or her intervention needs and involves all individuals who provide services to the child, including school personnel. (See *www.medicalhomeinfo.org* for more information on this model.) Typically, it is the pediatrician's office that serves as the child's medical home and helps the child and family access and understand additional needed services and resources. Ideally, school personnel are very involved in the medical home and in coordinating with other professionals to provide effective services in a family-centered format. Physicians who ascribe to the medical home model may have fairly in-depth knowledge of school-based services and be eager to collaborate with school professionals. We know of at least one pediatrician who has a medical home practice who regularly attends the individualized education plan (IEP) meetings of his patients and has a phone line dedicated to school personnel. Although this level of commitment to coordination with school professionals may be unusual, it is important for school-based professionals to remember that medical personnel typically do value input from school-based professionals.

ETHICAL AND LEGAL ISSUES IN HOME/SCHOOL COLLABORATION

Several ethical and legal issues warrant discussion because these are particularly relevant for interventions involving home/school collaboration. These include issues such as practicing within one's area of competence, protecting the confidentiality and other rights of students, and ensuring adequate informed consent. A comprehensive discussion of ethics and legal issues is beyond the scope of this book. For more comprehensive discussion of these issues, we recommend the text by Jacob and Hartshorne (2007) and the ethics codes published by the National Association of School Psychologists (NASP, 2000) and the American Psychological Association (2002).

Competence

For many school-based providers, integrating collaborative home/school interventions into their practice will mean using new skills or at least skills that they have not used since their training. Further, training and education vary widely across the disciplines commonly lumped together in school-based mental health providers. Even within specialty areas (e.g., school psychology, school counseling, school social work), training can be quite different from one program to the next. For example, one school psychologist may receive almost exclusive training and supervised experience in assessment, whereas another might receive in-depth training in intervention and consultation. Thus, some school psychologists will be prepared primarily for assessment, with little intervention experience and no background working directly with parents on intervention efforts, whereas others might have a great deal of intervention experience.

In general, ethical guidelines suggest that competence can be determined by training and supervised experience. Thus, attending a 2-hour workshop on cognitive-behavioral therapy (CBT) for selective mutism alone probably would not make someone competent to provide intervention unless he or she also had other relevant training and experience in similar populations (e.g., CBT for generalized anxiety). Some interventions have fairly clear guidelines about the training necessary to be considered competent, whereas others are vague. When in doubt, seeking peer consultation or supervision from a colleague is important, particularly when guidelines are limited or unclear, such as with new or emerging treatments. Ethical codes also indicate that practitioners should engage in ongoing continuing education efforts to maintain their competence. In addition, state educator licensing/credentialing boards typically require continuing education and training for renewal of licensure/certification to ensure that skills are up-to-date.

Further, ethics dictate that providers clearly and accurately portray their level of competence to clients. Families generally are not aware of the differences among mental health professionals (e.g., psychologists, psychiatrists, social workers, counselors), their various degrees and certifications, and the level and type of training they receive. Thus, for example, families will often ask their child's psychologist for an opinion about medication options or will turn to the school counselor to help interpret their child's psychological test results. In both cases, the most appropriate response would be for the clinician to let families know that their questions are outside his or her area of competence and to refer them to the appropriate professional. A parent may also ask more pointed questions about a provider's competence treating a specific problem, with a specific treatment modality. These questions can sometimes feel threatening or insulting, particularly for clinicians who are new to their field. However, such questions are very appropriate and reflect good consumerism on the part of parents; we often recommend that parents ask these types of questions when seeking services for their child in the community. Further, because many parents are not savvy mental health consumers or might feel uncomfortable directly asking about a clinician's competence, it is incumbent on providers to offer information about their competence, typically during the informed consent process. For example, during an informed consent process, a provider might say, "I am trained as a school psychologist and have been practicing for 1 year. My expertise is primarily in using behavioral interventions to help with behavior problems in the classroom and at home."

Professional Relationships

Most school-based mental health professionals are well aware of the importance of maintaining good relationships with their clients and coworkers, and these issues are discussed extensively in the various professional codes of ethics. A few issues warrant mention here because they are particularly relevant to collaborative home/school interventions. A primary example involves clarifying who the identified client or patient is for a particular intervention. This seems simple enough. However, by definition, collaborative interventions will include multiple parties. For example, a provider may be simultaneously working with a student and his or her teacher and parents. Thus, it is important at the outset to ensure that all parties involved know who the client is for a particular intervention. Ethical guidelines vary somewhat in their position on this issue. The American Psychological Association ethics code acknowledges that clinicians serve multiple clients and suggests clarifying the identified client at the outset of treatment. The NASP ethics code also notes that school psychologists serve multiple clients but states that the interests of the child/student are to be considered primary when a conflict of interest arises. Understandably, identifying who the client is can sometimes be confusing for children and families. For example, when using a behavioral parent training intervention, most of the direct work will be with the parents, attempting to improve their behavior management skills with anticipated benefits for the child. Parents may, therefore, assume that they are the primary client; however, professionals tend to see the child as the client in this type of intervention. At a minimum, the identified client should be clarified at the beginning of treatment and, for most readers of this book, the interests of the child/student will be considered primary.

Given that the child/student is considered to be the primary client in most school-based intervention work, NASP guidelines suggest that school psychologists provide students with a clear and understandable explanation of why services were requested, who will receive information about services, and possible outcomes. This is relevant here because generally students will not be the ones requesting a collaborative home/school intervention and their level of direct involvement will vary. Even when they are not directly involved (e.g., behavioral consultation for parents and teachers), this guideline suggests that students should be made aware of the intervention and anticipated results. For example, a school psychologist planning to implement a home/school intervention for school refusal might say, "As you probably know, we're concerned that you've been too nervous to come to school. So I'm going to meet with your parents and teacher to see if we can find some things that they might do differently to make that easier. I think that this will help you get back to school, but it will probably mean trying some new things that will be hard at first." The older the child and the more active the role he or she is expected to take in the intervention process, the more important it will be to have the child's buy-in regarding the intervention.

Professional Practice

Several relevant professional practice issues are addressed in ethics codes for school-based providers. The NASP guidelines require that providers use interventions that are research based and appropriate for the presenting problem. Although the American Psychological Association does not specifically state this, it notes that caution should be used with treatments that are considered experimental and it should be made clear to the client that research is limited. There are many examples of collaborative home/school interventions that are evidence based and easily justified. In particular, home/school interventions for externalizing problems tend to have significant data to support their use (see Chapter 4). For other presenting problems such as depression and anxiety, there are interventions with research to support their use but limited research on collaborative interventions specifically (see Chapter 5). When developing collaborative interventions to target these problems, providers will need to be more cautious and often extrapolate from supportive evidence for individual treatments. For example, cognitive behavioral interventions are generally supported in the treatment of depression, but data on working collaboratively with parents in setting up an intervention program for depression are less extensive.

Termination of services is another professional practice issue addressed by various ethics codes. Practitioners are required to terminate services when it becomes clear that a client no longer needs treatment or is no longer benefiting from treatment. When termination is anticipated, clients should receive reasonable preparation and efforts should be made to facilitate the ending of treatment. For example, in the school setting, a provider may anticipate that a family will no longer be able to receive services once the child advances out of his or her current school or that services will be interrupted (e.g., for summer vacation). The school-based clinician's responsibility would be to help the client prepare for the termination/interruption in services, such as offering a referral to another provider in the community or wrapping up services before the beginning of an expected school break.

NASP guidelines also address potential conflicts of interest for school psychologists who also have a private practice. The guidelines state that school psychologists in private practice are not to accept payment from clients who could receive similar services free of charge within the school system. This is particularly relevant here because many of the interventions discussed are traditionally offered in private clinical practice settings, and the scope of services offered in the schools is expanding. School-based providers should discuss with families what services they might be able to receive through the schools versus private practice and take precautions to avoid exploiting families seen in private practice settings.

Privacy/Confidentiality

Because it typically involves multiple parties, home/school collaboration also opens up potential problems with confidentiality. Ethical guidelines state that information shared by clients should remain confidential, except as required by law (e.g., child abuse or neglect, suspected harm to self or others). In work with children younger than the age of consent for mental health services, it is important to note that parents may request access to their child's mental health records. Of particular relevance for school-based professionals, the Federal

Educational Rights and Privacy Act (FERPA) protects the privacy of school records and allows parents the right to review their child's school records and request corrections if they believe that there are errors. FERPA does allow some provisions for releasing records to a new school when a child is transferring or to other school personnel who have a "legitimate interest" in knowing the information. Parents can also request in writing that information be released to other providers involved in their child's care (e.g., pediatrician, psychologist). It is important for school-based providers to remember that if they wish to receive information from non-school-based providers (e.g., physicians, community mental health professionals) parents must sign a release of information to allow the school clinician to receive this information and engage in ongoing collaboration with other professionals. Although FERPA is an educational law, other laws (e.g., Health Insurance Portability and Accountability Act) and professional ethical codes have mandates regarding privacy and sharing of information.

In the context of collaborative home/school interventions, it is important that all parties involved know the limits of privacy and confidentiality. This can become challenging when multiple players are included. For example, when working with a mother and teacher to address a child's anxiety, the mother may divulge that she and the child's father are planning to divorce. Should this be included in the child's records as it relates directly to her current problems? Should the teacher, who has been closely involved in the intervention, be informed of this? Most would probably argue that the answer to both of these questions is "No," although the answer might vary in different settings and according to parent preferences. At a minimum, this type of situation should be anticipated, and parents should know at the outset of an intervention how these situations will be handled and what their rights and their child's rights are.

Informed Consent

Parents and students should receive adequate informed consent to allow them to decide whether to take part in the intervention proposed. When a client is unable to provide legal consent (e.g., minors), providers are required to provide a description of the proposed intervention and seek the individual's assent in addition to obtaining consent from their legal representative (e.g., a parent or guardian). Legal requirements for informed consent vary by state. In general, informed consent should involve a discussion of confidentiality and its limits, the provider's training and areas of competence, a description of the proposed assessments and interventions (e.g., duration, course of treatment) and any relevant risks, and a description of alternatives. True informed consent is more than signing a piece of paper: This should be a process, with measures taken to ensure that participants know what to expect at each stage of treatment. For example, before starting to use extinction for a problem behavior (see Chapter 4), a provider might say, "It is very likely that when you quit responding, your child's behavior is going to get worse for a while before it gets better. Is that something that you're willing to try right now?" After spending a great deal of time in their field, it can be easy for professionals to overestimate how much clients will know about psychological and behavioral interventions. Although they may not ask, parents frequently have questions or misconceptions about mental health services. The informed consent process offers a chance to discuss what to expect as well as the limitations of our technology.

CHAPTER SUMMARY AND PURPOSE OF THE BOOK

Collaborative home/school intervention is a best practice worth striving for. However, as this chapter suggests, this approach will require an investment of time and energy. An important point that we hope has been conveyed is that the effort of working to involve parents more directly in the intervention process may be therapeutic for families in its own right and, at the very least, is likely to facilitate the success of any future intervention. Taking the initiative to address pragmatic barriers, acknowledging the difficulty of changing long-standing behavior patterns and listening to parents regarding their readiness to change, and reaching out to other providers all convey to families and the community how important a provider views families and their participation in the intervention process. With the current focus on empirically based treatments, it can be easy to become overly focused on technique and lose sight of these human elements.

In this book, we focus on how to involve parents in interventions that work. Many of the school-based programs that have empirical support and make use of parents are larger, comprehensive prevention programs. Although these programs are very valuable and have a clear place in supporting the social–emotional, behavioral, and academic needs of students, we also believe that school-based mental health professionals need more resources to most effectively intervene with youth who are already exhibiting significant problems. This book is intended to be a resource for school-based mental professionals who wish to work more collaboratively with parents in implementing evidence-based interventions for youth who are struggling with emotional, behavioral, or academic problems. We have drawn from the available literature to provide treatment plans for externalizing problems, internalizing problems, and academic problems that could be implemented within a school setting in collaboration with parents. Because of the focus on parent involvement, we have not attempted to discuss all evidence-based interventions within each of these categories, only those for which it is desirable and feasible to involve parents. Before turning to the specifics of intervention techniques, we first provide an overview of common emotional, behavioral, and learning problems in school-age children (Chapter 2) and then turn to the issue of assessment of these problems within a problem-solving context (Chapter 3). We then provide an overview of collaborative interventions for externalizing problems (Chapter 4), internalizing problems (Chapter 5), and academic problems (Chapter 6).

2

Introduction to Emotional, Behavioral, and Learning Problems in School-Age Children

Emotional and behavioral problems are common reasons for referral to mental health and educational professionals within the school system. Although the proportion of children who qualify for special services because of an emotional disturbance is relatively small, teachers frequently voice concern about emotional and behavioral problems and feel the least prepared to address these issues. Such problems can lead to disruptive classroom behavior, poor peer relationships, and difficulties with learning. School-based mental health professionals are, therefore, often asked to assist with the treatment of such problems in the classroom, and the potential impact of these interventions is tremendous. Additionally, a number of students, including many of those with emotional and behavioral problems, have academic difficulties that need to be addressed. In this chapter, we provide an overview to the issues related to the identification and treatment of emotional, behavioral, and learning problems in school-age children. In addition to describing some of the more common problems seen in children, we outline the need for mental health services and discuss the rationale for implementing services in school settings. This chapter is intended to help provide background knowledge and, along with Chapter 1, set the stage for the remainder of the book, in which we discuss assessment and intervention of these problems in a collaborative arrangement with parents.

OVERVIEW OF COMMON PROBLEMS

Emotional, behavioral, and learning problems in children have been defined and discussed in a variety of ways. One of the most frequently used methods is the classification of problems into different categories. This is the method used in the *Diagnostic and Statistical Manual of Mental Disorders* (DSM-IV; American Psychiatric Association, 1994) as well as in the federal special education guidelines (Individuals with Disabilities Educational Improvement Act of 2004 [IDEIA]). Although the DSM-IV is used infrequently in educational settings, it remains the most common way of describing and classifying disorders. Thus, it is important for school-based mental health professionals to have some working knowledge of the DSM-IV, even if they are not using DSM-IV diagnoses with children. A basic understanding of the DSM-IV will allow better communication with other mental health and medical professionals outside of the school system.

The DSM-IV classifies problem behaviors, including learning disorders, into different diagnostic categories. Some of these categories are more specific to children and adolescents and are listed in the section of the DSM-IV on *disorders usually first diagnosed in infancy, childhood, and adolescence*. There are 10 different categories listed in this section of the DSM-IV (see Table 2.1) and within each category there are specific disorders. For example, the category of attention-deficit and disruptive behavior disorders includes ADHD, conduct disorder (CD), oppositional defiant disorder (ODD), and disruptive behavior disorder not otherwise specified. In addition to the disorders listed in the chapter on childhood disorders, children and adolescents can be diagnosed with any of the disorders listed in the more "adult"-focused chapters of the DSM-IV. Particularly relevant to children and adolescents are the sections on mood disorders (including the depressive disorders) and anxiety disorders. Although the DSM-IV is commonly used when diagnosing or classifying children with emotional and behavior problems, its use is certainly not without controversy, and as noted previously, it is used much less frequently in school settings than in more traditional clinical settings.

When using special education guidelines to classify children, there is only one category that relates specifically to emotional and behavioral problems—emotional disturbance (ED)—and one that relates specifically to learning/academic problems—specific learning disabilities (SLD). As defined by IDEIA (34 C.F.R. sec 300.8), ED involves the following:

> A condition exhibiting one or more of the following characteristics over a long period of time and to a marked degree that adversely affects a child's educational performance:
>
> - An inability to learn that cannot be explained by intellectual, sensory, or health factors.
> - An inability to build or maintain satisfactory interpersonal relationships with peers and teachers.
> - Inappropriate types of behavior or feelings under normal circumstances.

TABLE 2.1. DSM-IV Disorders Usually First Diagnosed in Infancy, Childhood, or Adolescence

Mental retardation	Attention-deficit and disruptive behavior disorders
Learning disorders	Feeding and eating disorders of infancy or early childhood
Motor skills disorder	Tic disorders
Communication disorders	Elimination disorders
Pervasive developmental disorders	Other disorders of infancy, childhood, or adolescence

- A general pervasive mood of unhappiness or depression.
- A tendency to develop physical symptoms or fears associated with personal or school problems.

Emotional disturbance includes schizophrenia. The term does not apply to children who are socially maladjusted, unless it is determined that they have an emotional disturbance.

As can be seen, the ED category is somewhat of a "catch-all" category and includes a variety of different behaviors and symptoms. In addition to receiving services under the ED category, some students experiencing emotional/behavioral problems may receive services under other IDEIA categories. For example, children with ADHD who qualify for special education services are often served under the other health impaired category.

Children who experience significant academic problems (regardless of whether other problems are also present) may qualify for special education services under the SLD category. IDEIA (34 C.F.R. sec 300.8) defines an SLD as

A disorder in one or more of the basic psychological processes involved in understanding or in using language, spoken or written, that may manifest itself in the imperfect ability to listen, think, speak, read, write, spell, or to do mathematical calculations, including conditions such as perceptual disabilities, brain injury, minimal brain dysfunction, dyslexia, and developmental aphasia.

Specific learning disability does not include learning problems that are primarily the result of visual, hearing, or motor disabilities, of mental retardation, of emotional disturbance, or of environmental, cultural, or economic disadvantage.

In addition to defining problem behaviors by the diagnostic category or educational classification under which they fall, another common way to define and discuss emotional and behavioral problems is through empirically derived categories of behaviors. The most commonly used empirically derived categories are those of *externalizing problems* and *internalizing problems*. Externalizing problems are outer directed, such as aggression, "acting-out" behaviors, and hyperactivity. These behaviors are often described as behaviors that are disturbing to others rather than to the child him- or herself. Externalizing problems include symptoms of the DSM-IV disruptive behavior disorders as well as other problems that may not be part of a specific diagnosis or classification. In the research literature, the symptoms of these disorders are often referred to broadly as "conduct problems." As a group, conduct problems are among the most researched categories of childhood disorders. A substantial amount of literature suggests that conduct problems are stable over time for many children. About half or more of children continue to meet diagnostic criteria over time; those children who initially exhibit more severe symptoms are more likely to continue to exhibit symptoms over time (Loeber, Burke, Lahey, Winters, & Zera, 2000).

Internalizing problems are those that are more inner directed and cause significant distress for the child or adolescent. These problems include symptoms of DSM-IV mood and anxiety disorders as well as other behaviors that do not fall under a specific diagnostic category or classification (e.g., social withdrawal). Although there is less information on the stability of internalizing problems over time, based on the available literature, it appears that for a substantial subset of children, these disorders too are likely to continue. For example, in several studies in which the Child Behavior Checklist has been utilized to assess stability of psychopathology over time, researchers have noted significant continuity for both internalizing and externalizing symptoms (e.g., Stanger, MacDonald, McConaughy, & Achenbach, 1996; Visser, van der Ende, Koot, & Verhulst, 1999).

In addition to the externalizing and internalizing distinction, various authors have discussed other broad categories of problems in children. For example, Kazdin (2004) discusses three additional broad categories of disorders: substance-related disorders, learning and mental disabilities, and severe and pervasive psychopathology. Substance-related disorders include difficulties relating to the use/abuse of substances such as alcohol, tobacco, and illegal drugs. Learning and mental disabilities include problems associated with academic functioning, encompassing mental retardation and learning disabilities. Severe and pervasive psychopathology includes disorders that are considered to be long-term problems that cause impairments in numerous aspects of the individual's life, such as schizophrenia and autism.

In this book we have chosen to discuss the treatment of problems by the broad categories of internalizing problems, externalizing problems, and academic/learning problems, because these categories will likely make up the vast majority of cases that are seen by school-based mental health professionals. In addition, the focus of this book is on treatments that can be implemented in collaboration with parents; therefore, it seemed useful to emphasize these three areas because there are either existing treatments geared toward children with these difficulties that make use of parents (e.g., parent training for externalizing problems; family-based therapy for anxiety problems) or treatments that can be easily adapted to include parents playing a key role (e.g., interventions for academic problems).

Estimates of overall prevalence rates of mental health disorders in children are generally about 20%, although this varies depending on the population sampled, instruments used, and time frame considered. In a large-scale epidemiological study on children and adolescents (Costello, Mustillo, Erkanli, Keeler, & Angold, 2003), the 3-month prevalence rate of mental health disorders in children ages 9 to 16 was 13.3%. Slightly more boys (15.8%) than girls (10.6%) were diagnosed with a mental health problem. In terms of age patterns, children in the 9- to 10-year age group had the highest rate of diagnoses; there was then a slight decline through ages 11 and 12 followed by another increase. Costello et al. estimated that by 16 years of age 36.7% of children had met criteria for at least one DSM-IV diagnosis. In a study with younger children (ages 5–9; Briggs-Gowan, Horwitz, Schwab-Stone, Leventhal, & Leaf, 2000), it was estimated that almost 17% had a DSM-III-R disorder, with approximately 7% having an internalizing disorder and 12% an externalizing disorder. Boys were noted to be at higher risk for externalizing disorders than girls, with no differences noted for internalizing problems. A study of adults (Kessler et al., 2005) revealed that half of all cases of mental health problems start by age 14, with average age of onset being particularly low for anxiety (11 years) and impulse-control disorders, including ODD, ADHD, and CD (also 11 years). Thus, mental health problems in children and adolescents warrant concern and attention, not just because of the potential for current negative outcomes but also because of the high likelihood that symptoms will continue over time.

Although about a fifth of children nationwide have mental health problems, a much smaller number receive services under the special educational classification of ED. Only 7.9% of all students ages 6 to 21 receiving special education services fall under the ED classification (U.S. Department of Education, 2009). This makes up less than 1% of the total population of school-age children. Although it is not clear why there is such a large discrepancy between the total number of children with mental health problems and the number of children receiving school-based services within the ED category, it should be expected that there would be some discrepancy. By definition, children who are classified as ED must be underperforming academically. Although certainly a number of children with mental health problems do experience concomitant academic problems, many do not and even those who do may not experience them at a level required for an IDEIA classification. Thus, there are likely many children in our school systems who are not receiving special education services of any type but who are still in need of mental health services.

A larger portion of children receive special education services under the learning disability category than under the ED category. Approximately 4% of school-age children receive services in this category, making it the largest special education category: 46.4% of all children who receive special education services receive services under the SLD category (U.S. Department of Education, 2009). However, even though a large portion of children receive school-based services as SLD, estimates of the number of children who have learning problems are higher. For example, according to data obtained through the National Health Interview Survey (U.S. Department of Health and Human Services, 2009), 8% of children ages 3 to 17 have a learning disability; prevalence rates are higher in boys (10%) than in girls (5%). In a recent study using data from the National Survey of Children's Health, it was estimated that the lifetime prevalence of learning disability was 9.7%; children with special health care needs are more likely than others to have a learning disability (Altarac & Saroha, 2007). Other researchers have also found that children clinically referred for emotional and behavioral problems have a higher prevalence of learning disabilities than students in the general population (Mayes & Calhoun, 2006).

An even higher percentage of children experience significant difficulties in key academic areas that may hinder their performance in school and lead to lifelong difficulties. According to statistics published by the National Assessment of Educational Progress (NAEP, 2007a, 2007c), in 2007, 33% of fourth-grade students, 26% of eighth-grade students, and 27% of 12th-grade students scored below the basic level (defined as "partial mastery of the knowledge and skills that are fundamental for proficient work at a given grade"; p. 2) on reading assessments. In math assessments, 18% of fourth-grade students, 29% of eighth-grade students, and 39% of 12th-grade students scored below the basic level (NAEP, 2007a, 2007b). In writing, the NAEP, data indicate that 12% of eighth graders, and 18% of 12th graders are below the basic level (NAEP, 2008). Across all three of these academic areas, there were differences among ethnic groups, with Caucasian and Asian students scoring higher than African American, Latino, and Native American students. In addition, those students eligible for free or reduced-cost lunch had lower scores than children not eligible. In terms of gender differences, girls consistently scored higher than boys in reading and writing, and boys scored higher (but only by a slight margin) in mathematics. Given these data, clearly there are a number of children who are struggling academically who do not meet criteria for an SLD classification but who could likely benefit from interventions designed to increase their proficiency in academic skills.

PREVENTION AND INTERVENTION

In addition to formal diagnoses or significant levels of emotional, behavioral, and academic problems, there are children and adolescents who are considered to be at risk for the development of such problems. There is also an increasing recognition that anyone can develop significant emotional and behavioral problems, even those with no known risk factors. Given this, there is increased emphasis on prevention within the field of school psychology and mental health. Indeed, many argue that the role of psychology and mental health should not be restricted to reducing problems but should also include efforts to optimize functioning. This is consistent with the role of schools in general. Few would argue that schools should focus their efforts only on addressing learning problems, without attention given to optimizing the education for all of the eager and adept learners. There is abundant literature on the role of school-based services for early intervention, showing that prevention is a viable and important goal both clinically and economically (e.g., Gilliam & Zigler, 2000; Niles, Reynolds, & Roe-Sepowitz, 2008; Ou & Reynolds, 2006). Further, the literature on mental health and behavioral problems suggests that involvement of parents and coordination of services across setting are keys to effective prevention (Greenberg, Domitrovich, & Bumbarger, 2001). In addition to being a proactive approach to mental health, such prevention programs can help to reduce the stigma associated with the utilization of services and help to establish a community norm for parental involvement.

Although terminology varies, prevention programs are typically classified into one of three categories (e.g., see OSEP Technical Assistance Center on Positive Behavioral Interventions and Supports at *www.pbis.org*): *Primary* or *universal* programs are those offered to the general public or a whole group (e.g., a schoolwide antibullying campaign); *secondary* or *selective* programs are those offered to individuals or subgroups who are considered to be at risk by virtue of biological, psychological, or social risk factors (e.g., a social skills program for those identified as being rejected by their peers in a schoolwide screening); and *tertiary* or *indicated* programs are offered to high-risk individuals who do not meet diagnostic criteria for a disorder but who have detectable symptoms that place them at risk (e.g., a group intervention for youth with subclinical symptoms of depression). Of course, these categories are not mutually exclusive, and there are several prevention programs intended to address all three levels (e.g., the Triple P—Positive Parenting Program; Sanders, 1999, 2007).

These levels of prevention/intervention efforts are often represented through use of the triangle model presented in Figure 2.1 (e.g., OSEP Technical Assistance Center on Positive Behavioral Interventions and Supports, n.d.). As can be seen, the lower portion of the triangle accounts for the most children in a school setting: those who are not currently exhibiting significant emotional, behavioral, or academic problems. At this level, primary prevention would occur and would be focused on universal interventions for all students to reduce the number of new cases of problems. At the second level of the triangle are children who are considered to be at risk for developing problems. The focus here is on secondary

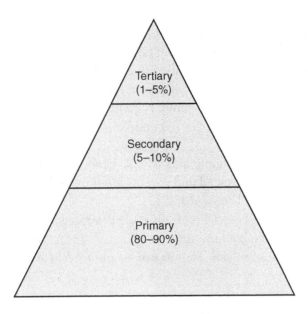

FIGURE 2.1. Prevention triangle.

prevention, in which students typically receive targeted group interventions. At the top of the triangle are children who are currently exhibiting significant emotional, behavioral, or academic problems and are in need of more intensive interventions, or tertiary prevention, geared toward reducing problematic behavior and increasing prosocial behaviors.

Social and Emotional Learning Programs

Social and emotional learning (SEL) strategies are becoming increasingly discussed and researched as a primary prevention strategies. As defined by the Collaborative for Academic, Social, and Emotional Learning (CASEL, 2008), SEL programs allow children to obtain competency in the following areas (p. 1):

- Self-awareness, including recognizing emotions.
- Self-management such as impulse control.
- Social awareness, including empathy and perspective taking.
- Relationship skills such as communication and conflict management.
- Responsible decision making, including adequate problem solving.

A number of programs targeting these areas have been developed (see *www.casel.org*). Most of these programs are intended to be implemented within the school setting, often by regular classroom teachers.

Research to date on SEL programs indicates that they can have positive benefits on a variety of factors, including decreased mental health problems, decreased substance use, increased school attendance, and increased academic achievement. Effects of these programs were noted to be more positive when programs were of longer duration, addressed behaviors in multiple settings (including the home setting), and had support from key leaders in the school setting (e.g., CASEL, 2008; Greenberg et al., 2003). Although some SEL programs do systematically involve families (e.g., PATHS: *www.preventionscience.com/ prevention-programs/paths/research-development.php*; Second Step: *www.cfchildren.org*) many do not (see CASEL, 2003, for a summary). Those that do involve families have three common themes, as identified by Patrikakou and Weissberg (2007):

- Communication between home and school: Parents are informed about what children are being taught at school and parents are provided with ideas for how to reinforce these skills in the home setting.
- Parent involvement at home: Programs include strategies and materials that can be used by parents in the home setting.
- Parent involvement at school: Parents are encouraged to attend school or classroom activities.

The CASEL web site also has a variety of resources for parents that practitioners may find useful, regardless of whether a schoolwide SEL program is in place. These resources include a packet with ideas for working with parents and a list of things parents can do at home to help their children develop social–emotional competency, including focusing on their children's strengths, talking about feelings, and helping children problem solve.

Although there are an increasing number of primary and secondary prevention programs, especially those that can be implemented in the school context, the interventions discussed in this book are aimed at the tertiary prevention level. We acknowledge that primary and secondary interventions, such as SEL programs, are important, and we encourage school-based mental health professionals to seek out resources and programs focused on these. However, with the focus of this book on parent-assisted interventions, the majority of these will be implemented with students already experiencing some problems. Parents can certainly be a key part of primary and secondary prevention efforts, and some of the interventions described in this book have been or could be adapted to fit within this model. However, given the more comprehensive nature of primary and secondary prevention programs, parent components are typically just one part of these programs, with more work being done within the school context. Therefore, we have focused our efforts on describing in more detail the specifics of interventions that can be implemented in collaboration with parents.

EVIDENCE-BASED PRACTICE

Another recent development within the psychology treatment literature, including school psychology, is an emphasis on *evidence-based practice* (EBP). The concept of EBP originated within the medical field, with David Sackett and his colleagues at the Centre for Evidence-Based Medicine being some of the key original proponents of EBP. Within psychology, one of the first steps toward formally discussing and defining EBP came in 1995 when Division 12 (Clinical Psychology) of the American Psychological Association developed criteria for what they termed "empirically validated treatments." This terminology was subsequently changed to "empirically supported treatments" (ESTs). Today the term "evidence-based practice" has become the more common term to reflect a broader definition of treatment methods that have empirical support. As originally outlined by Division 12, there were two categories of ESTs: well-established and probably efficacious. The criteria for ESTs as specified in this report and later modified slightly by Chambless et al. (1998) are summarized in Table 2.2. The criteria for ESTs are based on the outcomes of efficacy studies involving randomized controlled trials (RCTs), in which participants are randomly assigned to receive either the treatment being studied or no treatment (wait-list or control group) or an alternative treatment. Treatments conducted as part of RCTs are generally manualized and tightly controlled, with trained therapists delivering the interventions, often in a university

---

TABLE 2.2. Criteria for Empirically Supported Treatments

A *well-established* treatment is one that meets the following criteria:

 I. At least two good group design experiments demonstrating efficacy in one or more of the following ways:

   A. Superior to pill or psychological placebo or to another treatment.
   B. Equivalent to an already-established treatment in experiments with adequate statistical power (about 30 per group).

or

 II. A large series of single-case design experiments ($n \geq 9$) demonstrating efficacy. These studies must have:

   A. Used good experimental designs.
   B. Compared the intervention with another treatment as in I.A.

Further criteria for both I and II:

 III. Experiments must be conducted with treatment manuals.

 IV. Characteristics of the client samples must be clearly specified.

 IV. Effects must be demonstrated by at least two different investigators or teams of investigators.

A *probably efficacious* treatment is one that meets the following criteria:

 I. Two experiments showing that the treatment is statistically significantly superior to a wait-list control group.

or

 II. One between-group design experiment with clear specification of group, use of manuals, and demonstrating efficacy by:

   A. Superior to pill or psychological placebo or to another treatment.
   B. Equivalent to an already-established treatment in experiments with adequate statistical power (about 30 per group).

or

 III. A small series of single-case design experiments ($n \geq 3$) with clear specification of group, use of manuals, good experimental designs, and comparison of the intervention with pill or psychological placebo or another treatment.

Note. From Chambless et al. (1998). Copyright 1998 by the Society of Clinical Psychology, American Psychological Association. Reprinted by permission.

or other research setting. In addition, there are often strict inclusion and exclusion criteria regarding participation in RCTs, which historically have excluded individuals with more complex presentations of a disorder. In part, because of some of these issues, there has been debate as to whether efficacy studies and the resulting conclusions drawn are the best way to obtain and summarize data on what works in everyday practice, where clinicians are not working with a carefully chosen population following a specified treatment protocol.

More recently, the American Psychological Association 2005 Presidential Task Force on Evidence-Based Practice (2006) has expanded on the traditional definition of ESTs to more broadly incorporate interventions for which there is empirical support but that do not necessarily meet the EST criteria. As defined by the task force, *evidence-based practice in psychology* (EBPP) involves "the integration of the best available research with clinical expertise in the context of patient characteristics, culture, and preferences" (p. 273). Thus, rather than rely solely on RCTs to draw conclusions regarding what works and what does not, EBPP allows for the inclusion of a variety of research evidence in making informed practice decisions. As elaborated on by Spring (2007), evidence-based clinical practice can be viewed as a three-legged stool in which each of the three components are taken into account when determining the best course of action for an individual client. These "legs" consist of the best available research evidence; the client's values, characteristics, prefer- ences, and circumstances; and clinical expertise. Clinical decision making in an evidence- based practice model involves the integration of these legs to develop the best intervention for each individual client. Outcomes obtained from RCTs and other empirical research, including systematic empirical reviews, contribute to the best available research evidence but, in this model, are not the only pieces of information to be considered when developing evidence-based treatments. Clinical expertise involves a number of factors, including the ability to form a good interpersonal relationship with the client; the ability to assess, plan, and monitor in a treatment setting; and the ability to evaluate and apply research in a clini- cal context (American Psychological Association Presidential Task Force on Evidence-Based Practice, 2006; Spring, 2007). Client values and preferences involve taking into account cli- ent preferences for one type of treatment over another, clients' ability to access certain treat- ments, and clients' basic values (including those based on, e.g., religion, race). One of the key concepts in considering patient values and preferences is making sure to attend to the client as an individual and to develop treatment plans and goals with the individual needs of the client in mind. By emphasizing the individuality of clients, practitioners get away from the "one size fits all" idea. Of course, this is not to suggest that treatments that have no empirical support should be implemented just because a client expresses preference for such a treatment. It is important to remember that each of the three aspects of EBPP must be taken into account and balanced to provide the optimal treatment for each client.

Although much of the literature on EBP has been generic to the field of psychologi- cal practice, within the field of school psychology specifically the concept of EBP has also been drawing an increased amount of attention as evidenced by special journal issues (e.g., *School Psychology Quarterly*, Vol. 17, No. 4, 2002; *School Psychology Quarterly*, Vol. 20, No. 4, 2005) on the topic of EBPs in general (as with the 2002 issue) or specific evidence- based interventions (as with the 2005 issue on evidence-based parent and family interven- tions). In addition, a Task Force on Evidence-Based Interventions in School Psychology was created in 1998. This task force is a joint effort of Division 16 (School Psychology) of the American Psychological Association and the Society for the Study of School Psychology. It is also endorsed by NASP. As stated on their website (*www.indiana.edu/~ebi*), the mission of this task force is:

- To examine and disseminate the knowledge base on what prevention and intervention programs or approaches for children, youth, and families demonstrate empirical support for application in the school and community.
- To extend the knowledge base through facilitating sound research methodologies, technologies, and innovations.

To date, the task force has developed their *Procedural and Coding Manual* (see www.indiana.edu~ebi/projects.html) (in 2003), intended to be used to assist in the process of identifying, reviewing, and coding outcome studies to create summaries of evidence-based interventions. The task force has five different domains in which task force members are working to summarize treatments:

1. Academic intervention programs
2. Comprehensive school health care
3. Family intervention programs
4. Schoolwide and classroom-based programs
5. School-based intervention programs for social–behavioral problems

Although these domains and associated committees are in place and there are overviews of what each of these domains covers, reviews of evidence-based treatments within most of these domains are not yet available. However, in a 2005 special issue of *School Psychology Quarterly*, evidence-based parent and family interventions were summarized. In a series of articles, authors reviewed the research support for parent/family interventions across a range of populations and specific treatment methods, including early childhood family-focused interventions, parent involvement interventions, parent education, parent consultation, parent training, and family–school collaboration. As summarized by Ollendick (2005), some of the conclusions that can be drawn from the 115 studies reviewed across the different articles are as follows:

1. There is greater support for interventions that are part of a multicomponent package, those that are focused, and those that involve active collaboration among schools, parents, and students.
2. There are a number of methodological shortcomings in many of the studies reviewed, suggesting the need for more rigorous studies as well as the careful consideration of methodological problems when interpreting results.
3. The most effective treatments involved behavioral or cognitive-behavioral methods such as parent training, contingency management, and home/school notes.
4. The field needs to work toward identifying who is most likely to benefit from what intervention through examining mediators and moderators of treatment.

In an earlier publication not associated with the work of the task force, Rones and Hoagwood (2000) reviewed the effectiveness of school-based mental health services. They divided their review into several categories of behavioral issues, including emotional and behavioral problems, depression, conduct problems, stress, and substance use. Within each of these categories, the authors discussed universal prevention programs (those designed to prevent emotional and behavioral problems in all students) and indicated prevention programs targeted toward students already displaying significant symptoms. Within each of these areas, the authors identified a number of studies in which effective, as well as not-so-effective, interventions had been implemented within a school setting. Across programs, the authors identified five key components that included (p. 237):

1. Consistent program implementation.
2. Inclusion of parents, teachers, or peers.
3. Use of multiple modalities.
4. Integration of program content into general classroom curricula.
5. Developmentally appropriate program components.

Many of these points are in line with the conclusions drawn by Ollendick (2005). Based on these reviews, it is clear that effective interventions can be implemented within a school context and that parents and families may play an important role in maximizing the effectiveness of interventions.

Consistent with the American Psychological Association's initial criteria for empirically supported treatments, Division 53 (Child Clinical and Adolescent Psychology) and the Network on Youth Mental Health have developed a web site, Evidence-Based Treatment for Children and Adolescents (*sccap.tamu.edu/EST*), in which evidence-based treatments for anxiety disorders, depression, ADHD, and conduct/oppositional problems are discussed. It is important to note that the treatments summarized have been mostly evaluated in non-school settings. Although more research on the adaptation of these treatments to the school setting is needed, it seems likely that these interventions can be applied (perhaps with some modifications) in school settings.

It is important to keep in mind that these summaries of evidence-based interventions are only one part (one leg) of the EBP model. Thus, when developing treatment plans, practitioners need to integrate the information from these reviews with their clinical expertise and the preferences of the students and families they serve. To assist practitioners with developing a broader knowledge of the evidence available to support different interventions for externalizing, internalizing, and academic problems, each of the chapters in this book that focus on the treatment of these problems includes a review of some of the empirical support for the different treatment methods discussed.

NEED FOR SCHOOL-BASED SERVICES

As noted earlier, it is estimated that nationwide one in every five children has a mental health disorder, and these problems can have a significant and long-lasting impact on the child, his or her family, and society as a whole. Given the negative long-term outcomes associated with many emotional and behavioral problems, there is a clear need for services. Unfortunately, only a small portion of children and adolescents who are in need of mental health services actually receive them, currently estimated at about 20%. Although there have been somewhat inconsistent findings related to race/ethnicity and utilization of mental health services, several studies have noted lower utilization rates for African American and Latino youth compared with Caucasian youth (e.g., Elster, Jarosik, VanGeest, & Fleming, 2003; Kataoka, Zhang, & Wells, 2002). Angold and colleagues (2002) found that although Caucasian children were more likely to use specialty mental health services than were African American children, there was little disparity between groups in terms of school-based services. Children who are uninsured have been also noted to have lower utilization rates than those with public or private insurance (Kataoka et al., 2002). Of children who do receive mental health services, the majority receive services within the school setting (e.g., Rones & Hoagwood, 2000).

In addition to a lack of service initiation is the problem of premature termination of services. Estimates are that 40 to 60% of children terminate therapy prematurely (Kazdin, 1996). Early dropout has been related to a variety of factors, including the initial severity of child behavior problems (those children who have greater problem behaviors are more likely to prematurely terminate services; Kazdin, 1996) as well as a poor relationship with the therapist or the perception that therapy is not helpful (Kazdin, Holland, & Crowley, 1997). Although some of these individuals who drop out of therapy may have made some improvements, by definition premature termination means that these individuals were still in need of treatment.

Although it is clear that mental health services are underutilized initially and that many youth who access services do not continue with them, it is not clear exactly what factors contribute to this underutilization. Hypothesized reasons for low service use include the lack of recognition that services are available and effective, the cost of treatment, the stigma associated with receiving mental health care, and parent dissatisfaction with services. In addition, long wait lists for specialty child services may lead to the inability of children to receive needed services, even when these other barriers are not present (U.S. Department of Health and Human Services, 1999).

With schools as a location for mental health care services, many of the barriers to mental health care can be decreased. School-based services are free of charge, and there may be less stigma associated with receiving treatment in the schools (where it may not be as obvious what types of services are being provided) than in a community mental health clinic. In addition, even if parents are not aware of the availability of mental health services, other adults who are in contact with the child (e.g., teachers) are and can play an important role in making the initial referral for services. Of course, not all barriers are eliminated when providing school-based services. Parents may still not be interested in participating (or in having their child participate) and may still be dissatisfied with the services provided. In addition, a shortage of school psychologists and other school-based professionals with specialized training is frequently a barrier to provision of services in the schools. However, given that children spend a significant portion of their day in school and that the educational system is already the service entry point for the majority of youth who receive mental health services (Farmer, Burns, Phillips, Angold, & Costello, 2003), the schools seem like a logical place to attempt to extend services so that more children who are in need of mental health supports can receive assistance.

Although school-based mental health services can certainly fill a void in service access for many children, as noted in Chapter 1, it is important to keep in mind that some children may need services beyond what can be provided in the schools. Particularly for children with more severe emotional and behavioral problems, additional services and supports, such as medications, may be necessary to promote optimal functioning. It is important for school-based mental health professionals to know when to refer and to assist parents in the referral process. Although the schools are the most common place for children to access services, at least one study suggests that children who initially access services in the schools may be less likely to access mental health services provided in other venues, including specialty mental health settings and general medical settings (Farmer et al., 2003). We recognize that in some school systems professionals may be reluctant to refer for outside services because of the wording of state laws or the concern that the school district may be held financially liable for outside services. Some of these issues were addressed in more detail in Chapter 1, and we also attempt to address these in the three treatment-focused chapters.

CHAPTER SUMMARY

Emotional, behavioral, and academic problems are commonly seen in school-age children. Unfortunately, many children who exhibit such difficulties do not receive the needed help. School-based services, for children experiencing current problems as well as those considered at risk for such problems, are a viable means of getting services to the children who need them most. Empirical support for interventions, including those delivered in a school-based context, is growing. It is important for all mental health professionals, including those providing services in the schools, to stay current with regard to EBP and ensure that the interventions being delivered are those that are most likely to have a positive effect. In addition, ongoing progress monitoring as part of working within a problem-solving model, discussed more in the following chapter, is an important part of providing services in any context.

3

Assessment of Problems

As in other settings, assessment should be an integral part of good school-based interventions. Typically, an initial assessment in a school setting includes evaluation procedures (e.g., interviews, behavior rating scales) with parents, teachers, and the referred child/adolescent. Working in the schools also makes it easier to conduct direct behavioral observations. It is common for a multimethod, multi-informant assessment to reveal differences among raters. Parents, teachers, and children often have very different perceptions of child behavior. Even when a child is observed by multiple raters in the *same context*, discrepancies are common (e.g., differences between mother and father or between teachers). This should not be taken as an indication that one is right and the others are wrong. These differences likely reflect the varied thresholds that individuals have for identifying a behavior as problematic as well as the variability in behavior as a function of context.

In addition to determining the scope and severity of a child's behavior problems, initial assessments have several purposes, including (1) developing a working relationship with parents, teachers, and children; (2) identifying and prioritizing problems to be addressed in treatment; and (3) providing a baseline measure that will serve as a reference point for determining treatment success. The importance of developing a working relationship with key parties should not be underestimated, particularly in collaborative interventions. Given that the various parties involved are likely to have somewhat different perceptions of the child's behavior, it is important to know those views before making treatment recommendations. For example, a teacher who does not identify a child's inattention as a problem may not be willing to invest time and energy in developing or implementing an intervention. However, the teacher may be more willing to participate in an intervention plan once he or she learns that the child's attention problems get in his or her way in other classes, at home, and with peers. The final "product" of an assessment is usually a feedback/intervention planning meeting, ideally with parents and teachers present (as well as the child if appropriate), and a written summary of the evaluation findings that also provides direction for treatment.

Although the traditional view of assessment is as a one-time task to identify a problem, we strongly believe that assessment should be conceptualized as an ongoing process. By evaluating the problem presence and severity throughout the course of an intervention with all involved parties (parents, teachers, children), we can know whether the intervention is having the desired effect and make any modifications needed. This approach provides a nice reference point for parents and school staff who may lose sight of how much a child has gained with treatment. It also helps prevent the continuation of an ineffective intervention over a lengthy period of time. Receiving such ongoing feedback makes it much more likely that parents and teachers will be willing to invest their time and energy in collaborative interventions.

In this chapter, we discuss each of the commonly used assessment techniques. In addition, we focus on how the use of these methods can help facilitate parent involvement in the assessment and intervention process. Before we turn to specific techniques, though, we first provide an overview of assessment from a problem-solving perspective. This model is one that we believe should guide the ongoing assessment process from the initial identification of the problem to the evaluation of whether the chosen intervention is having the desired effect.

ASSESSMENT FROM A PROBLEM-SOLVING MODEL

When using a problem-solving model, we are less interested in gathering data to justify a label (e.g., emotionally disturbed) or diagnosis (e.g., depression, ADHD) and more interested in collecting information to be used in developing the treatment. This encompasses a range of data, from determining what the problems are and why they are occurring, to the later steps of evaluating whether the intervention is having the intended impact. Although diagnoses may help inform treatment decisions (e.g., we know that there are interventions with empirical support for addressing externalizing problems, such as ADHD), they rarely lead to the selection of specific treatment methods. The problem-solving model is intended to provide a targeted assessment, linked directly to the selection of treatment methods for children with a continuum of needs. Not all children require the same level and intensity of supports. Therefore, a problem-solving approach can be used to identify the needs of individual students and to match the interventions and resources utilized to the intensity of problems that students exhibit (Tilly, 2002).

Deno (2002) defines problem solving as an "approach to intervention" in an "effort to eliminate the difference between 'what is' and 'what should be' with respect to student development" (p. 38). In other words, the assessment is intended to determine where a student is currently functioning (i.e., "what is") and where we expect the student to function (i.e., "what should be"). Expected functioning may be obtained from academic benchmarks or normative data regarding children's behaviors and social skills. As described later in this chapter, many different methods of assessment can be utilized within the problem-solving approach, including interviews, observations, rating scales, and self-report measures. These strategies can also be utilized as part of conducting a functional assessment to help determine why the problem behavior is occurring.

A variety of problem-solving models have been discussed in the literature. In general, these models address four questions:

1. What is the problem?
2. Why is the problem occurring?
3. What should be done to address the problem?
4. Did the intervention work? (Tilly, 2002).

We discuss each of these steps next. These steps and the process outlined below are also consistent with Sheridan's Conjoint Behavioral Consultation model (Sheridan & Kratochwill, 2008; Sheridan et al., 2005) discussed in Chapter 1.

What Is the Problem?

The process of identifying the problem (i.e., the discrepancy between "what is" and "what should be") generally starts with a referral from someone who has noticed that a child is not performing as expected, either academically or behaviorally. For example, a teacher might note that a child is not talking (when appropriate) during class or free time, whereas the child's peers engage in frequent verbal dialogue with each other and with the teacher. The initial referral can come from a variety of sources, including teacher, parent, child/adolescent, or other professional. Within the schools, referrals typically come from teachers but may also be initiated by parents. For example, parents might notice that their child is withdrawn, has few friends, and seems to have difficulties interacting with peers in social situations. As discussed in detail in Chapter 1, school-based clinicians aiming to build more collaborative relationships with parents may initially need to encourage parents to seek their assistance because parents may not be aware that there are professionals within the schools who can help develop interventions for emotional and behavioral problems.

When school-based professionals receive a referral, the individual who expressed the concern generally provides some information regarding the problem (e.g., "Bryan won't talk in class"), but more information is needed to clarify the specific problems to be addressed. In addition, referrals are typically initiated by one individual, a parent *or* a teacher rather than a parent *and* a teacher. To help facilitate collaboration between the key individuals in a child's life, individuals who were not part of the initial referral should be involved in the process of clarifying the nature of the problems and identifying the child's strengths. Most likely, this will occur via a variety of methods, including interviews, observations, and rating scales. In a problem-solving interview, the professional will speak with a parent and teacher to obtain information relevant to the specific behaviors of concern that prompted the referral, the settings in which these behaviors occur, and the expectations regarding appropriate behaviors/desired changes in behaviors. As noted, parents and teachers may have different points of view on some (or all) of these issues. For example, a parent may report that her child is defiant and talks back at home while the child's teacher reports that the child is friendly and compliant in school. Alternatively, a teacher may report that a child has difficulties interacting with other children on the playground while the child's parents report no problems with peer interactions. Such discrepancies in reporting are attributable to several factors. Indeed, children (and adults, for that matter) do sometimes behave very differently in different settings. This likely reflects the multiple environmental contingencies that might differ across settings (e.g., contextual cues, modeling, adult and peer reactions), each with the potential to shape and maintain a child's behavior. Adult informants will also have different thresholds for identifying a behavior as problematic. Whereas one parent or teacher might appreciate a child's outspoken and assertive nature, or at least find this behavior to be within the range of "typical" behavior, another could easily define these behaviors as disruptive or defiant. Thus, neither a parent's nor a teacher's report of a problem behavior should be discounted. Instead, the professional should explore what differences might be present that would lead to discrepant reporting; this, in turn, may help when interventions are developed. In addition to interviews, observations and rating scales may help clarify the problems of concern.

Why Is the Problem Occurring?

In determining why the problem is occurring, the goal is to develop working hypotheses about the precipitants of a behavior and what might be maintaining it. These hypotheses are generated via an examination of the information obtained during problem identification, with additional data gathered to clarify the function or purpose of the behavior. The hypothesized functions of the problem behaviors should inform decisions about the interventions that would be most likely to remediate the behaviors of concern. At this stage, it is important to realize that a child's behavior may serve different functions at home and at school or even across different contexts within the same setting. For example, problem behaviors at home may be exhibited to gain parental attention, whereas problem behaviors at school may be exhibited to escape from an aversive task.

An important question to address at this phase of the problem-solving process is whether the child's problems represent a skill deficit (the child *cannot* do the task or perform the behavior) or a performance deficit (the child has the skills but *won't* perform the task or behavior). If the child's difficulties represent a skill deficit, then the intervention will need to focus on teaching the child the specific tasks or behaviors needed. For example, a boy may not be engaging in social interactions with peers because he does not know how to perform basic social skills such as initiating a conversation, asking to join in a group activity, and so on. In such a situation, teaching of these skills would be an important first step. In another scenario, a girl may not be engaging in appropriate social interactions because she is reinforced for her inappropriate behavior (e.g., instead of asking to share a toy, she grabs the toy and then plays with it). In this case, the focus would be on changing the reinforcement the child receives so that she is reinforced for asking to share and is not allowed to play with a toy if she obtains it through grabbing.

What Should Be Done to Address the Problem?

After the problem has been clearly identified and functional hypotheses have been generated, an intervention to address the problem is developed. The intervention should be based on data obtained at the earlier stages of the problem-solving process and clearly tied to the identified functions of the behavior. The intervention should target the discrepancy identified between the problem and the desired outcome. Interventions may be implemented in just one setting (at home or at school); however, for the intervention to be maximally effective, it is often necessary to engage parents and teachers in the process. In addition, engaging parents and teachers facilitates greater home/school collaboration and makes this process the norm. Even if the problem behavior is occurring exclusively in one setting, involving parents and teachers can still be beneficial. For example, if the problem is school based (e.g., the child is not turning in homework even though it is being completed at home), the intervention might involve a system whereby the child receives reinforcement at home for turning in homework at school. Such an intervention involves communication between parents and teachers to ensure the child is receiving reinforcement as appropriate.

Did the Intervention Work?

Once an intervention has been put in place, we must determine whether it is having the desired effect: Is it changing the target behavior? Or, as examined based on our definition of problem solving, is the intervention closing the gap between "what is" and "what should be"? When attempting to answer this question, typically data collected during the problem identification phase (i.e., the baseline data) are compared with data collected during the intervention phase. Data may be displayed graphically (see Figure 3.1 for an example) to help determine whether the behavior is changing in the desired direction. If the interven-

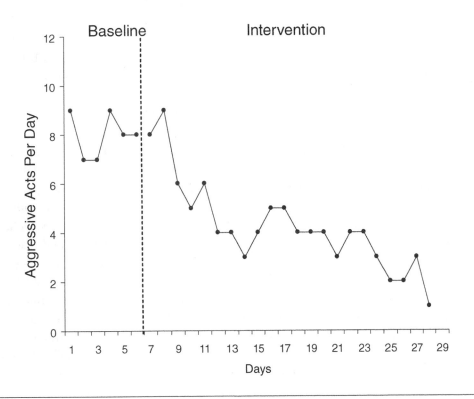

FIGURE 3.1. Graphic example of intervention results.

tion is not having the intended effect, the practitioner works to figure out why. For example, perhaps the intervention was not implemented as intended, the hypotheses regarding the functions of the behavior were incorrect, or the wrong problem was targeted. If the intervention is having the desired effect, then typically that intervention is continued and the practitioner continues to track progress over time. Again, information from both parents and teachers should be obtained to assist in determining whether an intervention is having the desired effect. Practitioners should also assess with all parties involved whether an intervention is having any unintended negative effects.

ASSESSMENT METHODS

In the following sections, we discuss some of the more common assessment methods and techniques that can be used to assist with the problem-solving process when engaging in collaborative assessment and intervention. Often one will not need to use all of these methods but should pick and choose those that are most appropriate in helping to identify the problem. In gathering assessment information, it is important to obtain information from all critical individuals, including the child's parents and teachers, as well as the child him- or herself when appropriate. This is especially true when the goal is to develop collaborative interventions across the home and school settings.

Interviews

Interviews are often conducted as a first step in the assessment process. Interviews can be helpful in gathering a variety of information in a relatively short period of time. They allow the evaluator to obtain a better understanding of the problems of concern as well as background information that may be relevant to placing the behaviors in a broader context. At the outset of an assessment, the interview will often be relatively broad, with the intent being to collect information that will provide an overall view of the child and a formulation of his or her current difficulties. Later, interviews are likely to be much more focused, such as when collecting information needed for a functional behavioral assessment. By necessity, interviews often become almost exclusively focused on problems the child is experiencing. However, it is also important to ask about the child's strengths and positive attributes and about situations in which the child functions well. Obtaining information on these behaviors enables one to highlight the positive characteristics of a child for parents and teachers—features that often get lost when the conversation focuses on problem behaviors—and to learn what serve as reinforcers for a child and in what situations he or she does well.

Regardless of who initiates the referral (parent or teacher), both should be interviewed to determine their perceptions of the problem as well as the child's strengths. Parents and teachers may be interviewed together but, in general, are interviewed separately because of both practical constraints (e.g., time, scheduling) as well as the desire to collect accurate, detailed information from each source. In addition, depending on the age of the referred child, he or she may also take part in an interview. Involving parents from the beginning in the interview process is particularly important in helping facilitate a collaborative relationship. In addition, having information from both the teacher and parents allows the professional to have a better understanding of the full range of the child's behavioral functioning. Parent and teacher interviews can be utilized to obtain background information on the child as well as information that will facilitate the problem-solving process (i.e., specific information on the behaviors of concern and the antecedents and consequences of these behaviors). In Form 3.1 (at the end of the chapter) we provide an example of a problem-solving interview that could be utilized with both parents and teachers.

Parents, teachers, and students all have relevant and often slightly different information to share in an interview. Although there are exceptions (e.g., children in foster care), parents typically have the longest track record with their child. They are likely in the best position to describe a child's developmental history, medical background, and psychosocial history (e.g., stressful life events, family constellation, and other relevant sources of support). The long-term view of a parent is informative in determining whether a given behavior represents a change in function versus an ongoing concern and provides a history of what has and has not worked for dealing with ongoing concerns. Parents also have the advantage of seeing their child in multiple settings (e.g., home, neighborhood, church), which contributes to a functional understanding of the child's behavior. An example of a parent interview that can be utilized to collect background information is presented in Form 3.2 (at the end of the chapter).

In contrast, teachers will generally have a relatively short-term perspective that is specific to the school setting (e.g., classroom, playground). However, teachers have the advantage of contact with a large sample of children who are roughly the same age as the target child (i.e., the child's classmates, previous students). This, along with their educational background, generally gives teachers a good sense of typical child development, common problems, and effective solutions. Because they see children along with their same-age peers, teachers may be more aware of a child's social functioning than parents, including, for example, who the child sits with at lunch, whether the child has friends to play with at recess, and whether he or she is among the first or last to be picked for group activities. A sample teacher interview that can be used to collect background information on a child's school functioning and behavior is presented in Form 3.3 (at the end of the chapter).

Finally, students can provide information about their own behavior that may not be readily apparent to others. For example, even fairly young children can provide subjective information about their own moods (e.g., sadness, anxiety) and motivations, which can be more difficult for parents and teachers to observe. At a minimum, children can offer information about their likes and dislikes, which will be relevant when choosing reinforcers for a behavioral intervention. As discussed by Merrell (2008), interviews with children should generally cover the following areas:

- *Intrapersonal functioning*, including information on feelings, eating/sleeping habits, understanding of reason for referral/interview.
- *Family relationships*, including information regarding relationships with parents and siblings, perceived family conflict/support, family routines.
- *Peer relationships*, including report of friendships, activities enjoyed with friends, problems experienced in social situations.

- *School adjustment*, including information on academic achievement, favored/less favored teachers and academic subjects, involvement in extracurricular activities.
- *Community involvement*, including information on involvement in community-based activities (sports, clubs, church) and relationships with others in these contexts.

McConaughy (2005) discusses child interviews in detail and provides examples of questions that may be used to obtain information related to these broad categories. Because these questions can become quite detailed and vary considerably based on the child's age, presenting problem, and responses, we have not attempted to include a standard child interview form in this chapter. We encourage readers wanting more specifics on child interviews to consult McConaughy's book.

Observations

Observations are commonly used in school settings to obtain a direct picture of the behaviors in question. Schools are an ideal place in which to conduct observations because the evaluator has access to children in their natural environment. Because observations provide direct access to a behavior (at least in terms of externalizing behaviors), they require less inference to draw conclusions regarding behaviors than do other methods of assessment. Observations can also provide valuable information regarding the context in which a problem behavior occurs, including the antecedents and consequences of a behavior. Such information can be used when conducting a functional assessment of the behavior in question, as discussed later in this chapter. Direct observation also may earn the evaluator a bit of credibility in the eyes of teachers and parents, demonstrating that the professional has taken the time to come and see a child's behavior in person. Although behavior observations can provide valuable information, they do have limitations. One drawback is that they are time consuming. Typically, an observation is conducted for 30 to 60 minutes and focuses on just a few behaviors. In addition, often more than one observation of a child is conducted to help ensure the reliability of data over time. Another limitation of observations is their relative lack of utility outside the school setting. Although potentially useful, formal home observations are less feasible, because it is generally not practical for school-based professionals to go to a child's home to observe his or her behavior and the potential for reactivity to being observed is much greater. However, observational techniques can still be used to gather data in the home setting; the nature of the observation just changes, as discussed later.

Observations can be conducted by a variety of individuals. The school psychologist (or other school-based mental health professional) is often the one to conduct more structured observations in the classroom setting. However, parents and teachers can also conduct observations of a child's behaviors. It is important to keep in mind, though, that only some observation techniques are easily used by parents and teachers, who cannot always devote their full attention to the observation process, as is required with many observational techniques. Gathering observational data from both home and school can provide useful information and provide a picture of the problems across settings.

When conducting observations, several types of recording techniques can be used. One of the most basic techniques is the *event or frequency recording* method. When using this method, the observer codes the number of times the behavior occurs during the observation period. This technique is useful for behaviors that have a discrete beginning and end and that may happen infrequently. For example, hitting behavior may occur only two or three times a day, but even at a low frequency this behavior is considered problematic. Because this method is easy to use, parents and teachers can often use this method when tracking behaviors. For example, a parent might track the number of times a child hits her brother from the time the child gets home from school until dinnertime. Likewise, the child's teacher could record the number of times a child hits his or her classmates during the school day (or a portion thereof). Form 3.4 (at the end of the chapter) is a sample log that could be used by parents or teachers to track behaviors.

Duration recording is used when there is a concern regarding how frequently the behavior occurs. When using duration recording, the observer records how long a behavior lasts. For example, the observer might code the time length of a temper tantrum. Temper tantrums that last only 5 minutes are likely of less concern to parents and teachers than those that last 45 minutes. This method is also easy to use, although, as with event/frequency recording, it is important that the behavior has a discrete beginning and end. This method may also be easily used by parents and teachers when the concern is how long a behavior is occurring.

Interval recording techniques are typically used for more structured observations and are not as easy and user-friendly as the event and duration methods. Thus, it is unlikely that parents or regular education teachers would be asked to use these methods. Instead, these would be used by the mental health professional or special education teacher. One of the most common recording techniques is *partial-interval recording*. In this method, the observation time period is divided into brief time intervals. For example, a 30-minute observation period could be divided into 60 30-second intervals. If the behavior of interest occurs at all during an interval, the observer makes a mark to indicate the behavior occurred. Typically, an observer will code several behaviors in a single observation period (e.g., out of seat, talking to peers, hitting peers). Form 3.5 (at the end of the chapter) contains a sample interval recording log. To obtain comparative information, the observer should code behaviors of several of the child's peers in addition to the target child. To do this, the observer might choose three comparison peers and rotate through them so that during each interval the observer is only coding the behavior of two children (the target child and one of the comparison peers). This makes the observation session more manageable than trying to code the behaviors of four different children at once. Behaviors can also be coded using a *whole-interval technique*. In such a method, instead of marking the behavior as occurring if it is observed at all during the interval (as with partial interval recording), the behavior is marked as having occurred if it lasts throughout the entire interval (e.g., for the entire 30 seconds). *Momentary time sampling* is another interval recording technique. When using this method, the observer notes whether the behavior occurs only at the end of the time interval (e.g., every 30 seconds).

When conducting observations, it is important to operationally define the behaviors to be recorded. For example, instead of simply coding "off-task" behavior, this behavior should be more clearly defined or broken down into several clearly definable behaviors. Off-task behavior might include talking audibly to peers, being out of one's seat, and putting one's head on the desk. When defining behaviors, it is also important for the observer to keep in mind what he or she will actually be able to observe. For example, an observer might define off-task behavior as the child "breaking eye contact with his/her seatwork." However, it is unlikely that the observer will be able to actually observe every time the child breaks eye contact with his or her work.

Rating Scales

Behavior rating scales are commonly used in school settings to obtain information on a variety of behaviors in an easy, quick format. Rating scales are typically categorized as either "broad-band" or "narrow-band" measures. Broad-band measures contain items used to evaluate a range of problem behaviors. These measures often have externalizing and internalizing composite scores as well as a number of subscale scores, each measuring a different area of problem behavior. Narrow-band measures are more focused and assess just one problem area, such as ADHD. Many rating scales have parallel parent and teacher versions that make them helpful for gathering similar information across settings and raters. Next, we discuss some of the more commonly used rating scales, although this is by no means an exhaustive list of rating scales, because an increasing number of psychometrically sound instruments are available.

Broad-Band Rating Scales

Broad-band measures can be helpful in screening for many of the common problems a child might be experiencing. However, because within each subscale or problem area items are limited, they may be less helpful in gathering in-depth information on a specific problem area.

Achenbach System of Empirically Based Assessment (ASEBA). The ASEBA includes the Child Behavior Checklist (CBCL; intended to be completed by parents) and its parallel teacher report version, the Teacher's Report Form (TRF), which are some of the most commonly used rating scales available. This system also includes a parallel self-report form, the Youth Self Report, for youth ages 11 to 18. There are preschool versions (CBCL 1½-5 and Caregiver–Teacher Report Form for children ages 1½ to 5; Achenbach & Rescorla, 2000) and school-age versions (for children 6–18; Achenbach & Rescorla, 2001) of both the parent and teacher forms of this scale. The CBCL/TRF each contains 112 problem items, which are rated on a 3-point scale. A total score as well as internalizing and externalizing composite scores are obtained. Eight main empirically derived syndrome subscale scores are provided as well as six DSM-oriented scales. The preschool versions have the same composite scores and contain six empirically derived syndrome subscale scores on the caregiver version and seven on the parent version; five DSM-oriented scales are included on both forms. Table 3.1 provides a summary of the subscales on the CBCL/TRF. The CBCL and TRF have substantial data to support their technical soundness. As reported in the CBCL/TRF manuals, reliability and validity of these measures are strong.

TABLE 3.1. Child Behavior Checklist/Teacher's Report Form Scales

School-age version	Preschool version
Composite scores	
Total score	Total score
Internalizing	Internalizing
Externalizing	Externalizing
Syndrome scales	
Anxious/Depressed	Emotionally Reactive
Withdrawn/Depressed	Anxious/Depressed
Somatic Complaints	Somatic Complaints
Social Problems	Withdrawn
Thought Problems	Attention Problems
Attention Problems	Aggressive Behavior
Rule-Breaking Behavior	Sleep Problems (parent version only)
Aggressive Behavior	
DSM-oriented scales	
Affective Problems	Affective Problems
Anxiety Problems	Anxiety Problems
Somatic Problems	Pervasive Developmental Problems
Attention Deficit/Hyperactivity Problems	Attention Deficit/Hyperactivity Problems
Oppositional Defiant Problems	Oppositional Defiant Problems
Conduct Problems	

Behavior Assessment System for Children—Second Edition (BASC-2; Reynolds & Kamphaus, 2004). The BASC-2 is another commonly used broad-band rating scale. The BASC system contains parallel parent and teacher forms as well as a self-report form that can be completed by children ages 8 to 18. The parent and teacher forms are each subdivided into forms for three age ranges: preschool (ages 2–5), children (ages 6–11), and adolescents (ages 12–21). Each form has a variety of subscale and composite scores, as outlined in Table 3.2. Psychometric properties of the BASC across raters and ages are strong and support the use of this scale in the assessment of children and adolescents.

Conners—Third Edition and Conners' Comprehensive Behavior Rating Scales (CBRS) (Conners 3; Conners, 2008a; Conners' CBRS; Conners 2008b) are recent updates of the Conners' Rating Scales—Revised (Conners, 1997), a set of broad-band measures frequently used in the schools. With these updates, the Conners 3 focuses more exclusively on symptoms associated with ADHD and the Conners' CBRS is a more comprehensive scale with a large number of subscales (see Table 3.3) including those that directly address DSM-IV

TABLE 3.2. Behavior Assessment System for Children—
Second Edition Scales

Composite scores

Externalizing
Internalizing
Adaptive Skills
School Problems (teacher child and adolescent versions only)
Behavioral Symptoms Index

Subscale scores

Hyperactivity
Aggression
Conduct Problems (child and adolescent versions only)
Anxiety
Depression
Somatization
Adaptability
Social Skills
Functional Communication
Leadership (child and adolescents versions only)
Study Skills (teacher child and adolescent versions only)
Activities of Daily Living (parent version only)
Attention Problems
Learning Problems (teacher child and adolescent versions only)
Atypicality
Withdrawal

disorders. As with the CBCL and the BASC, there are parallel parent and teacher versions of both the Conners 3 and Conners' CBRS (for ages 6–18), as well as a self-report version for ages 8–18. The manuals for these scales present extensive information on the reliability and validity of these measures.

Early Childhood Symptom Inventory–4 (ECI-4; Gadow & Sprafkin, 1997b, 2000)/ Child Symptom Inventory–4 (CSI-4; Gadow & Sprafkin, 2002)/Adolescent Symptom Inventory–4 (ASI-4; Gadow & Sprafkin, 1997a, 1998). These symptom inventories were developed to reflect DSM-IV criteria for a variety of emotional and behavioral disorders in children and adolescents, including internalizing disorders (e.g., separation anxiety disorder, social phobia), externalizing disorders (e.g., oppositional defiant disorder, conduct disorder), developmental disorders (e.g., Asperger's Disorder), and other disorders (e.g., tic disorders). The ECI-4 is designed for children ages 3 to 5, the CSI-4 for children ages 5 to 12, and the ASI-4 for adolescents ages 12 to 18. In addition, there is a self-report measure (Youth's Inventory–4) for children ages 12 to 18. Each inventory has a parent and teacher version, which can be scored based on a symptom count method or a symptom severity score. As reported by the scales' authors, the reliability and validity of these measures are adequate. Relative to the other measures reviewed here, the normative samples for these scales are relatively small (e.g., the normative sample for the CSI-4 parent form is 552 children).

TABLE 3.3. Conners' Comprehensive Behavior Rating Scales

DSM-IV-TR Symptom Scales

ADHD–Inattentive
ADHD–Hyperactive/Impulsive
Conduct Disorder
Oppositional Defiant Disorder
Major Depressive Disorder
Manic Episode

Generalized Anxiety Disorder
Separation Anxiety Disorder
Social Phobia
Obsessive–Compulsive Disorder
Autistic Disorder
Asperger's Disorder

Content Scales

Emotional Distress
Academic Difficulties
Hyperactivity/Impulsivity
Physical Symptoms

Defiant /Aggressive Behaviors
Perfectionistic and Compulsive Behaviors
Violence Potential

Validity Scales

Positive Impression   Negative Impression   Inconsistency Index

Narrow-Band Rating Scales

Narrow-band rating scales are useful in obtaining more information about a specific problem of concern. For example, there are a variety of narrow-band rating scales intended to help assess for symptoms of ADHD and other externalizing disorders. Some of the more commonly used scales are discussed next.

Attention-Deficit Disorder Evaluation Scale—Second Edition (ADDES-2; McCarney 1995a, 1995b). The ADDES-2 includes both a 46-item parent report form and a 60-item teacher report form, with normative data available for children ages 4 to 18 for the school form and ages 3 to 18 for the parent form. For each respondent version, a total score as well as two subscale scores (reflecting inattentiveness and hyperactivity–impulsivity) are obtained. Psychometric properties of these measures are strong, as reported by the scales' author.

ADHD Rating Scale–IV (DuPaul, Power, Anastopoulos, & Reid, 1998). This is an 18-item measure that contains the DSM-IV criteria for ADHD in a rating scale format. Items fall onto two factors (inattentive and hyperactive–impulsive), and a total score is also obtained. Normative data for both parent and teacher ratings for children and adolescents ages 5 to 18 have been developed. The test authors report high reliability and validity for this measure.

ADHD Symptoms Rating Scale (ADHD-SRS; Holland, Gimpel, & Merrell, 2001). The ADHD-SRS is a 56-item measure developed to help evaluate the severity of ADHD symptoms in children and adolescents ages 5 to 18. Items fall onto two factors (inattentive and hyperactive–impulsive), and a total score is also obtained. Items are rated on a 5-point frequency of behavior scale (range *behavior does not occur* to *behavior occurs one to several times an hour*). Both parents and teachers can complete the ADHD-SRS and separate norms are provided for home and school raters. Psychometric properties of the ADHD-SRS are strong as reported by the scale authors.

Eyberg Child Behavior Inventory (ECBI) and Sutter–Eyberg Student Behavior Inventory–Revised (SESBI-R; Eyberg & Pincus, 1999). The ECBI (36 items) and SESBI-R (38 items) were developed to assess the frequency and severity of problem behaviors in children ages 2 to 16. Both measures have an Intensity scale, on which respondents indicate on a 7-point scale how often the behavior occurs, as well as a Problem scale, on which respondents answer "yes" or "no" to indicate whether they view the behavior as a current problem. As reported in the manual, psychometric properties of these scales are strong, and these measures are sensitive to treatment changes.

Social Skills Improvement System (SSIS; Gresham & Elliott, 2008). The SSIS Rating Scales (an update of the Social Skills Rating System; Gresham & Elliott, 1990) were designed to assess social skills and related behaviors in the home and school setting. Separate forms for parents and teachers of children ages 3–18 are available and there is also a self-report (student) form for children ages 13–18. The SSIS Rating Scales assess social and related skills across three areas: Social Skills, Competing Problem Behaviors, and Academic Competence. Psychometric properties of the SSIS Rating Scales are strong and the rating scales can be used in conjunction with other parts of the SSIS, including an Intervention Guide (for targeted intervention) directly tied to the Rating Scale results. A Performance Screening Guide (which can be used to screen an entire class or school for social skills and related problems) and a Classwide Intervention Program (for universal intervention) are also part of the SSIS system.

School Social Behavior Scale—Second Edition (SSBS-2; Merrell, 2002b)/Home and Community Social Behavior Scales (HCSBS; Merrell, 2002a). The SSBS-2 and HCSBS were developed to assess social competence and antisocial behavior in children ages 5 to 18. The SSBS-2, intended for completion by teachers or other school personnel, contains 32 items that measure social competence and 32 items that measure antisocial behavior. Each of these composite areas has three subscale: Peer Relations, Self Management/Compliance, and Academic Behavior are the social competence scales; Hostile/Irritable, Antisocial–Aggressive, and Defiant/Disruptive are the antisocial behavior scales. The HCSBS also contains the same two composite scales (each with 32 items) but each scale has only two subscales: Peer relations and Self-Management/Compliance for the social competence scales; Defiant/Disruptive and Antisocial–Aggressive for the antisocial scales. As reported in the test manuals, both the SSBS-2 and HCSBS have strong reliability and validity.

Scales of Adaptive Behavior

Scales of adaptive behavior are commonly used when evaluatting children for possible developmental delays, including mental retardation and pervasive developmental disorders. They can be a helpful part of an assessment battery because youth with such concerns may have concomitant behavioral problems. Next we briefly discuss two commonly used measures of adaptive behavior.

Vineland Adaptive Behavior Scales—Second Edition (VABS-II; Sparrow, Cicchetti, & Balla, 2005). The VABS-II was developed to obtain information that might be helpful in the diagnosis of mental retardation and developmental delays. This system includes a survey interview form and parent/caregiver rating form for individuals ages birth to 90 and a teacher rating form for children ages 3 to 21. Domains include communication, daily living skills, socialization, and motor skills, with an optional Maladaptive Behavior Index. As reported in the manual, psychometric properties of this system are strong.

Adaptive Behavior Assessment System—Second Edition (ABAS-II; Harrison & Oakland, 2003). The ABAS-II was developed to assess adaptive functioning in individuals with suspected mental retardation or developmental delays. Various forms are available for children and adults ages birth to 89, with forms completed by parents, teachers, and the individual adolescent/adult. Composite scores are obtained for conceptual, social, and practical domains. As reported in the manual, the ABAS-II has strong psychometric properties.

Self-Report Measures

As noted, some broad-band rating scale systems have parallel self-report measures for children/adolescents to complete. In addition to these broad-band measures are a variety of narrow-band self-report instruments, many of which are intended to help assess for the presence of symptoms related to anxiety and depression. Fewer self-report measures are available to assessment externalizing constructs, because youth are often considered to be inaccurate reporters of these symptoms. Several of the commonly used narrow-band band self-report measures are discussed next.

Children's Depression Inventory (CDI; Kovacs, 1992). The CDI is a 27-item measure intended to assess the severity of depression in children ages 7 to 17. In addition to a total score, five subscale scores can be obtained: Negative Mood, Interpersonal Problems, Ineffectiveness, Anhedonia, and Negative Self Esteem. Psychometric support for the CDI is generally strong, as reported by Kovacs (1992). However, Myers and Winters (2002) note in their review article that this measure has several weaknesses, including poor discriminant validity producing a high false-negative rate and poor construct validity (perhaps measuring a more general state of distress rather than depression specifically).

Reynolds Child Depression Scale (RCDS; Reynolds, 1989)/Reynolds Adolescent Depression Scale—Second Edition (RADS-2; Reynolds, 2002). The RCDS (for children in grades 3–6; ages 8–12) and RADS-2 (for adolescents ages 11–20) are parallel forms to assess the severity of depression in children and adolescents. Each instrument consists of 30 items. Whereas the RCDS and the original version of the RADS were unidimensional, the RADS-2 contains four subscales (Dysphoric Mood, Anhedonia/Negative Affect, Negative Self-Evaluation, Somatic Complaints) in addition to a total depression score. Psychometric properties of the RCDS and RADS-2 are strong; however, more data on the discriminant validity of these measures are needed (Myers & Winters, 2002).

Multidimensional Anxiety Scale for Children (MASC; March, 1997). The MASC is a 39-item self-report measure of anxiety intended to be completed by children and adolescents ages 8 to 19. This instrument measures total anxiety as well as symptoms based on four main scale: Physical Symptoms (Tense Symptoms, Somatic Symptoms), Harm Avoidance (Perfectionism, Anxious Coping), Social Anxiety (Humiliation Fears, Performance Fears), and Separation/Panic. In addition, an Anxiety Disorders Index as well as an Inconsistency Index (to identify random or careless responding) are included. As reported in the manual, reliability and validity of this measure are strong.

Functional Behavioral Assessment

A functional behavioral assessment (FBA) involves determining the functions, or purposes, that a behavior serves. Once these functions are identified, interventions are tailored to (1) allow the child to achieve similar functions via more adaptive behavior and (2) make it less likely that the function will be served by the maladaptive behavior. In a functional assessment, the relationship between the behavior of concern and the antecedents and consequences of this behavior are examined. Within this framework, there are three potential functions of a behavior: (1) attention (including peer and adult attention as well as positive and negative attention) and access to desirable activities or objects; (2) escape or avoidance from undesirable activities; and (3) sensory stimulation (Steege & Watson, 2009). Of course, these are not mutually exclusive, and a single behavior might have multiple functions. Steege and Watson (2009) describe three types of FBA: indirect functional behavioral assessment, direct descriptive functional behavioral assessment, and functional behavioral analysis.

In indirect FBA, assessment methods such as rating scales and interviews are used to obtain information and describe the problem behaviors. This information is then used to develop hypotheses regarding the relationships between the behavior of concern and the antecedents and consequences of the behavior. Steege and Watson (2009) suggest that, because the data obtained from these indirect measures are not as reliable as data obtained from direct methods, this method not be used on its own when attempting to determine the function of a behavior. They recommend that these indirect methods be used initially as a first step when conducting FBAs and that the information obtained from these methods then be used to help guide and inform the use of direct FBA approaches.

The direct descriptive FBA takes this procedure one step further and utilizes behavioral observation methods to obtain data regarding the behaviors of concern and the associated antecedents and consequences. When utilizing this method, the observer would note (1) when the behavior occurred, (2) what was happening immediately before the behavior (antecedent), (3) what happens after the behavior (consequences), and (4) what effect the consequence had on the behavior. Form 3.6 (at the end of the chapter) is an example of a functional assessment log that could be used for such an observation. For example, Jason's mother sought help for him based on complaints from his teacher that Jason was engaging in excessive talking out in math class. When Jason was observed in his classroom, it was noted that soon after math instruction began, Jason began to shout out answers (incorrect ones) and make fun of other children who provided correct answers. The teacher provided Jason with several warnings to cease this behavior or be sent to the principal's office; these warnings produced no increase or decrease in the behavior. Eventually, Jason was sent to the principal's office, where the principal reported that Jason was well behaved. Both Jason's teacher and the principal reported that this pattern of behavior is typical, with Jason being sent to the principal's office following his persistent verbal outbursts in math class. From this observation (and the information obtained from the teacher and the principal), we might hypothesize that the function of Jason's behavior is to escape from math class. Verbal warnings had little effect on the behavior—thus, it seems unlikely the behavior is attention driven—but Jason's escape from the classroom environment appears reinforcing; he continues to behave inappropriately in math class, knowing he will be sent to the principal's office.

FBA procedures can be used to confirm the relationships noted in the first two types of FBA. When conducting a functional analysis, the professional both manipulates and observes the behavior of concern in an attempt to empirically test the function of a behavior. Because this method can be quite time intensive and often involves attempting to elicit a problem behavior (e.g., providing attention for acting-out behaviors to empirically test whether attention is maintaining this behavior), FBA is not used very often in regular education settings. Instead, a combination of the first two types of functional assessment methods is generally used.

It is important to conduct a functional assessment of the problem behaviors both at school and at home when developing cross-setting interventions; as noted earlier, the function of the behavior may vary across settings. Once the function of a behavior is determined, the mental health professional can design an intervention that specifically targets this function. For example, with Jason, the intervention might involve preventing Jason from escaping math class for his verbal outbursts. Instead, Jason would be required to stay in class and may receive an in-class consequence and/or a consequence at home (positive or negative depending on his behavior). In addition, in the classroom, Jason might be allowed to "escape" and engage in a more enjoyable activity after he has completed a certain number of math problems if no verbal outbursts occurred during math class (e.g., visiting the principal after math class is completed). Functional assessment can be invaluable in ensuring that the correct purpose of the behavior is targeted and that the designed intervention does not inadvertently increase the problematic behavior (e.g., sending a child to the principal's office when escape is the identified function of the behavior).

Curriculum-Based Assessment Methods

As discussed later in Chapter 6, academic problems, including issues related to homework completion, are common concerns and can be an important area to target for intervention. Although there are numerous ways to assess academic problems, the method that fits best with the problem-solving model is curriculum-based assessment (CBA). CBA methods involve test strategies that are tied to a student's curriculum. Curriculum-based measurement (CBM) is a type of CBA that uses specific tasks to assess student performance in reading, spelling, math, and written expression (Shinn, 2002). As outlined by Shinn, the following are tasks typically used within a CBM framework:

- *Reading:* Have the child read aloud from a passage for 1 minute. The number of words read correcting during this time is the summary variable used.
- *Math:* Students complete math work sheets over a 2- to 5-minute period. The number of digits correct is calculated.
- *Written language:* Students are provided with a story starter and asked to write for 3 minutes. The number of words written, words spelled correctly, and/or word sequences are calculated.
- *Spelling:* Students write words as dictated for 2 minutes. The number of correct letter sequences and words spelled correctly are counted.

All of these tasks are brief measures of fluency that are sensitive to change and can be administered repeatedly to help assess change in a student's academic performance.

One specific system of CBA that is widely used within the schools is DIBELS (Dynamic Indicators of Basic Early Literacy Skills). This system was developed by researchers at the University of Oregon to assess several of the "big ideas" in basic literacy skills. As outlined on the DIBELS official homepage (*dibels.uoregon.edu*), these include:

- Phonological awareness.
- Alphabetic principle.
- Fluency with connected text.

Within each of these areas, measures of academic progress have been developed and validated. These include:

- *Initial sounds fluency:* a measure of phonological awareness in which the child is shown four pictures and is asked to point to the picture of the word that begins with a certain letter.
- *Phoneme segmentation fluency:* a measure of phonological awareness in which the child is asked to verbalize the individual phonemes in words of three to four phonemes that are presented orally.
- *Nonsense word fluency:* a measure of alphabetic principle in which the child is shown a nonsense word on a piece of paper and asked to say the word or the individual letter sounds of the word.
- *Oral reading fluency:* a measure of accuracy and fluency with connected text in which the child is asked to read aloud for 1 minute from a passage.
- *Retell fluency:* a measure of comprehension that is meant to supplement the oral reading fluency measure and provide a check on how much the child comprehends.
- *Letter naming fluency:* a measure that provides an assessment of risk in which students are asked to identify randomly presented letters.

The DIBELS system provides benchmark goals and indicators of risk for children in kindergarten through third grade and estimated benchmark goals and indicators of risk for students in grades 4 through 6. Children who are determined to be at risk for reading difficulties would be targeted for intervention to improve their skills. The DIBELS web site contains probes that can be used as well as benchmark/risk indicators that can be used for comparison purposes.

Norm-Referenced Academic Achievement Measures

Although CBA methods fit best within a problem-solving model, especially when assessment is considered an ongoing process to determine not only whether there is a problem but also whether an intervention is working, norm-referenced assessments of achievement are still commonly used in school settings. These include broad measures of academic achievement, such as the Woodcock-Johnson III—Tests of Achievement (Woodcock, McGrew, & Mather, 2001) and the Wechsler Individualize Achievement Test–Second Edition (Wechsler, 2001), as well as more specialized measures such as the Comprehensive Test of Phonological Processing (Wagner, Torgesen, & Rashotte, 1999), the Test of Written Language–Third Edition (Hammill & Larsen, 1996), and the KeyMath Test–Revised (Connolly, 1988). These measures are often used in education assessments to evaluate students' strengths and weaknesses, to determine whether they may have a learning disability, and to evaluate whether students qualify for additional service (e.g., special education, gifted programming). Norm-referenced measures have the advantage of a large and heterogeneous normative sample and rigorous psychometric testing (often representing several years of test development) to establish reliability and validity.

Recently, the reliance on norm-referenced measures for making educational placement decisions has been criticized (e.g., Fletcher, Francis, Morris, & Lyon, 2005) Although a detailed review of these issues is beyond the scope of this book, a few points warrant mention as they relate to collaborative home/school interventions. One concern is simply that norm-referenced measures do not reliably and validly indicate which children have learning problems. In addition, norm-referenced tests typically lack sensitivity to treatment effects and are, therefore, not particularly useful for monitoring students' response to intervention. By necessity, norm-referenced measures tap a variety of skills to ensure adequate breadth. However, this means that they are less able to evaluate specific skills that are the focus of intervention. This may give the appearance that students are not making progress, despite significant gains in fundamental skills. This can be a source of frustration for parents and teachers alike and can mask the effectiveness of intervention.

Given these strengths and weaknesses, norm-referenced tests are thought to be most useful for initial screening, when a broad assessment is needed to establish a child's skills in a range of educational domains. In monitoring response to intervention and schoolwide gains, CBM methods are more likely to provide a sensitive indicator. These measures have the additional advantage of being easily understandable for most parents. It is much easier for most parents to see that their child went from reading 10 grade-appropriate words in 1 minute to reading 20 words than to interpret a change in standard scores or percentiles.

CHAPTER SUMMARY

Assessment is an important part of developing interventions. By obtaining a thorough and clear understanding of the problem behaviors a child is exhibiting and the function that these behaviors might serve, the school-based mental health professional will be in a better position to develop interventions that are most likely to lead to a reduction in the discrepancy between "what is" and "what should be." In addition, the clinician can utilize the assessment process to bring parents, students, and teachers together to form a collaborative relationship. This relationship should help facilitate the implementation of the most effective interventions. We strongly recommend that in conducting assessments school-based clinicians follow a problem-solving model so that assessment informs not only the identification of the problem but also the development of a treatment plan and the ongoing evaluation of this treatment plan. By utilizing assessment in this manner, clinicians are likely to make good use of their assessment time and obtain data that are meaningful in addressing the problem behaviors that children exhibit.

FORM 3.1

Problem-Solving Interview

Describe the behaviors of concern.

How long have these behaviors been occurring?

What behavior(s) would you like to see in place of these problem behaviors?

In what setting(s) do the problem behaviors typically occur?

In what setting(s) are the problems behaviors typically not present?

Who is present when the problem behaviors occur?

(cont.)

What typically immediately precipitates the problem behaviors?

What is your response to the problem behaviors? What effect does this have on the behaviors?

What are others' responses to the problem behaviors? What effects do these have on the behaviors?

What have you tried that has worked to decrease the problem behavior and/or increase appropriate behaviors?

What have you tried that has not worked?

Parent Interview Form

General Background

Child's name: _____

Age: _____ Birth date: _____ Sex: _____ Grade: _____

Who is currently living at home with the child?

    Mother: _____   Natural   Foster   Step   Adoptive

    Father: _____   Natural   Foster   Step   Adoptive

    Other children:

Name	Age	Sex	Relationship to child

    Other adults:

Name	Relationship to child

Parents' marital status: _____

If separated: Name of other parent: _____

                 Involvement with child: _____

Who referred you? _____

Who is your child's primary care provider/pediatrician? _____

Presenting Problems

What are the primary problems your child is having? _____

_____

_____

_____

When did these problems begin? _____

    If the problems have changed over time, please describe changes and general time
    frames for changes: _____

_____

How often are these problems occurring? _____

Describe the impact these problem behaviors have on your family: _____

_____

(cont.)

Family Background

Home schedule of:

Mother_____

Father_____

Typical school day for child:

_____

_____

_____

What time does your child typically go to bed? _____ And actually fall asleep?_____

What time does you child typically wake up?_____

Has your child or family experienced any recent stressful events (e.g., deaths in the family, relocation) or ongoing stressors (e.g., financial problems)?   Yes_____   No_____

If yes, please describe: _____

_____

Are there any psychiatric conditions that run in the family (e.g., depression, ADHD)?

Yes_____   No_____

If yes, please describe: _____

Child Developmental, Medical, and Mental Health History

Were there complications during your pregnancy or delivery of your child? Yes___   No_____

If yes, please describe: _____

_____

Was your child delayed in reaching developmental milestones (e.g., talking)? Yes_____   No____

If yes, please describe: _____

_____

Does your child have any current health problems?   Yes_____   No_____

If yes, please describe: _____

_____

Is your child currently on any medications?   Yes_____   No_____

If yes:

Medication	When prescribed	Who prescribed	Effect
_____	_____	_____	_____
_____	_____	_____	_____
_____	_____	_____	_____

List any prescription medications your child has been on in the past: _____

_____

Has your child had any hospitalizations, emergency room visits, or significant illnesses?

Yes_____   No_____

If yes, describe:_____

(cont.)

60

Has your child ever received mental health services?   Yes_____   No_____

    If yes, describe (include when received, length of therapy, name of provider, and perceived helpfulness of services):_____

_____

Academic and Social History

Current school:_____   Teacher:_____

Past schools attended: _____

Teacher reports of academic progress:_____

Is your child receiving special education services?   Yes_____   No_____

    If yes, please describe: _____

Does your child receive any other type of special help in school?   Yes_____   No_____

    If yes, please describe: _____

Does your child have behavioral problems in school?   Yes_____   No_____

    If yes, please describe: _____

_____

Describe your child's relationships with his/her peers: _____

Assessment of Behavior Management

Who ordinarily disciplines your child? _____

How is your child disciplined? _____

_____

How often is your child disciplined? _____

What type of discipline is most effective? _____

_____

What has been tried that has not worked? _____

_____

Do parents agree on discipline? _____

Current Concerns/Positives

What are your top three concerns at this time?

_____

_____

_____

Name three things you think your child does well.

_____

_____

_____

FORM 3.3

Teacher Interview Form

Child's name: _____

Teacher's name: _____

School: _____ Grade: _____

What are your primary concerns regarding this child? _____

_____

_____

_____

How long have you noticed these problems? _____

    If the problems have changed over time, please describe changes and general time
frames for changes: _____

_____

How often are these problems occurring? _____

What have you tried that has helped with these problems? _____

_____

_____

What have you tried that has not helped? _____

_____

_____

Is this child currently on any medications? Yes_____ No_____ Don't know_____

    If yes, what, if any, effects (positive or negative) do you attribute to the medication?_____

_____

How is this child progressing academically? Describe any difficulties the child is having, favorite/
less favorite subjects, etc.: _____

_____

_____

Is this child receiving special education services? Yes_____ No_____

    If yes, please describe: _____

(cont.)

Does this child receive any other type of special help in school?   Yes_____   No_____

If yes, please describe: _____

Does this child have attendance problems?   Yes_____   No_____

If yes, please describe: _____

Describe this child's relationships with his/her peers, including how he/she interacts with peers in classroom, on playground, etc.:_____

_____

What activities does this child enjoying doing at school?_____

_____

What does this child do well?

_____

_____

_____

Behavior Observation Log

Day	Time	Behavior 1 _____	Behavior 2 _____	Behavior 3 _____
Example: Monday	**Example:** 10–11 A.M.	**Example:** III	**Example:** I	**Example:** IIIIII

FORM 3.5

Interval Recording Log

Behavior 1—Out of Seat: Child's buttocks lose contact with seat of his/her chair.

Behavior 2—Talking to Others: Child engages in audible conversation with peers.

Behavior 3—Physical Aggression: Child hits, kicks, or otherwise physically attacks others.

Interval	Target Child			Comparison Peer		
	Behavior 1	Behavior 2	Behavior 3	Behavior 1	Behavior 2	Behavior 3
1a						
1b						
2a						
2b						
3a						
3b						
4a						
4b						
5a						
5b						
6a						
6b						
7a						
7b						
8a						
8b						
9a						
9b						
10a						
10b						
11a						
11b						
12a						
12b						
13a						
13b						
14a						
14b						
15a						
15b						

Functional Assessment Log

Setting of behavior	Antecedent (What happened immediately before the behavior?)	Behavior (Description of behavior)	Consequence (What happened immediately after the behavior?)	Outcome (What happened following the consequences?)

4

Interventions for
Externalizing Problems

Some of the most common problems for which school-age children are referred to mental health professionals are those that involve externalizing, or acting-out, behaviors. These problems include aggression, noncompliance with rules and instructions, off-task behavior, inattention and hyperactivity, and defiance. Teachers often make referrals for children exhibiting such behaviors after observing these problems in their classrooms. Parents may notice these behaviors at home, but initially opt to seek assistance from their child's pediatrician or other health care provider rather than a school-based professional. As noted in Chapter 3, determining whether a child's behavior problems are exhibited across settings is considered an important first step. This is particularly relevant to externalizing problems because for some (e.g., ADHD), presence across settings is a diagnostic requirement. For other behaviors (e.g., aggression), manifestation across settings is an important indicator of severity. From a treatment perspective, abundant data show that intervening in just one setting (e.g., only in the home) may produce improvements in the child's behavior in that context, but generalization to other settings is limited if these settings are not specifically targeted (e.g., Drugli & Larsson, 2006; Webster-Stratton, Reid, & Hammond, 2004). Even when behavior problems are restricted to one setting, it can be beneficial to have both parents and teachers involved in an intervention (e.g., as with home/school notes discussed later in this chapter).

Although school-based mental health professionals have not historically involved parents extensively when developing treatment plans for children with externalizing problems, we believe that they are in an ideal position to reach out to parents and assist them with difficulties they may be encountering at home and involve them in the intervention process. In this chapter we begin by reviewing some of the evidence-based treatments for externalizing problems and then outline several treatment methods that could be implemented by school-based clinicians in collaboration with parents. Most of these treatments are short term in nature, making them well suited to implementation by school-based clinicians, who often have limited time to conduct interventions. We conclude this chapter with a discussion of

TABLE 4.1. Interventions for Externalizing Problems

Intervention	Description	Developmental level
Behavioral parent training	An intervention in which the clinician works with parents to address problematic behaviors. Parents are taught to use positive reinforcement to increase prosocial behaviors and discipline, such as time-out, to decrease problematic behaviors. Can be delivered in an individual or a group format.	Typically used with preschool and elementary school-age children. Adaptations can be made to use similar methods with older children, though research with this age group is limited.
Collaborative problem solving	Clinician works with parent and child together to resolve issues in a collaborative manner. Focus is on helping parents identify antecedents of "explosive" behaviors and collaboratively work to find ways to address problem.	All ages, though less applicable for very young children or those with limited verbal skills.
Home/school contingencies	The clinician works with parents, teachers, and child to identify problem behaviors within the school setting, develop a tracking method for these behaviors, and identify contingencies that parents can use at home based on school behavior. The home/school note system is a specific example of this type of intervention.	All ages; although most research is with elementary school-age children.
Problem-solving skills training	Children are taught to apply cognitive problem-solving skills to difficult situations that often lead to inappropriate behaviors. Parents are less directly involved but can help children learn to apply to problem-solving steps.	Typically used with children ≥ 8 years; however, some programs for preschool-age children.

consulting with non-school-based professionals to help families receive the comprehensive, integrated services they may need to address their difficulties. Table 4.1 summarizes the techniques covered in this chapter.

Case Vignette

Julie is a 9-year-old Caucasian girl who resides with her mother, father, and two younger siblings. Julie was diagnosed with ADHD when she was 6 and began taking Adderall to manage her symptoms. Although she has shown some improvement in her behavior (e.g., improved concentration, reduced hyperactivity), Julie still experiences some difficulties both at home and at school. Defiant behaviors are a key area of concern. She frequently refuses to complete her chores and other household tasks when asked. The morning routine is particularly difficult, and her mother has become very frustrated with the amount of time it takes Julie to get ready for school. When her mother asks her to complete a task, Julie often responds with statements such as "No! I won't do it and you can't make me!" Although Julie's mother uses some reasonable and age-appropriate discipline techniques (e.g., time-out, removal of privileges), she acknowledges that these are not used consistently. At school Julie's teachers report similar problems. Although Julie is not as openly defiant in the classroom, she often does not follow through with instructions until they are repeated numerous times. In addition, both at home and in school, Julie is very talkative, often interrupting and talking over others, and occasionally verbally mocking her mother, teacher, and peers. This has caused frustration for her parents and teachers and has led other children to avoid interacting with Julie.

EVIDENCE-BASED INTERVENTIONS FOR EXTERNALIZING PROBLEMS

Interventions for externalizing behavior problems (often referred to as "conduct problems" in the literature), such as those exhibited by Julie, have received more research attention than interventions for most other childhood emotional and behavior disorders. There are several excellent reviews of this literature (Eyberg, Nelson, & Boggs, 2008; Weisz, Hawley, & Doss, 2004). In general, research supports the use of behaviorally based interventions for externalizing disorders, both in home and school settings. These include a variety of behavioral parent training programs (e.g., parent–child interaction therapy: Brinkmeyer & Eyberg, 2003; the Incredible Years: Webster-Stratton & Reid, 2003a; Oregon parent management training: Forgatch, Bullock, & Patterson, 2004), other family-based interventions (e.g., multisystemic therapy: Henggeler & Lee, 2003), and group and individual interventions for children and adolescents (e.g., problem-solving skills training: Kazdin, 2003). In addition, school-based interventions, including contingency management programs and academic interventions, have been demonstrated to have positive effects for children with externalizing problems (e.g., DuPaul & Eckert, 1997). In addition to empirical support for psychosocial interventions, there is also support for the use of stimulant medications to treat ADHD (e.g., MTA Cooperative Group, 1999) and some evidence supporting the use of psychiatric medications to treat related conduct problems (Collett, Scott, Rockhill, Speltz, & McClellan, 2008). In this section, we review the empirical support for these interventions. In the following sections, we provide more details on interventions for externalizing problems that can be implemented in collaboration with parents.

Behavioral Parent Training

There is an extensive literature base supporting the use of behavioral parent training for conduct problems in the home. Several behavioral parent training models have been developed and tested with a broad range of child and parent participants. Parent training has been evaluated in children with specific DSM-IV diagnoses (e.g., ODD, ADHD), those with broadly defined conduct problems, and those considered to be "at risk" for developing conduct problems based on demographic or other risk factors (e.g., low socioeconomic status).

In a meta-analysis of studies examining the effects of behavioral parent training, Maughan, Christiansen, Jenson, Olympia, and Clark (2005) concluded that behavioral parent training was effective in reducing behavior problems in children, with effect sizes in the small to moderate range (i.e., weighted effect sizes of 0.30 for between-subjects designs, 0.68 for within-subject designs, and 0.54 for single-subject designs). In an earlier meta-analysis, Serketich and Dumas (1996) also found support for the effectiveness of parent training in reducing problematic child behaviors, with a large overall effect size ($d = 0.86$). In both of these reviews, the authors found that outcome varied as a function of both methodological and participant variables. For example, Maughan et al. found that effect sizes were smaller in studies using random assignment, although Serketich and Dumas did not find a significant relationship between random assignment and effect sizes. In both studies, the age of participants was related to effect sizes. Serketich and Dumas reported a significant relationship ($r = .69$) between effect sizes and child age, indicating that parent training was more effective with older children (although the average age of children in the studies included in their meta-analysis was just over 6 years). Maughan et al. also found differences related to age, although with a slightly different trend. They found smaller effect sizes for children ages 6 to 8 compared with those ages 3 to 5 and 9 to 11 in between- and within-group studies. Although further research is needed to sort out the variables that moderate and mediate outcome, these meta-analyses provide clear support for parent training as an effective intervention in reducing externalizing behaviors in children.

A few of the more popular evidence-based parent training programs include Webster-Stratton's Incredible Years (Webster-Stratton & Reid, 2003a) and Eyberg's parent–child interaction therapy (PCIT; Brinkmeyer & Eyberg, 2003). These two programs as well as the Triple P—Positive Parenting Program (Sanders, 1999), which takes a tiered prevention/intervention approach, are briefly reviewed next.

Webster-Stratton's Incredible Years is a multicomponent program that includes a group parent training component, an individual child-focused component, and a teacher consultation component. The parent training portion of this program is a videotape-based program aimed at parents of young children. The parent training program consists of two components: BASIC and ADVANCE. In the BASIC component, parents take part in 13 to 14 2-hour weekly group sessions. Parents are first taught to increase their positive attention to their children through use of child-directed play, praise statements, and incentive programs. Discipline, including ignoring, time-out, and logical and natural consequences, is then covered. Throughout the training, videotape-based models are used to illustrate the concepts being covered. The ADVANCE portion of the program covers more parent-specific skills, including personal self-control, communication skills, problem-solving skills, and strengthening social support and self-care (Webster-Stratton & Reid, 2003a). Webster-Stratton and her colleagues have conducted numerous studies on this program. These results support the effectiveness of the Incredible Years program in reducing behavior problems in children and increasing the use of effective discipline skills in parents both immediately after treatment and for up to a year posttreatment (e.g., Webster-Stratton, 1998; Webster-Stratton et al., 2004).

PCIT is an individually based parent training program aimed at parents of young children. In this program, parents are first taught to use a child-directed interaction, in which parents use play skills to implement positive attending and communication skills, including praise, reflection, imitation, description, and enthusiasm. Following mastery of these skills, parents are then instructed on the use of parent-directed interaction skills. These include the use of clear, effective commands and a time-out procedure (Brinkmeyer & Eyberg, 2003). There have been a number of studies published on the effectiveness of PCIT. Following participation in this program, parents have reported a decrease in child behavior problems as well as parenting stress. Parents have also been observed to interact more positively with their children (Schuhmann, Foote, Eybert, Boggs, & Algina, 1998). Outcomes of PCIT have been noted to maintain over time for many families, even over the course of 3 to 6 years (Hood & Eyberg, 2003). Researchers have also noted improvements in children's behaviors following the use of an abbreviated form of PCIT, in which parents attend five in-person sessions alternated with five phone consultations (Nixon, Sweeney, Erickson, & Touyz, 2003).

The Triple P—Positive Parenting Program is a comprehensive parenting program that is aimed at prevention of behavior problems (Sanders, 1999). The program incorporates five different levels of prevention/intervention and is geared toward parents of children from birth to age 12. The first level, Universal Triple P, is an informational level geared at all parents. Information regarding parenting is shared through media outlets, tips sheets, and so on. At the second level, Selective Triple P, parents are provided with one to two sessions, typically in a primary care setting, involving "anticipatory developmental guidance" for children who are considered to be at risk for behavior problems. At the third level, Primary Care Triple P, a four-session intervention, is implemented for parents whose children have mild behavior problems. At this level, parents are provided with information as well as specific intervention strategies to address the problems of concern. The fourth level, Standard Triple P/Group Triple P/Self-Directed Triple P, involves an eight- to 10-session parent training program for parents who are considered to have children who have specific problems but do not meet diagnostic criteria for a behavior disorder. Specific parenting skills such as attending to positive behaviors and the use of time-out to decrease inappropriate behaviors are covered. This program can be covered in an individual, group, or self-directed (using a parenting workbook) format. The fifth level, Enhanced Triple P, offers support to families in which the parents are experiencing additional difficulties (e.g., marital problems, depression). As reviewed by Sanders (1999), there have been a number of studies that support the efficacy and effectiveness of the Triple P program, particularly the Level 3 parenting program. For example, Sanders, Markie-Dadds, Tully, and Bor (2000) compared the enhanced, standard, and self-directed behavioral family interventions to a wait-list control group. Positive results were obtained for both the enhanced and standard programs. Although there were some positive outcomes for families in the self-directed program, the results for this component were more mixed, especially immediately postintervention. An evaluation of the Primary Care Triple P program (Turner & Sanders, 2006) also demonstrated positive effects immediately postintervention and at a 6-month follow-up.

Other Family-Focused Interventions

Collaborative problem solving (CPS; Greene & Ablon, 2006) is a newer intervention program that also has a focus on working with parents and has received some empirical support. Although CPS shares with parent training the focus on involving parents in the intervention process, the focus in CPS is helping parents and children jointly solve problems rather than helping parents apply behavioral contingencies to better manage the child's behavior. In support of CPS, Greene et al. (2004) conducted a study with 47 children between the ages of 4 and 12 who had a current diagnosis of ODD and symptoms of either bipolar disorder or major depression. Children and their parents were randomly assigned to either receive behavioral parent training or CPS. Significant decreases in oppositional symptoms were noted at the end of treatment and at a 4-month follow-up for all children, with effect sizes somewhat larger for children in the CPS group. Thus, this study supports the use of CPS. However, to date this is the only published study on this intervention method. Although more data are needed to help clarify the effects of CPS, this intervention seems promising and involves parents as key individuals in addressing the problems children are exhibiting, making it well suited for implementation by school-based mental health professionals.

Multisystemic therapy (MST; Henggeler & Lee, 2003) is another evidence-based intervention for externalizing problems. MST is geared toward children who engage in "severe and willful misconduct," including juvenile offenders and those with serious psychiatric problems. MST utilizes an intensive family systems approach to treatment in which the focus of therapy is on how systems (including the home, school, and community) affect each other, the identified client, and his or her family. The delivery of MST involves a variety of interventions used as needed, including family interventions, peer interventions, school interventions, individual interventions, medications, and family social support. MST therapists have a very low caseload (four to five families at one time) and are very involved with the families they serve; in fact, they are continuously available to provide services. There is considerable support for this intervention method, with studies demonstrating decreases in substance use, decreases in rates of rearrest, decreases in externalizing problems, and improvement in family functioning (Henggeler & Lee, 2003). Given the time-intensive nature of this therapy, it is not feasible for school-based mental health professionals to implement this intervention. However, because of the focus of MST on all systems in which an adolescent is involved, it may be helpful for school-based mental health professionals to have some basic knowledge of this intervention in case they work with MST therapists in providing school-based interventions for youth.

Child-Focused Interventions

In addition to interventions that focus on working collaboratively with parents to address children's conduct problems, there are a variety of other interventions for conduct problem that have empirical support but do not focus primarily on working with parents. Problem-solving skills training (PSST) is one of these interventions. In this intervention, the therapist works with the child individually to help the child apply cognitive problem-solving steps to interpersonal situations (Kazdin, 2003). Although parents are not the focus of this type of treatment, they are still involved via periodic joint sessions to learn how to help facilitate the child's use of the problem-solving steps, mainly through praise. In addition, PSST is often combined with behavioral parent training (Kazdin, 2003). Kazdin and his colleagues have conducted several randomized controlled trials (RCTs) using PSST. In two studies, PSST was compared with a relationship-based therapy. In both studies, PSST led to greater reductions in problem behaviors at home and at school and an increase in prosocial behaviors compared with the relationship-based therapy (Kazdin, Bass, Siegel, & Thomas, 1989; Kazdin, Esveldt-Dawson, French, & Unis, 1987b). These results were noted immediately after treatment and maintained at a 1-year follow-up. Other studies have evaluated the efficacy of PSST in combination with behavioral parent training. Kazdin, Esveldt-Dawson, French, and Unis (1987a) noted that the combination of PSST and parent training resulted in fewer behavior problems at posttreatment than a contact control condition in a sample of children receiving inpatient psychiatric services. In a study comparing PSST alone, parent training alone, and the combination of these treatments, all treatments led to reductions in behavior problems at posttreatment, but children in the combined group demonstrated the greatest changes at posttreatment and at a 1-year follow-up (Kazdin, Siegel, & Bass, 1992). More recently, Kazdin and Whitley (2003) explored the addition of a parent problem-solving model to PSST and parent training. Although children in both groups (with and without the parent problem-solving component) improved, the problem-solving component increased treatment efficacy.

Another child-focused treatment program is the Dinosaur School, developed by Webster-Stratton and colleagues as part of the Incredible Years program. As with the parent training component of the Incredible Years program, the Dinosaur School makes use of videotaped vignettes that are used in group settings to address the social, emotional, and cognitive deficits that young children with conduct disorders exhibit. Areas covered include emotional literacy, friendship skills, and problem solving (Webster-Stratton & Reid, 2003b). RCTs of this program have provided support for the use of this program with children ages 4 to 8. For example, in a study comparing parent training only, child training only, parent training plus child training, and a wait-list control group, children in all three treatment groups improved. Children who received the training demonstrated more improvement on measures of problem solving and conflict management than those who did not participate in the child training component. Parents who received parent training rated their children as having fewer behavior problems and interacted more positively with their children than those parents who did not receive parent training. These results were maintained at a 1-year follow-up, with children in the combined condition having the most significant improvements in behavior (Webster-Stratton & Hammond, 1997). Although improvements were noted by parents and children, teachers did not report improvements in behaviors. Thus, Webster-Stratton and colleagues (Webster-Stratton et al., 2004) conducted an evaluation of these treatment components with an added teacher training component. Families were randomly assigned to one of six conditions: parent training only; parent training plus teacher training; child training only; child training plus teacher training; parent, child, and teacher training combined; and a wait-list control group. In the teacher training component, teachers received 4 days of group training covering classroom management, promotion of positive relationships, and strengthening of social skills. Two school-based consultations for each child were also provided. In comparison to the control group, improvements on the majority of parenting measures were noted for all groups receiving parent training. Improvements on child measures (conduct problems, social competence with peers) were noted for most treatment groups. However, child social competence with peers improved only for those children who took part in the child training group. Improvements on the teacher measure (negative classroom management) were noted in all groups except the parent training only group. Results were maintained at a 1-year follow-up. The authors note that as a single treatment parent training had the most positive effects; however, the domains of functioning were impacted differently by the various treatments.

Classroom-Based Interventions

Classroom-based interventions have also been found to be effective in remediating externalizing problems in the school setting. DuPaul and Eckert (1997) conducted a meta-analysis of school-based interventions for ADHD. Studies were classified in one of three intervention categories: academic intervention, contingency management, and cognitive-behavioral. Overall, their findings indicate that school-based interventions are effective, with contingency management and academic interventions being more effective than cognitive-behavioral strategies in improving children's classroom behavior.

Stage and Quiroz (1997) conducted a meta-analysis of interventions to decrease disruptive classroom behaviors. They evaluated a variety of behaviorally based classroom interventions as well as other interventions (e.g., parent training, individual counseling). Results indicated a moderate overall effect size ($d = 0.78$). Effect sizes for specific behaviorally based classroom interventions ranged from moderate (e.g., $d = .53$ for response cost) to large (e.g., $d = 0.90$ for token economies, $d = 0.95$ for differential reinforcement). Overall, the results support the use of some of the most commonly used classroom behavioral management techniques.

As noted, Webster-Stratton and her colleagues (Webster-Stratton et al., 2004) have evaluated a school-based intervention as part of their Incredible Years program, with positive effects noted in the school setting with the addition of a teacher training component.

Psychiatric Medication

Medications may also benefit children who present with externalizing problems. In particular, children with ADHD may benefit from stimulant medications (e.g., Ritalin, Concerta, Adderall). The Multimodal Treatment Study of ADHD (MTA) is one the largest randomized controlled studies conducted to date on the effectiveness of medication for ADHD. Results from this study indicated that, in treating the core symptoms of ADHD, stimulant medications or a combination of stimulant medications and behavioral interventions were more effective than behavioral interventions alone or standard community care (MTA Cooperative Group, 1999). Although there is significant evidence to support the effectiveness of medications for children with ADHD, there are fewer studies on the use of medication with children with conduct problems who do not have ADHD (Collett et al., 2008). There is some evidence suggesting that stimulant medications may also be effective in reducing symptoms associated with conduct problems, even in the absence of a formal diagnosis of ADHD (e.g., Pappadopulos et al., 2006). Other medications, including clonidine and risperidone, have also been used in the treatment of conduct problems (often in association with comorbid disorders such as ADHD), with a handful of studies supporting the effectiveness of these medication treatments (e.g., Connor, Barkley, & Davis, 2000; Reyes, Buitelaar, Toren, Augustyns, & Eerdekens, 2006; Snyder et al., 2002).

Summary of Interventions for Externalizing Problems

In summary, a number of interventions for externalizing problems have garnered significant empirical support in the research literature. The psychosocial treatments for externalizing problems share a variety of common elements, including

- A social learning orientation/format, including modeling of skills in session, role plays or practice with feedback in session, and "homework" assignments to practice skills outside of session.
- A focus on changing environmental contingencies in place, often through a focus on creating changes in adults behaviors (e.g., parents and teachers).
- A dual focus on increasing adaptive behaviors and decreasing maladaptive/inappropriate behaviors.

In the following sections, we focus on some of these intervention techniques that have empirical support and that can be implemented by school personnel in collaboration with parents. In some instances, school personnel (e.g., teachers, aides) may also be involved. However, we have not included discussion of interventions that focus exclusively on the school setting.

BEHAVIORAL PARENT TRAINING

As noted previously, behavioral parent training has a significant amount of empirical support and is a commonly used intervention for children with externalizing problems. Although there are a number of specific behavioral parent training programs (e.g., Eyberg's PCIT, Barkley's Defiant Children, Webster-Stratton's Incredible Years), they share a similar structure and focus. In this section, we outline how parent training could be conducted by school-based mental health professionals. We do not focus on one particular behavioral parent training program but have drawn from the existing programs for our discussion.

Overview of Parent Training

The focus of parent training is to work with parents to reduce problematic behaviors that youth are exhibiting and to increase positive, prosocial behaviors. To meet these goals, parents are instructed in the use and application of behavioral principles and methods that have been found to be effective in reducing problematic child behaviors. In general, these methods involve positive reinforcement of appropriate behaviors and mild discipline for inappropriate behaviors. Although the intervention is focused on changing the child's behavior, parents are seen as key players in this process. In fact, the change in child behavior comes through changes parents make in their responses to the child's behaviors. Thus, although the child is the identified target client, the bulk of the intervention work is done directly with the parents rather than the child. In fact, although the child is present in most individual parent training sessions, when parent training is conducted in group settings, it is usually only the parents who are present.

Although we typically talk about involving the parents of a child in session, in reality it is often only one parent (usually the mother) who attends sessions. Currently, there are a lack of data on whether paternal involvement in parent training increases the effectiveness of the intervention; however, involving fathers in the treatment is recommended (Tiano & McNeil, 2005). By involving both parents, there is a greater possibility of consistency within the home, and the greater the consistency, the more likely a child is to change his or her behavior in all situations at home. In addition, by involving both parents, they can provide support for one another as they implement the interventions within their home. Because many of the difficulties that parents experience with parent training models involves the actual implementation of skills, having a supportive partner in the home may help alleviate the stress, guilt, worry, and so on that parents may be feeling related to the implementation of the skills learned in treatment sessions.

Most behavioral parent training programs follow a two-part model initially developed by Hanf (1969). In this model, parents are first taught to attend to and praise positive behaviors the child exhibits. In the second part, parents are taught to effectively use discipline skills such as time-out and removal of privileges. Although some studies (e.g., Eisenstadt, Eyberg, McNeil, Newcomb, & Funderbunk, 1993) suggest that the order of presentation of these parts do not matter, most practitioners prefer to implement the positive part first. This allows the parent to build a stronger relationship with the child, potentially reducing the need for discipline and facilitating the effectiveness of some discipline techniques. For example, "selective ignoring" is unlikely to be successful if the child receives a low level of parent attention even when he or she is behaving appropriately.

Most available parent training models use a social learning approach and active methods of training in which the following steps are implemented:

- Didactic instruction/description of the use of the skill.
- Modeling of the skill.
- Parental practice of the skill in session, with feedback provided by the therapist.
- Parental practice of the skills at home.

The modeling of the skills in session can take several forms. Often the practitioner will model skills for the parent using the referred child. However, particularly in group parent training programs, videotaped models may be used. By modeling skills for the parent, the therapist can put into action what was described to parents. This is especially important because the skills sound simple and straightforward to many parents, but their implementation can get complex. In addition, the fact that parents practice the skills in session and receive feedback from the therapist is important in ensuring that parents understand and can perform the skill. Some therapists combine the modeling and practice portions by videotaping parents interacting with their child and then having parents view the video to better understand how they are applying the skills with their child. By having the parents practice skills learned in session, the therapist can provide feedback to the parent before the parent begins to implement the skill at home. This can help prevent confusion regarding how a skill was to be implemented or difficulties with the implementation of a certain skill.

Behavioral Targets/Appropriate Applications

Behavioral parent training is typically used when a child's presenting problems involve noncompliance, defiance, and other problems within the broad category of externalizing problems. The majority of parent training programs developed and supported with empirical data focus on children in the 2- to 12-year age range. Some programs are specifically targeted at younger children, whereas others cover this broader age range. For example the Incredible Years program was developed specifically for preschool-age children and PCIT targets children ages 2 to 7. However, programs such as Barkley's Defiant Children (Barkley, 1997) targets the 2- to 12-year age range. Fewer programs have been developed for older children, with Barkley's Defiant Teens program (an upward extension of the Defiant Children program; Barkley, Edwards, & Robin, 1999) being a noteworthy exception. However, the vast majority of research on parent training is focused on children, and it is not clear how well these outcome data would apply to adolescents.

Parent variables are another important consideration. Because parent training methods make active use of parents in the intervention process, parent characteristics must also be examined before deciding whether this treatment will have a high likelihood of success. For example, parents who are experiencing significant psychopathology of their own or who are having marital problems may not be the best candidates for parent training, and some data support the notion that parents with such difficulties will experience less success in parent training programs (e.g., Kazdin, 1995; Kazdin & Wassell, 1999). Because parent-related factors can have an impact on the outcome of parent training, it is important for practitioners to ask about such factors during the intake process. When a parent is experiencing his or her own mental health problems, a referral to an appropriate community-based mental health professional may be important before the implementation of parent training.

Parent training can be conducted in individual and group formats. The majority of established parent training programs are tailored to individual use. However, given that school-based mental health professionals must serve a large number of children/families and engage in a variety of different activities, group parent training will likely be more feasible to implement in the schools. The main difference in the implementation of group and individual parent training is that when conducting group parent training the child is typically not present. Thus, the practitioner must make greater use of modeling and role plays to allow the parents to observe and practice the skills being presented. In addition to the cost- and time-effectiveness of group-based parenting training, such programs may also benefit parents via the inherent support and interaction from other parents built into this program format.

Conducting Parent Training

In the following sections, we outline a parent training program that may be implemented in a school-based context in either a group or an individual format. Although the program presented here is not identical to any of the previously mentioned parent training programs, it follows the same model as other behavioral parent training programs with empirical support (e.g., Incredible Years, PCIT). As should be clear from the descriptions provided previously, there is significant overlap among all behavioral parent training programs. We have taken the common elements of these programs and present them here.

Explaining Behavioral Principles

During the first session, we recommend spending time discussing behavioral principles with parents. Because parent training is based on the application of behavioral principles, we believe it is important for parents to have an understanding of why they are applying certain methods and why we expect these methods will work. As part of the discussion on behavioral principles, parents are introduced to the concepts of reinforcement for appropriate behaviors and extinction (ignoring) and punishment for inappropriate behaviors. Thus, this first session helps "set the stage" for concepts to be discussed in later sessions.

When covering behavioral principles, it is important that the clinician not lecture to the parents. Although the nature of this material may be a little "dry," the practitioner's job is to engage the parents and get them discussing their experiences with the different principles covered. In Form 4.1 (at the end of the chapter) we provide a handout that may be given to parents to facilitate the discussion of behavioral terms. When discussing the terms included in the handout, clinicians should attempt to engage parents in an active discussion about how they see these different principles at work with their children. For example, in a parent training group, clinicians could have parents engage in a group discussion regarding experiences they have had with ignoring behaviors and outcomes they have seen in their children.

Positive Reinforcement for Appropriate Behavior

Following the introductory session, the idea of praising children for appropriate behaviors is introduced. The skills for parents to learn at this stage are typically taught in a play-based format. In session parents are instructed on the use of skills that will facilitate a positive, child-focused interaction during a special playtime with their child. Developing positive reinforcement skills within a play-based context allows parents to begin to build a stronger relationship with their child and provides the child with needed reinforcement for appropriate behaviors. Often parents of children with behavior problems have a strained relationship with their children, and parents may even be avoiding interacting with their children or ignoring appropriate behaviors in favor of attending (typically in a negative manner) to the inappropriate behaviors the child displays.

Parents are asked to set aside time each day to play with their children and to use this time to practice skills of attending and positive reinforcement. Different parent training programs recommend different lengths of this special playtime (ranging from 5–20 minutes). To our knowledge, there are no data on the optimal length of time for these activities. Likely more important is that parents choose a duration that they can commit to, during which they can provide a high level of engagement. Thus, we recommend having parents commit to engaging in these play activities for just 5 minutes a day. During the playtime, the parent is to completely focus his or her attention on the child and describe what the child is doing ("You're drawing a blue circle"), reflect comments the child makes (child: "It's not a circle, it's a cookie"; parent: "Oh, a cookie! That looks yummy"), and praise the child for appropriate behaviors ("Thank you for sharing your crayons with me"). Parents are instructed to not ask questions, to not give commands, and to not be critical of the child. The rationale is that questions, commands, and criticism detract from the positive, child-focused nature of the interaction.

In addition to facilitating the development of a stronger parent–child relationship, this special playtime also allows parents to practice the skills of attending and positive reinforcement. By focusing on these skills exclusively during this special playtime, it is hoped that parents will overlearn these skills and apply them more in day-to-day interactions with their child.

When introducing these skills, parents are provided with a handout on the play-based skills that includes examples of how these skills might be implemented (see Form 4.2 at the end of the chapter). The clinician should discuss the specifics presented in the handout with the parents and encourage them to think about when they can engage in this playtime, what toys they can use, and so on. In individual parent training, theses skills are then modeled by the clinician and the parent practices the skills while receiving therapist feedback. In group parent training, the format of this modeling and practice must be altered some because children will not be present. Videotaped models can be used to illustrate the concepts and promote discussion among parents. For example, we have used videotaped models of both "good" and "bad" examples of this playtime. In our discussion of these models, we ask parents to focus on the differences in the child's behavior as a result of the parent's behavior during the playtime (e.g., the child is more engaged in the "good" model). We also identify and discuss with parents some of the specific listening skills that are exhibited by the model (e.g., reflection, praise) as well as some of the problems seen in the "bad" model (e.g., directing the child's play). An alternative to videotaped models is to have the clinician model with a parent acting as child. Once the skills have been modeled, parents practice these skills. In an individual setting, this is done with the referred child. However, in group settings, typically parents will practice the skills with one another. We have found that adults are generally not very adept at playing the part of the child, making this practice particularly artificial. However, we believe such practice is better than no practice and still helps facilitate parents' effective use of these skills. Parents are then instructed to practice these skills at home with their child and report back in the next session on how the playtime went, including challenges faced and problems encountered.

With older children, there will likely need to be some adaptations in terms of how the specifics of these principles are applied. The play-based context typically used for teaching these skills works well for most children younger than 12, but with adolescents the play situation will typically seem child-like and condescending. Parents should still be instructed to use the same basic attending skills (particularly praise) but to do so by joining in with the child in an activity in which he or she is already engaged or by looking for instances throughout the day when positive reinforcement can be delivered.

Ignoring

Ignoring is a skill that is easy to talk about and one that can be quite effective but it is *very* difficult for many parents to implement consistently. (As noted earlier, spending some quality time with a very whiny, demanding child makes this readily apparent.) Although most parent training programs discuss ignoring, many do so in a brief manner folded in with other topics. Although some, such as McMahon and Forehand's (2005) program, do address ignoring more directly. Especially in a group parent training setting, in which it is impossible to individually problem solve with every family the difficulties they might be having implementing skills, we believe it is important to cover this as a discrete topic. Ignoring is a component of other aspects of parent training (e.g., ignoring minor misbehavior while engaged in special playtime; ignoring crying when in time-out), and ensuring that parents understand this concept can be key to the effective implementation of the parenting program. To facilitate the discussion of ignoring, parents are provided with a handout that specifically covers this skill (Form 4.3 at the end of this chapter), and the contents of this handout are discussed with parents in session.

Many parents are alarmed at the fact that they are being asked to ignore misbehavior. However, they should be reassured that only certain misbehaviors are to be ignored; others require consequences to be applied. The behaviors that make the most sense to ignore are those that involve tantrums or tantrum-like behaviors such as crying, whining, and yelling. Often these behaviors are done for attention or to attempt to gain access to a desired activity or object. For example, a child might cry when he is told he cannot have candy in the grocery store. Ignoring prevents the child from gaining access to what he wants and the behavior is not reinforced, as long as ignoring is done correctly. Parents should be instructed on what ignoring is—and what it is not. Although this seems fairly straightforward, we have had many parents tell us they are ignoring and then demonstrate their "ignoring" skills by continuously telling their child to stop or repeatedly asserting, "I am not going to talk to you while you're acting like this!" We have come to refer to such behavior as "pseudo-ignoring." To truly ignore, parents need to not attend in any manner to their child. In essence, they should act as though their child is not there. This means no talking to the child, no staring at the child, no giving the child "looks," and so on. Talking encompasses all types of verbal exchanges, including nagging statements (e.g., "Remember, I'm not going to let you have that candy if you keep asking me for it"). Once the behavior has ceased, the parent should be instructed to look for an appropriate behavior to praise (e.g., "Thanks for walking next to me while we are shopping. It's fun to have you along"). It is very important that parents do look for behaviors to praise so that there is a contrast in the parental attention children receive for positive behaviors versus negative behaviors. If children are not praised for appropriate behaviors, then parents are essentially ignoring both appropriate and inappropriate behaviors.

It is important to note that ignoring can be quite difficult for parents, especially in public situations. Even when ignoring might be the optimal strategy, parents may not be able to commit to implementing this method. We feel that it is better not to implement selective ignoring if the parent does not believe he or she can follow through. The risk of attempting an ignoring strategy but ultimately giving in is that a variable reinforcement schedule is created, which is much more difficult to extinguish. Thus, it is important to talk with parents about ignoring and help them identify behaviors and situations they truly can ignore—and respect their input when they indicate that they will not be able to ignore in certain situations. Having parents prioritize behaviors/situations in which they will use ignoring and gradually implement ignoring procedures can be one way to approach use of this important strategy.

Giving Effective Commands

Once parents are able to implement the positive attending skills with relative fluidity and understand the principles of ignoring, the use of effective commands is introduced. Typically, in parent training programs, discipline techniques are first practiced in response to child noncompliance. By helping parents issue effective commands first, there is a greater likelihood the child will comply, but also it allows the parent to be clear on his or her expectations for the child. Too often commands are issued as requests ("Can you take out the trash for me?") or in another manner that makes it difficult for children to comply (e.g., multiple commands given at once, commands given repeatedly before the child has a chance to comply). In discussing effective commands, the clinician can provide the parents with a handout on commands (Form 4.4 at the end of the chapter) and discuss the points presented.

Effective Discipline

Once parents understand how to provide commands effectively, they are instructed on the use of effective discipline techniques. Time-out is the most commonly recommended technique for younger children. However, many parents report that they have tried time-out and "it doesn't work." Therefore, it is important for the clinician to be able to "sell" time-out and convince parents to try this method, done the way discussed in session. We typically recommend that time-out be used with children at least up to age 10. For children ages 10 to 12, we recommend utilizing time-out if certain conditions are met: The parent can physically pick up the child, the child has some past experience with time-out, and the parents are committed to trying time-out. If these conditions are not met, we typically recommend utilizing a combination of job card grounding and privileges (discussed later in this chapter).

When discussing time-out in session, parents should be provided with the handout covering the use of time-out (Form 4.5 at the end of this chapter), and the key points should be discussed in session. In individual parent training (with the child present), time-out is explained to the child and then attempts are made to get the child in time-out in session. In group parent training, without the child present, these steps are not possible. However, parents should be instructed to explain time-out to their children at home. This explanation should include where the time-out location is, what behaviors will result in the child getting sent to time-out, and how the child needs to behave in order to be released from time-out (e.g., sitting quietly). In group parent training sessions, parents can practice providing these explanations and then can practice with each other the motions of sending a child to time-out. Of course, such practice will not mirror the real issues parents will face in using time-out at home. Such issues include the child leaving the time-out location, having a tantrum while in time-out, and so on. Thus, it is important to have a follow-up discussion on time-out when parents return to the next session. In this session, parents can share with each other their successes in implementing time-out as well as the difficulties they faced. The clinician can facilitate this discussion and help parents problem solve difficult situations.

One of the most common problems parents face in the use of time-out is that the child will not stay in the time-out location. Different parent training programs deal with this issue differently, and based on currently available data, there is no one "right" way to address this issue. We typically recommend having the parent stand close to the time-out location so that the parent can immediately replace the child in the time-out location if the child attempts to leave. However, when doing this, it is important that the parent not reinforce the child for attempting to leave time-out by giving the child extra attention, chasing the child, and so on. Initially, some children may view being repeatedly placed back in time-out as a "game." With consistent, quick, and calm responding, the child will eventually lose interest in this "game" and remain in time-out for at least a brief period of time. This can take some time initially, though, so parents must be prepared for this and have the time and resources available to wait out a child. For example, if there are other children in the home who will require the parent's attention in the interim, how will this be dealt with? Problem solving these issues with parents ahead of time is key to making this procedure work. Another common method of dealing with a child who leaves the time-out chair is the use of a "back-up room," as is currently recommended by the PCIT program. If the child leaves the time-out chair, the child is taken to a time-out room and closed in the room for 1 minute. Following this the child is returned to the time-out chair. The room used must be devoid of reinforcing items (e.g., no toys should be present) and should obviously be a place where the child can be enclosed without any safety concerns.

Job card grounding (as described in Form 4.6 at the end of the chapter) is an alternative discipline method that is typically recommended for older children. This method of discipline was initially developed and described by Christophersen (1998) and while grounding is not a central part of many behavioral parent training programs, it has been used by others (e.g., Barkley et al., 1999). Job card grounding can be applied in situations in which one would use time-out or can be used for more serious misbehaviors. In this method of discipline, parents are instructed to create five to 10 jobs that can be done around the house and write the steps of these jobs on index cards. These should be jobs that the child is physically capable of doing and completing within 10 to 15 minutes and that the child can safely complete. They should also be jobs that do not have to be done immediately or within a certain time frame (e.g., washing the dinner dishes and taking out the trash would not be appropriate given that they are time-sensitive). When the child misbehaves, he or she is given a job to complete. Until the job is completed, the child is grounded; grounding lasts only as long as it takes him or her to do the chore. Thus, with this method, the child has some measure of control over his or her grounding time. Although parents can define the specific activities from which the child is grounded, these typically include TV, video game, computer (except for homework purposes), and phone privileges.

Using privileges to manage behavior can also be an effective method of discipline as well as a way to reinforce appropriate behaviors. Parents have several options on how to set up such a program. Parents might tie privileges to certain behaviors. For example, if a child sets the table for dinner, he or she is granted the privilege of watching 30 minutes of TV after dinner. In combination with providing privileges for appropriate behavior, parents may also choose to take away privileges for inappropriate behavior. Privileges that would be taken away are those that the child has access to on a regular basis. For example, if a child is automatically allowed to watch 2 hours of TV per day, he or she might lose TV time for not performing an expected chore or for engaging in inappropriate behaviors (e.g., hitting a sibling). Typically, parents will use a combination of granting privileges for positive behaviors and taking away privileges for inappropriate behaviors. See Form 4.7 (at the end of this chapter) for a handout describing the use of privileges and a work sheet to list positive behaviors, chores, rewards, and privileges.

In addition to more comprehensive privilege programs, parents may use smaller reinforcement/privilege programs. For example, if a child has difficulty getting ready for school in the morning, the parents might develop a program targeted specifically to correct this. Parents will compile a list of required behaviors (e.g., get dressed, eat breakfast, brush teeth) and tie the reward program to the completion of these behaviors. The reward could be delivered immediately (e.g., if the required behaviors are completed by a certain time, the child is allowed to play a board game with the parent before school) or the child could work toward a larger reward. For example, if a child wants a certain music CD, he or she could earn points or tokens toward this reward. A grab bag reward program is another option. In this reinforcement program, items or activities that are reinforcing to the child are written on pieces of paper and put into a container (e.g., paper bag, decorated can). If the child completes the required tasks, he or she is allowed to draw from the grab bag and receive the reward noted on the slip of paper.

Common Obstacles/Troubleshooting

Although parent training can be a very effective intervention for children exhibiting externalizing problems, it is not uncommon to encounter certain obstacles in implementing this intervention. One of the first obstacles frequently observed involves parent expectations: Some parents are unaware of what to expect when they seek assistance for their child and may have the attitude that "It's my child who has the problem, so why do I need therapy?" It is important to sell parents on parent training as an effective intervention from the beginning, because the success of this intervention depends on their active participation. Emphasizing that you need parents' help in creating behavior change can be an effective way of overcoming this obstacle. For example, we often tell parents that we see them as "cotherapists" in the process: We have the expertise in behavioral interventions; they have the expertise on their child and their home situation. We also focus on parents as individuals who are much more important—and have a much greater impact—in their children's lives than clinicians. Encouraging parents to commit to trying this intervention briefly (e.g., three to four sessions) may increase their initial buy-in. Once they begin to see results from the intervention, they are often willing to engage in additional sessions. Motivational interviewing (as discussed in Chapter 1) can also be useful in helping engage parents in the parent training process.

Another common obstacle encountered with parent training involves parents who view the program as overly negative (e.g., sending a child to time-out after every instance of non-compliance). Parents often feel guilty and feel that the use of regular discipline may negatively impact their relationship with their child. Several points warrant special emphasis. One is that children appreciate consistency and structure. Thus, although a child is certain to dislike time-out or job card grounding, knowing that the parent will consistently provide a consequence for misbehavior is important. In addition, the positive part of the parent training program is designed so that parents have a positive foundation of interacting with their child before beginning the discipline component. It is important to emphasize to parents that as long as their ratios of positive to negative interactions favors the positives (e.g., a 5:1 ratio of positives to negatives is often recommended, although there is no empirical support for this specific recommendation and it may be hard for parents to achieve this), children will not feel overly "punished."

The success of parent training depends a great deal on parents completing their "homework" and implementing the principles discussed in session at home (e.g., having special playtime with their child). A common problem is that parents do not implement these skills at home. This can occur for a variety of reasons, including parents not fully being sold on the intervention, lack of time, lack of understanding of the how to implement the skills, lack of resources (e.g., no one to watch a younger child when attempting to have special playtime with the target child). As skills are being introduced, it is important to problem solve with parents as much as possible to try to anticipate and prepare for some of these problems. For example, when discussing special playtime, parents should think about when they can commit to this quality time, what they will do with their other children, and what problems they expect to encounter. Along these lines, it is important for the clinician to understand and appreciate real obstacles a parent may face in implementing these skills. For example, a single parent who is caring for multiple young children may not be able to repeatedly replace a child in time-out when first practicing this skill at home if all of the children are present and in need of attention (e.g., an infant who needs to be fed). In situations such as this, exploring different options with parents is important to determine what will work. For example, maybe time-out can first be used only after other children are in bed, perhaps a back-up room will be used instead of replacing the child in time-out, or maybe there is a grandparent or friend who can assist the parent initially. There are typically multiple solutions to any given situation, so it is important that clinicians be flexible in finding the solution that is the best fit for the family while still ensuring the application of effective behavioral methods.

Although parent training is a home-focused intervention by definition, there is ample support for the use of the same principles in behavioral interventions for the classroom setting. Thus, when school-based mental health professionals are working with parents of children with externalizing problems, they should consider whether similar behavioral interventions can be applied in the classroom. This will likely be particularly important for children who exhibit problems across both the home and school settings.

COLLABORATIVE PROBLEM SOLVING

Although there are significant data to support the effectiveness of behavioral parent train-ing, it does not work for all families and in all situations. Researchers have developed and evaluated other interventions targeted at children with externalizing problems. CPS is one of those interventions. This mode of intervention still involves working with the parents and the child together. However, the focus is on helping them resolve issues in a collaborative manner. As noted, there is some empirical support for this intervention, but there are still only a limited number of published studies on CPS at this time. Practitioners should keep this in mind and be alert for additional empirical studies on CPS.

In their text on CPS, Greene and Ablon (2006) provide specifics on the background of CPS and methods for implementing it in a variety of settings, including the schools. In con-trast to parent training, which places greater emphasis on the consequences of behaviors, the CPS model focuses on the antecedents of the child's "explosive" behaviors. The idea is that by learning what predicts explosive behaviors parents and children can then engage in a CPS process to resolve the problem. The first step in the CPS process is to identify skill deficits that are leading to dysfunctional behaviors as well as triggers associated with these behaviors. To identify pathways and triggers, it is recommended that the clinician conduct a situational analysis in which the parent is asked to describe instances of child misbehavior. The clinician's goal is to make sense of the information the parent is describing to develop specific hypotheses about which pathways are leading to the child's explosive behaviors. Greene and Ablon identify five pathways, each involving an area of cognitive deficits that can lead to explosive behaviors:

- *Executive skills,* including difficulties with transitions and difficulty remaining calm.
- *Language-processing skills,* such as difficulty expressing thoughts.
- *Emotion regulation skills,* including sad, anxious, irritable behaviors.
- *Cognitive flexibility skills,* such as concrete thinking, insistence on routine.
- *Social skills,* such as misreading social cues and unawareness of how his or her behavior affects others.

Once pathways and triggers are identified, parents can learn to predict explosive episodes and use CPS skills to decrease them.

Greene and Ablon (2006) define the CPS steps as follows:

- Empathy.
- Defining the problem.
- Invitation.

These steps can be used in a proactive manner (to head off an anticipated problem) as well as in an "emergency" manner (to deal with an immediate problem), although it is preferable that parents use skills proactively.

Empathy is used to help acknowledge the child's concern and to help define the problem as perceived by the child. An empathetic dialogue might begin with "I've noticed you haven't been very happy when I drop you off at school." As part of the empathizing, parents should attempt to more clearly figure out why the child is having problems—as Greene and Ablon put it, asking "What's up?" Once the child's concerns are clear, the parents can provide additional empathetic statements. For example, to the "What's up?" question, the child might respond with "I'm worried you're not going to remember to pick me up at the end of the day." The parent might then respond, "So, what you're worried about is me not coming back to get you once I drop you off. I can see how that would be upsetting."

In the second step of defining the problem, the parent brings in his or her concern. Thus, both the child's concerns and the parent's concerns should be clear. At this step, the clinician may need to help parents define their concerns so that there is something for the parent and the child to work on. For example, using the prior scenario, the parent might begin by saying, "I don't want Joshua to be upset when I drop him off at school." The clinician may then further clarify by asking, "What specific concerns do you have about Joshua being upset?", to which the parent may then respond, "Well, when he gets too upset he just starts tantruming and screaming and won't stop. I have a hard time getting him in the school so he's late to school and disruptive to the class when he gets there, and I'm late for work."

Once concerns from both sides are identified, the parent invites the child to brainstorm ideas for how to solve the problems in a way that is agreeable to both the child and the parent. Greene and Ablon (2006) emphasize using "Let's" in this invitation. For example, the parent may say to the child, "Let's think of some ideas for how we can solve this problem." Although multiple solutions may be generated the final solution needs to be "feasible, doable, and mutually satisfactory" (Green & Ablon, 2006, p. 60).

Throughout their discussion of CPS, Greene and Ablon (2006) distinguish this method (Plan B) from two other methods parents typically use in attempts to change children's behaviors. Plan A involves parents imposing their will and insisting that things be done a certain way. Plan C involves parents reducing or removing their expectations for the child to behave in a certain manner. Greene and Ablon believe that Plan A responses can increase explosive child behaviors and, therefore, do not advocate for the use of Plan A techniques. Although Plan C is not part of the problem-solving process, Greene and Ablon do indicate that parents can decide ahead of time to pursue Plan C with some behaviors. If the parent decides that there really is not a concern or a problem with a behavior the child is exhibiting or an activity the child wants to do, then there is not a problem (and, therefore, nothing to solve), so the parents can simply remove the expectations of this behavior or activity. For example, parents may initially have expressed concern that their child insists on doing her homework while listening to music but, after some discussion of the situation and recognition that the homework is being completed, the parents decide this situation is not a problem. Greene and Ablon are careful to differentiate Plan C from giving in (which occurs after insisting something be done a certain way) or ignoring.

As noted earlier, Greene and Ablon (2006) discuss the use of CPS in the schools as well as in the home. Thus, school personnel interested in using CPS can potentially use the same intervention for their work with parents as well as with teachers and other school personnel if the child is having problem behaviors across settings. Engaging the parents and school personnel together in the CPS efforts may be helpful in obtaining a complete, integrated picture of the child's problem behaviors as well as in promoting and maintaining home/school communication.

HOME-BASED CONTINGENCIES FOR SCHOOL BEHAVIOR

Parents should be viewed as integral to the solution of any school-based problems children may be exhibiting. However, often we look for solutions only within the schools, where teachers and other school personnel often have limited time and resources. Involving parents in the intervention process can increase the opportunities for positive outcomes. One of the home-based contingency methods that has been discussed at length in the research is the home/school note program (e.g., Jurbergs, Palcic, & Kelley, 2007; Kelley, 1990; Kelley & McCain, 1995). In such a program, the practitioner works with the teacher and parent together to develop a system for tracking behaviors at school (typically done by the teacher) and rewarding positive behaviors at home (done by the parent). Such a program not only takes some of the burden of the program implementation off the teacher but also helps facilitate ongoing home/school collaboration. The steps involved in developing an effective home school program include (1) identifying target behaviors; (2) developing a method to track behaviors; and (3) identifying and applying home-based contingencies.

Identifying Behavioral Targets

Home/school contingency programs can be used for almost any problematic behaviors exhibited in the classroom. However, because the teacher will need to be able to track and note the presence and absence of the behaviors, the behaviors targeted should be ones that are easily identifiable to the teacher, even when he or she is engaged in active teaching in the classroom. The behaviors should also be specific enough that the child knows what is expected and the parent knows what is being tracked. For example, "on task" is likely too broad of a behavior to include on a home/school note. Instead, specific behaviors that make up "on task" should be identified. For example, if the child is having difficulties staying seated, this specific behavior could be included. Alternatively, if the child's off-task behavior includes talking to peers at inappropriate times, this would be a suitable behavior to include. In general, we recommend that only three to five behaviors be included on a home/school note. The inclusion of more behaviors can become problematic for the teacher recording the behaviors and overwhelming for the child, who is attempting to make behavioral changes. If there are a number of behaviors the teacher wishes to target, the note can be revised once certain behavioral targets are met. For example, in a home/school note program to increase "staying seated," once the child is remaining in his or her seat at an acceptable rate, this behavior can be removed from the note and replaced with a new behavioral goal. In choosing which behaviors to include in the note initially, those that are most problematic to the child's successful learning (or the learning environment of others) should be targeted. However, it is also important to include behaviors for which there is a good chance the child will be successful. Behaviors should be worded positively when possible as positive wording can help make it more clear what the child is expected to do. For example, instead of tracking "gets out of seat," the target behavior can be "stays in seat when expected."

Tracking Behaviors

Once behaviors are identified, a tracking sheet can be developed. This tracking sheet will be used by the teacher to record the occurrence of behaviors and will be sent home to the parents (via the child) so the parents know what consequences to provide to the child. The tracking sheet should cover the entire school day unless there is a reason to target a specific part of the day. For example, if the child is only having difficulties in certain classes, the behaviors might only be tracked during these classes. Assuming the behaviors will be tracked over the entire school day, the day is divided into segments by either time periods (e.g., hour by hour) or class periods (e.g., English, Math, Science). For each period, the teacher is asked to mark whether the child engaged in the behavior. In Figure 4.1 we provide an example home/school note that might be used with Julie (our child described in the clinical vignette at the beginning of this chapter). Form 4.8 (at the end of the chapter) is a blank home/school note.

The teacher can simply be asked to record "yes" or "no" as to whether the behavior occurred or did not occur during each time interval. Alternatively, the teacher may respond with a numerical rating (e.g., 1 = *behavior never occurred*; 2 = *behavior occurred some*; 3 = *behavior occurred frequently*). Although the yes–no method may be easier for a teacher to use, the numerical rating allows the teacher to consider more variability in a child's behaviors, and this method may be more sensitive to change because of the increased ability to reflect behavior variability. Ideally, when the teacher marks whether the behavior occurs, the teacher also provides some quick feedback to the student. This can help keep a student on track by acknowledging successes and pointing out areas of difficulty before the end of the school day, when the child has no chance to correct behavior for that day. However, this does need to be kept brief because of the teacher time that would be required for more extensive comments. A statement such as "Julie, you did a great job following my directions, but you need to work a little harder on not talking to your classmates when you are supposed to be doing seatwork" would provide feedback to the student while taking little time away from the teacher's ongoing classroom duties.

Home-Based Contingencies

A key part of the home/school note system is the delivery of home-based contingencies. At the end of each school day, the child brings the note home and receives a reinforcer from his or her parents for meeting a certain predetermined criterion. To determine the criterion, first the total number of possible points must be calculated. For example, if three behaviors are being rated as "yes" or "no" across seven class periods, the total number of points possible would be 21 (1 point for each "yes"). Next, an appropriate reinforcement criterion must be established. In general, it is best to have this criterion be one that the child can have some success with initially. The criterion can then be increased if the child is easily meeting

DAILY SCHOOL NOTE FOR: Julie

Date: January 9th (Thursday)

Julie _____ is responsible for presenting this form to his/her teachers at the end of each time period, and he/she is responsible for bringing this form home each evening. Each teacher is responsible for initialing in the appropriate column.

Required for evening privileges: 14/21 _____

Class time

	9:00–10:00		10:00–11:00		11:00–11:45		12:15–1:00		1:00–2:00		2:00–3:00		3:00–3:35	
	Y	N	Y	N	Y	N	Y	N	Y	N	Y	N	Y	N
1. Interacted appropriately with peers.														
2. Talked only when appropriate/expected.														
3. Responded to teacher's instructions.														

FIGURE 4.1. Example of a home/school note for Julie.

89

it every day. We might first set the criterion at 14 of 21 points. Thus, the child only receives the reinforcer if she earns 14 points. In addition, parents might set a low-end criterion for access to everyday privileges after school. For example, if the child does not receive at least 4 points, she loses TV and video game privileges for that afternoon. If the child receives 4 to 12 points, she earns no reinforcer but also loses no privileges.

The reinforcer that the child receives at home should be delivered immediately, but a longer term reward system can also be utilized. For example, the child may earn a small reinforcer immediately (e.g., extra computer time, playing outside with Dad) and be able to save points toward a larger reward (e.g., the purchase of a new video game, dinner out with Mom and Dad). If the child is earning points toward a larger reward, the points earned each day need to be delivered immediately and a clear tally of points kept in a prominent location (e.g., a chart on the refrigerator). In general, it is probably best to avoid using delayed reinforcers with younger children and older children who lack the cognitive skills necessary to appreciate delayed gratification.

Troubleshooting

Several common problems can be encountered with home/school note systems that will reduce the effectiveness of such programs if not addressed immediately. A frequent problem is that the note does not make it home with the child to the parents. Clearly, when this occurs, the parents are unable to determine whether the child has earned a reinforcer for the day. To prevent this problem, it is important to include a contingency for the note not coming home; for example, no note counts as no points and the child loses access to certain privileges at home that evening. Initially, it is important for the parent to ask about the note when the child comes home and not wait for the child to present the note, which may not happen even if the note did make it home. By asking for the note, the parent emphasizes its importance. A system at school might also be set up to address this problem whereby the teacher would remind the child to put the note in the take-home folder or backpack, to bring home.

Another common problem is that parents do not consistently follow through and provide immediate reinforcement for a positive note. Clearly, if the reinforcers are not delivered as promised, the purpose of the system is defeated. Most children are quick learners, and once they find that bringing home the note makes little difference, they will change their behavior accordingly. Thus, it is important to stress to parents the importance of providing the reinforcers immediately. If parents or the teacher report that the system is not working, the application of the reinforcers should be one of the first issues examined. We have seen parents fail to follow through on promised rewards, leading to children who were initially excited about the home/school note plan ceasing to be interested and doubting that they will ever be able to earn a promised reward. To make the delivery of rewards easy for parents, the clinician should discuss with the parents the identified rewards and ensure that the parents can actually provide these on a regular basis. Some rewards may initially seem easy to deliver but get more burdensome on parents if given on a daily basis. For example, if the child wishes to go to the skate park (requiring Mom or Dad to drive) as a reward, this may get difficult for the parents if they do not have the time to do this on a regular basis. In addition, keeping reinforcers more simple may help avoid child negotiators, who may try to "work the system" via bargaining for a more complex reinforcer (e.g., "I'm only going to work to get to go to the skate park. I don't care about extra computer time at home.")

Problems may also be encountered at the school end of the home/school note. The most common problems are that teachers either fail to mark the note or fail to provide appropriate feedback for the child as they are recording behaviors. In both cases, initial discussion with teachers to get their buy-in and providing an explanation of the goals of the program are helpful. In addition, it is important that teachers have input on the behaviors that are chosen to track and that they feel confident they will be able to track these behaviors on a daily basis. Often when teachers report that the system is taking too much time and that they are not able to track behaviors, clarifying expectations can help. Teachers sometimes believe they need to provide lengthy feedback to students each time they mark the note. This is not the case and, in fact, lengthy feedback should be discouraged. The teacher should be encouraged to provide very brief feedback as noted previously, taking no longer than a couple of seconds to do so.

Regardless of where the problem originates, ongoing communication among the parents, teacher, and mental health professional is important in keeping the system working. It is the clinician's job to facilitate this communication. Thus, the clinician should not assume that his or her job is done once the home/school note system is set up and in place. Instead, the clinician should check in with the parent, teacher, and child on a regular basis (especially initially) to identify and troubleshoot problems before they become so large that they undermine the whole program. In addition, the clinician should facilitate the tracking of progress to ensure the home/school note system is having the desired impact. This tracking could simply involve looking at the note each day and graphing the number of instances of each behavior to determine whether the behaviors are changing in the desired direction.

COLLABORATING WITH PARENTS IN THE CONTEXT OF CHILD-FOCUSED TREATMENTS

As noted earlier, some of the treatments for externalizing problems that have empirical support involve working directly with children. Kazdin's problem-solving skills training and Webster-Stratton's Dinosaur School program, which also involves some instruction on problem solving, both have been evaluated and noted to produce positive results. Often these programs are offered in conjunction with behavioral parent training, and as noted earlier, it does appear that the combined approach is superior to intervening with children individually (e.g., Kazdin et al., 1987a, 1992; Webster-Stratton et al., 2004). Although these child-focused treatment programs do not involve extensive collaboration with parents, they do still make use of parents in promoting positive child changes. In addition, these problem-solving interventions are time-limited and can easily be implemented in a school setting by trained mental health professionals such as school psychologists. In this section, we provide a brief overview of these programs and highlight how parents can be involved.

Overview of Problem-Solving Skills Interventions

PSST interventions involve teaching children to apply cognitive problem-solving steps to situations in which they frequently encounter difficulties responding with appropriate behaviors. Because this treatment is more cognitively based, it is typically used with older children/adolescents (e.g., ages ≥ 8 years). However, as noted earlier, Webster-Stratton's Dinosaur School program is intended for use with young children. PSST can be an effective intervention for children who react quickly and impulsively to situations and for those who have thinking errors in their responses to situations. Although different problem-solving programs phrase the specific problem-solving steps somewhat differently, the steps commonly noted are as follows:

- *Identifying the problem.* At this initial stage, children are taught to sort through the aspects of a problem situation. For example, although a child experiencing conflict with a teacher might initially define the problem as "She's not fair!", with further discussion, an underlying problem—that the child is having difficulty understanding directions and is reluctant to ask for clarification—may be revealed.
- *Identifying alternative solutions to the problem.* Once the problem is clearly identified, children are asked to generate possible solutions. Children should be encouraged to generate as many solutions as possible. Often children initially have some difficulties generating alternative solutions and may need assistance from the clinician in session. Additionally, if the child fails to spontaneously generate any prosocial solutions to the problem, the clinician will want to suggest possible positive solutions. At this stage, however, it is important that solutions not be judged by the clinician.
- *Evaluating the outcomes of the different solutions.* Once multiple solutions are generated, the child evaluates the possible outcomes of each. The clinician may need to initially assist the child in this process, especially in terms of more delayed consequences of a certain action. For example, a child may decide that pushing another child off a swing is a good way to get a turn at swinging ("If I push him off, I get to use the swing right away") but may fail to see the longer term consequences (e.g., having to go inside for the rest of recess for violating playground rules; other children not wanting to play with the child).
- *Choosing a solution to implement.* After the outcomes of each potential solution are evaluated, the child chooses the solution to implement.
- *Evaluating the success of the chosen solution.* At this final stage, the child evaluates whether he or she chose the best solution for the identified problem. For example, what really happened when the chosen solution was put in place: Was the outcome positive or negative?

Children (and their parents) can be provided with a handout detailing these steps (see Form 4.9 at the end of the chapter for an example) so that children can first learn the basic steps of problem solving. Children are then taught to use the problem-solving skills in session. Initially, these skills are often practiced within the context of game situations. For example, the child and the clinician might play a game of checkers and use the problem-solving skills to help them decide which moves will be the best moves to make (Kendall & Braswell, 1985).

When children are first practicing these skills in session, they are encouraged to say each of the steps out loud. This way, the clinician can ensure that the child is going through all the appropriate steps. Eventually, the child moves to whispered speech and then internal speech.

After the skills are practiced in game situations, children begin to practice these skills in hypothetical social situations. The clinician brings in examples of social situations in which these skills may be used and asks the child to respond to the situation using these skills. Following this or conjointly, skills are applied to the child's real-life situations. In addition to working through situations in session, the child is encouraged to apply these skills to situations he or she faces. Typically, the child is assigned homework of applying these skills and recording in writing what occurred when these skills were used.

Involving Parents in PSST

Although PSST is a child-focused intervention, parents can be integral in making this intervention successful. We suggest involving parents from the beginning and making them aware of the problem-solving steps as soon as they are taught to the child. As the child is asked to apply these steps outside of session, parents can prompt the child to use the steps and can assist the child if he or she misses steps. Encouraging parents and children to come up with a covert signal to help remind the child to use the steps can be helpful. For example, we have worked with children and their parents who have used various hand signals or gestures (e.g., a time-out signal, pulling on an ear) as well as verbal signals (e.g., "PS"). It can also be very helpful for parents to provide positive feedback (verbal and/or tangible reinforcers) when they notice the child using the problem-solving steps. Because children often have an easy time applying the skills in session but a harder time applying them in real situations in the "heat of the moment," parent involvement may help children generalize the skills to real-life settings.

Parents can also help generate the real-life problem situations to be discussed in session. Often children have a hard time remembering the specifics of situations. Having parents write down situations as they occur throughout the week and providing these to the clinician at the beginning of session can be a good way to develop a number of real-life situations for use in in-session role plays.

Although parent involvement can be very helpful when conducting PSST, it is important that the parents not nag the child about his or her use of the skills. Parents should serve as a coach for the child by offering reminders and positive feedback for using the skills. By checking in regularly with the parents and with the child about parents' involvement, clinicians should be able to quickly identify any difficulties with the parental involvement component and problem solve these with the parent and child together.

Teachers, too, can help children as they are practicing the problem-solving steps. Teachers may not be able to provide as much coaching and feedback as parents; however, teachers can help generate applied examples for the child and clinician to discuss in session. In addition, teachers can help cue students to implement the problem-solving skills in the classroom and provide positive feedback for the use of target skills.

COLLABORATING WITH OTHER PROFESSIONALS

Schools are their own communities and can be insular places. It is important for school-based mental health professionals who are working with children with externalizing problems and their families to remember that there are outside resources they can use to help a child whose needs exceed the resources available in the schools. In addition, there are nonschool professionals who may value input from the school in the process of making diagnostic or treatment decisions. Each of these is discussed next. In order for the school-based professional to collaborate with outside professionals, it is important for the clinician to know what and who the community-based resources are. Having knowledge of community-based psychology clinics, private mental health practitioners, and health professionals (e.g., pediatricians) will help ensure that the school-based professional does communicate with outside resources. It may be helpful for the school-based professional to have in-person meetings with some of the community-based professionals. Such meetings can help demystify the treatment process at the different locations for all parties involved. In addition, such face-to-face meetings allow for the establishment of a professional relationship, which can help facilitate later communication.

When to Refer

Referrals to community-based professionals may occur for a variety of reasons. These include situations in which there are problems of concern not directly related to the child but that may be impacting the child or the parent's effectiveness at home. For example, we mentioned earlier in this chapter that parents who are struggling with their own psychological issues or who have significant marital conflicts are often not ideal candidates for parent training. In such cases, the school psychologist may suggest to the parents that they seek assistance from a community-based mental health professional to work on these issues. How this referral is made is important. Obviously, the school-based professional does not want to offend the parent. In general, we believe it is best for clinicians to approach parents from the point of view that they are interested in what is best for the child. It is also important to incorporate information that parents have already provided into the rationale for this referral. For example, when making a referral for marital therapy, the school psychologist might state, "You've mentioned several times that you and your husband argue frequently about a variety of matters, including finances, discipline of your children, and how to spend free time. You also told me when we met initially that you weren't very happy in your marriage. It might be helpful to you and your husband to talk to someone about the difficulties you are facing currently. If you and your husband can improve your relationship and communication skills, it will be easier for you to present a united front when disciplining Brittany. If you're interested, I can provide you with some names of professionals who specialize in couples work." When providing referrals, it is important that several referral sources be provided if available (in smaller communities this may not be possible), and the school psychologist should not be perceived as endorsing one option over another. In addition, the school psychologist should never threaten to make school-based services contingent on the parent seeking additional help.

In addition to referring parents to outside resources for their own issues, school-based professionals may also refer children and their families to outside professionals. Often this may occur when a problem is perceived as outside the area of expertise of the school-based professional. For example, if the school-based professional is conducting parent training with parents of a young adolescent and it is revealed that this youth has a drinking problem, a referral would likely be made because most school-based professionals do not have experience and expertise in treating addictions. Although we believe it is important for school psychologists to be viewed as comprehensive mental health providers, we recognize that not all school psychologists will have the necessary training and background needed to work with the variety of problems that might be presented. Thus, knowing one's limitations and knowing when to refer is important. The same can be said about clinicians outside the school: Not all mental health providers are equipped to work with children with addictions, so it is important to refer to appropriate individuals.

School-based mental health professionals may also refer when there is a question about whether medications may help a child's problems. This is true with all mental health problems but is particularly relevant in the treatment of externalizing disorders where medications are a common component of a comprehensive treatment program. For example, if a child has been diagnosed with ADHD and the school-based professional is involved in setting up a home/school note system, a referral might also be made to the child's pediatrician to evaluate whether medications would be appropriate. In making such a referral, the school-based professional needs to be careful with his or her wording. It should never be stated or suggested that a child must be on medication to remain in school or for the school psychologist to continue working with the family. In addition, the school psychologist should not word the referral to make it sound like he or she thinks the child should be on medication; rather, the referral is made to the physician to determine whether medications might be appropriate. For example, this type of wording should *not* be used: "Mark is having a lot of problems attending in class. Given his ADHD diagnosis, I really think he should be on Ritalin. Why don't you talk with your doctor to see about getting a prescription." Instead, wording along these lines should be used: "As you know, Mark is having a lot of problems attending in class. I'm hopeful the home/school note system we've developed will target some of this. However, in the interest of exploring all of your options, you might want to consult with your doctor to see if she thinks medications would be appropriate for Mark given our concerns with his behaviors."

When making referrals to outside professionals, school-based professionals should ensure they are doing so in a manner consistent with federal laws as well as laws in the states in which they provide services. School district policies related to referrals must also be considered. At the federal level, the 2004 special education law (IDEIA) contains a provision that prohibits school personnel from requiring children obtain a prescription for any medication as a precondition of attending school or receiving special education evaluations or services. Additional language indicates that this prohibition should not be construed as preventing school personnel from sharing information with parents regarding a student's academic or behavioral functioning or from referring a child for special education services (Klotz & Nealis, 2005). In addition to this provision in IDEIA 2004, the House of Representatives passed a stand-alone bill (Child Medication Safety Act of 2005, HR 1790) that would prohibit school personnel from requiring that children obtain a prescription for any psychotropic medications as a precondition for attending school or receiving school-based services. Although this bill was referred to the Senate, the Senate did not vote, and the bill never became law. In addition to these federal laws, some individual states have passed similar laws. Thus, it is important for school psychologists to be familiar with the laws in states in which they work to ensure they are in compliance with these regulations.

Ongoing Collaboration

In addition to referring families to outside resources, school-based mental health professionals are also in an excellent position to engage in ongoing collaboration with outside resources. In particular, and as introduced and discussed briefly in Chapter 1, the relationship between schools and physicians has received considerable attention, particularly in the context of prescribing stimulant medications to children diagnosed with ADHD. Physicians are often mystified by the school process and may be unsure what services a child is receiving, what services are available to a child, and how a child accesses services. School-based professionals can help facilitate the collaboration needed between all relevant parties (parents, school personnel, and medical personnel) when developing treatment programs for students with behavior problems. School-based information can assist a physician in making decisions regarding medications, and information the physician can provide to school-based professionals can help in understanding the effects—the negative as well as positive—that might be seen from a medication. In addition, if a child is receiving school-based and medical services, the school psychologist can help ensure the treatments are coordinated by providing feedback to all involved parties and being involved in discussions related to changes in treatments (e.g., the physician may attempt to reduce medication dosages if a behavioral intervention plan is working at school and at home).

One area in which school input can be particularly important is when physicians are attempting to titrate the dosage of a stimulant medication to find the level that produces the best behavioral outcomes with the fewest side effects. School personnel can be involved by tracking behaviors of concern (e.g., hyperactivity) as well as behaviors indicative of possible side effects (e.g., tics, lethargy). These data are then shared with the prescribing physician, who utilizes the information in making dosing decisions. When setting up such a collaborative program, the school psychologist, other relevant school personnel (e.g., classroom teacher), parent, and physician should identify key outcomes that they wish to see changed with the use of medication. A tracking system would be developed and behaviors tracked as the physician begins prescribing the medication. The combined information regarding targeted behavioral goals as well as side effects will help inform the physician as to whether the dosage (or even the type of medication) needs to be altered (DuPaul & Carlson, 2005).

Although ongoing collaboration with a child's physician can be an important part of a comprehensive intervention program, this often does not happen or happens to a lesser extent than would be ideal. In a recent survey, the majority of school psychologists reported engaging in monitoring medication effects. However, school psychologists also reported a number of barriers to their involvement in this task, including time, accessibility of physicians, and physicians' perceptions of school psychologists' role in this task (Gureasko-Moore, DuPaul, & Power, 2005).

In addition to consulting with medical professionals, school-based mental health professionals may also consult with community-based mental health providers. If a child is receiving services outside of the school for problems that have a school-based component, it can be important for the service provider and school personnel to communicate regarding expectations for the child's behavior at school and intervention options that may be available at school to support the work of the community-based professional.

CHAPTER SUMMARY

Externalizing problems are some of the most common reasons children are referred for services, especially in the school-based setting, in which these behaviors are likely to be disruptive to the class. Because externalizing problems often manifest in the home as well as the school setting, clinicians implementing interventions for these problems are in an ideal position to facilitate a collaborative relationship with parents. As noted throughout this chapter, there are numerous interventions for externalizing problems, but almost all require the involvement of adults in a child's life to be maximally effective. Thus, when faced with designing treatment programs for such problems, clinicians should work to involve these key individuals in the treatment plan. In addition, because the psychosocial treatments of externalizing problems are relatively short term in nature, they are ideal interventions for implementation by school-based professionals, who are often pressed for time with their multiple duties and high caseloads.

Common Behavioral Terms

Children's behaviors are greatly influenced by the responses their behaviors receive from others, particularly parents. Understanding how your behaviors can influence your child's behaviors can lead to a better understanding and better management of your child's behaviors. Below are some common terms we use when discussing behaviors.

ABCs of Behavior

A =**antecedent**—what is happening *before* a behavior occurs.

B = **behavior**—the actual behavior that occurs.

C = **consequence**—what happens *after* the behavior occurs.

To help illustrate these definitions, here are a couple of examples:
- A: You are getting dinner on the table and set a glass of milk in front of your child.
- B: Your child cries and says, "No, I don't want milk. I want soda."
- C: You take the milk away and give your child soda.

In this example, the consequence of the child's crying was that he received his desired beverage. Receiving a desired consequence increases the chance the behavior (crying, demanding) will occur again.

Now let's look at the same antecedent and behavior but with a different consequence.
- A: You are getting dinner in the table and set a glass of milk in front of your child.
- B: Your child cries and says, "No, I don't want milk. I want soda."
- C: You say to your child, "Milk is what we drink at dinner" and ignore his crying.

In this example, the child did not get his desired beverage and, therefore, is less likely to cry in the future to get what he wants.

These examples illustrate several important behavior principles:

Reinforcement

Positive Reinforcement—When positive reinforcement is applied, we increase a behavior by giving a desired consequence (**reinforcer**). Because different children find different things reinforcing, it is important to determine what your child likes in order to decide what will be effective reinforcers. Reinforcers can include toys and money but also attention and praise. Even some things we consider unpleasant can be reinforcers. For example, most children are reinforced by parental attention, and for many children even negative parental attention (yelling) may increase behaviors. Reinforcers should be given as soon as possible after a behavior occurs for them to be most effective. It is also important to remember that you can positively reinforce behaviors you don't want to reinforce. In the first scenario above, the child was positively reinforced for crying (he received his desired consequence of being able to have soda at dinner).

(cont.)

Negative Reinforcement/Escape—Escape involves increasing a behavior by removing something perceived as unpleasant. Frequently, the use of escape increases negative behaviors. For example, a child who does not like math class may act out during class and get sent to the principal's office. In this case, being sent to the principal's office is reinforcing because the child gets to escape from math (an unpleasant activity). This child is then more likely to act out in math class in the future.

Often parents and children get in a pattern of negative reinforcement. For example, your child may whine to get out of cleaning his or her room (escape a negative task). Because whining is unpleasant to you, you give in and allow your child not to clean the room. The next time your child whines, you will be more likely to do the same thing because you have been negatively reinforced (the unpleasant whining stops) for giving in. In addition, your child has been negatively reinforced by your withdrawal of the aversive task. Thus, your child is more likely to whine again in the future.

Extinction

Extinction can be used to decrease behaviors. This involves ignoring (and, therefore, not reinforcing) a behavior. For example, if your child cries and whines every night to get soda at dinner and you had been giving in and allowing soda but then you start ignoring your child's pleas, eventually your child will stop asking for soda because he or she is no longer reinforced for this behavior.

Extinction Burst

It is important to remember that when you begin to ignore behaviors that you had been attending to, the behaviors almost always get worse before they get better. This is called an "extinction burst." However, if you continue to ignore the behaviors, they will stop. It is very important that you continue with the ignoring, even as the crying and whining worsen. If you initially ignore these behaviors but give in when they become too annoying, your child learns he or she can get what he or she wants if he or she cries/whines long enough.

Differential Reinforcement

We can often change children's behaviors by reinforcing them for something we approve of and ignoring misbehaviors. This is called "differential reinforcement." For example, when your child is whining for soda at the dinner table, ignore this behavior. Once he or she does any other appropriate behavior (e.g., taking part in the dinner conversation, eating his or her vegetables), reinforce (praise) your child for it quickly.

Punishment

Punishment is used to decrease behaviors by delivering an undesirable consequence following the occurrence of a behavior. The best type of punishment to use is "response cost." When using this method, the child loses a reinforcer (i.e., something positive and desirable) when he or she engages in inappropriate behavior. For example, a child may lose TV privileges if he or she does not complete certain chores.

FORM 4.2

Increasing Your Child's Good Behavior

To increase your child's good behaviors, it is important to reinforce these behaviors by paying attention to them. Although this may sound like an easy thing to do, it is important to practice positive attending skills. The best way to do this is in a one-on-one play setting with your child where your child is allowed to "lead" the play. Below are guidelines for implementing this one-on-one time.

1. **Choose a time.** Choose a 5- to 15-minute time each day to play with your child. This should be a time period in which you can play one-on-one with your child and not be distracted or interrupted by other children, household duties, etc. It's best to be consistent with the time, so try to choose a time that will work every day.

2. **Choose appropriate toys.** Choose three to four different toys to play with during these special play times. These toys should be constructive toys that your child enjoys (e.g., blocks, Legos, Lincoln Logs).

3. **Use child-directed statements.** As you begin playing with your child, use the following type of statements. These help you focus your attention on your child.

   a. **Descriptions:** Describe out loud what your child is doing, being as specific as possible.

      Examples of descriptions include:
      "You put the green triangle on top of the red square."
      "It looks like you are drawing a cat with the purple crayon."
      "Look at that tower—you have the blocks stacked so high."

   b. **Reflections:** When your child speaks, reflect back to the child what he or she said. Try not to repeat exactly what your child said but to reflect the general message of the child.

      Examples of reflections include:
      Your child says, "Look, I'm building a house—just like Grandpa's house." So you say, "You're building a house and it is blue, just like Grandpa's house."

      Your child says, "I'm going to use the blue marker because that is my favorite color." You say, "You're going to color with the blue marker. I agree that blue is a pretty color."

   c. **Praise:** Verbally praise your child for appropriate/positive behaviors. Try to be as specific as possible with your praise statements.

      Examples of praise statements include:
      "Look at how high you stacked your blocks. You're doing a great job being slow and careful with your building."
      "Thanks for giving me a crayon to draw with. I appreciate how you are sharing your toys."

(cont.)

d. **Join in/imitate:** Join in your child's play, while still allowing your child to lead the activity. For example, if your child is drawing, you can draw too but allow your child free access to the crayons.

e. **Be enthusiastic and genuine:** All of your statements should convey to your child that you are interested and excited about what he or she is doing. Use voice inflection and comments to show your enthusiasm, and make sure your comments sound genuine and not forced or sarcastic.

Examples of enthusiastic/genuine statements include:
"Wow! Look at that great picture. You have drawn a lovely house."
"Look how high you have stacked your blocks! That's such a tall tower!"

4. **Avoid directive statements.** This playtime is intended to be child focused. By avoiding directive or critical statements, you keep your focus on what your child is doing and allow your child to lead the play activities. During your playtime, you should refrain from the following:

a. **Asking questions:** For example, "What are you building? Is that a barn for your horse?"

b. **Giving commands:** For example, "I think you should build a barn for your horse."

c. **Being critical:** For example, "That's a barn? It doesn't really look like one."

Questions, in particular, can be hard to avoid. Although questions may seem harmless (and it is certainly appropriate to ask your child questions outside of this playtime context), questions serve to lead the play or conversation in the direction in which you want to go and require the child to respond to you. Therefore, to keep this playtime child directed and focused, it is important to refrain from asking questions.

5. **Dealing with misbehavior.** Occasionally, your child may misbehave during this special playtime. If this misbehavior is minor, simply turn and look away from the child. Once your child's behavior is appropriate again, immediately attend to your child. If the misbehavior continues or if the original misbehavior was severe, simply tell your child playtime is over.

How to Effectively Ignore

1. Decide what behaviors you will ignore. Keep in mind that not all behaviors should be ignored. For some behaviors, you will need to apply consequences. Aggressive behaviors are one category of behaviors that should not be ignored. Ignoring is best used for minor misbehaviors, especially those that involve crying, yelling, whining, pestering, etc.

2. When the behavior occurs, tell your child in a matter-of-fact voice, "I'm not going to talk to you when you ... " and label what the child is doing. Tell the child this only once. Avoid lecturing because this typically reinforces (i.e., increases) the child's negative behavior.

3. Ignoring means that you remove **all** attention from your child. You should not communicate or talk with your child in any way. This means avoiding eye contact as well as not talking to your child at all. This sounds very simple but can be very hard to do.

4. Remember that often when you ignore a behavior (especially one that you had attended to before) it will get worse before it gets better. Be prepared for this and **do not give in.**

5. To help you ignore, it can be a good idea to engage in another task (e.g., reading, making dinner) so that you can distract yourself from your child's negative behaviors. If you need to (and your child will be safe), you can leave the immediate area (e.g., if the child is in the living room, go into the kitchen).

6. Once your child stops engaging in the negative behavior, be sure to praise him or her for an appropriate behavior. For example, if your child stops crying and begins doing a puzzle, you can say, "Great job putting that puzzle together. That looks like a lot of fun." Be sure to be genuine in your praise.

Giving Effective Commands

You may be able to improve your child's compliance simply by altering the manner in which you give commands to make them as effective as possible.

1. **Only give commands when you can follow through.** Save commands for situations in which it is important that a command to be given. Make sure you can and do provide consequences for compliance/noncompliance.

2. **Get your child's attention before giving the command.** Say your child's name, make eye contact with your child, etc. Make sure you are in close proximity to your child when you give a command.

3. **Give commands your child is capable of completing.** Commands involving tasks that are too difficult for your child to do physically (e.g., putting an item away on a high shelf) or too difficult for your child to understand should be avoided.

4. **Be direct and simple.** Use a polite, matter-of-fact tone of voice. Do not phrase commands as questions or suggestions. For example, instead of saying, "Would you like to turn off the TV now?", say, "Please turn off the TV."

5. **Give one command at a time.** Children may have difficulties following through with multiple-step commands. If there is a series of tasks your child needs to complete, give one command at a time with a consequence for compliance/noncompliance after each command.

6. **Tell your child what to do.** Instead of telling your child what not to do ("Don't yell"), tell your child what to do ("Please use your inside voice").

7. **Make limited use of explanations.** Often children ask for explanations or rationales simply to avoid complying with a command (e.g., "Why do I have to put my toys away now?") If explanations are used, make sure they are brief and provided either before the command ("We're going to the park. Please put your cars away") or after the child complies with the command ("Please put on your cars away.... [child complies] Thanks for putting your cars away like I asked. I needed you to put them away so we can go to the park.")

8. **Give choice commands if possible, especially with older children.** If your child can make a choice, let him or her know that in the command (e.g., "Please put on your sneakers or your sandals").

Effectively Using Time-Out

Time-out is an effective method of reducing your child's inappropriate behaviors, especially when used in conjunction with positive attention for appropriate behaviors. To effectively use time-out with your child, follow the guidelines below:

1. **Give an appropriate command.** Always give appropriate commands in a firm, directive manner. (See Giving Effective Commands handout.)

2. **Wait 10 seconds.** After giving a command, wait 10 seconds for your child to comply. You may count silently to yourself but avoid counting out loud.

3. **If your child does not comply within 10 seconds, restate the command.**
   If your child has not begun to comply within 10 seconds, you should say firmly,
   "If you don't _____ [insert command], then you will go to time-out."
   After giving this warning, wait another 10 seconds for compliance.

   When using time-out for a misbehavior other than noncompliance (e.g., breaking a set rule), send the child to time-out immediately and do not use this warning statement.

4. **Send/take child to time out.** If, after a warning, your child has not started to comply with your command within 10 seconds, say calmly and firmly, "You did not do as I asked, so you must go to time-out" and immediately take your child to the time-out location. The child should not be allowed to argue, belatedly comply with the command, or stall in another manner. Initially, you may need to lead your child to the time-out location or pick up your child and place him or her in time-out. Once your child is in the time-out location, say firmly, "Stay there until I tell you to get out."

5. **Do not attend to the child.** Once your child is in time-out, do not give him or her any attention. Do not talk to the child, do not remind the child why he or she is in time-out, do not respond to the child's pleas, etc. When the child has remained in the time-out for the appropriate amount of time (see page 2 of this form), return to the child and say, "You may get out of time-out now."

6. **Restate the command.** After your child gets out of time-out, repeat your original command. If the child complies, praise him or her. If the child does not comply, repeat the time-out sequence.

7. **Praise appropriate behavior.** Watch for your child's next appropriate behavior and praise him or her for it.

(cont.)

Frequently Asked Questions about Time-Out

Where Should My Time-Out Location Be?

For young children, time-out in a chair is the preferable method. The chair should be an adult-size dining room-type chair. It should be placed far enough away from all objects (including walls) that the child cannot kick or hit anything while in the chair. There should be nothing reinforcing that the child has access to from the chair (e.g., TV, radio). The time-out chair should be placed in a location that you can observe (e.g., in a hallway, at the edge of a room). Note, though, that a chair is not necessary for an effective time-out. Time-out is more of a state of being (i.e., no reinforcement provided) than a specific place.

How Long Should My Child Stay in Time-Out?

The general rule of thumb is that children should remain quiet and calm in time-out for 1 minute per year of age, not to exceed 5 minutes. However, when initially using time-out, this is typically too much to expect so plan on working up to this. When time-out is first used, it is common for children to cry, whine, scream, etc. for long periods of time. If this occurs, once your child has been quiet for a few moments (10–30 seconds), release your child from time-out. Gradually you can increase the amount of time you require your child to remain quiet.

What If the Child Leaves the Time-Out Chair?

It is not uncommon for children to test the limits when parents first begin to use time-out. Children will often leave the chair and may do so immediately after being placed in time-out. If this happens it is important to immediately return the child to time-out. Each time the child gets out, you should return the child to the chair. The first couple of times you return the child, state in a firm, calm voice, "You need to stay in time-out until you are quiet." When first using time-out (when it is most likely the child will leave the chair), it is a good idea to stand right next to the chair (but do not look directly at the child or do anything to give the child attention). That way, you can immediately put the child back in time-out as soon as he or she leaves the time-out chair. Children who squirm, bounce, roll around, stand, etc. in the chair should not be considered out of time-out. This behavior should simply be ignored.

What Should I Do If My Child Says He or She Needs to Get Out of the Chair?

The child is not to leave the time-out chair to use the bathroom or get a drink until his or her time is up and he or she has completed the task that was asked of him or her. If your child is permitted to do so, he or she will come to use this demand as a means of escaping from time-out on each occasion he or she is placed there. Simply ignore all requests your child makes.

FORM 4.6

Job Card Grounding

Job card grounding is a discipline method that can be used as an alternative to time-out—especially with older children for whom time-out may no longer be appropriate. Below are guidelines on how to set up this program:

1. Create a detailed description of 5 to 10 household jobs that your child can safely do. Your child should be able to complete each job in approximately 15 minutes. Make sure the jobs are not ones that have to be completed immediately. For example, washing the dinner dishes would not be an appropriate job because this is something that could not wait for several days if your child does not immediately complete the job. More appropriate jobs would be ones that can wait and ones that can be done repeatedly (e.g., dust furniture, vacuum, clean the bathroom).

2. Write a detailed description of each job on a separate card. The steps should be specific enough that your child knows what to do without asking you for additional guidance. For example, "Dusting the Living Room: remove all books from the coffee table, spray the table with dusting spray, wipe with a clean rag until there are no streaks, replace books, repeat for side tables and TV table."

3. When your child breaks a rule, give him or her one to three jobs to complete, depending on the severity of the rule broken. Your child should draw the cards randomly from a container (e.g., plastic container, paper bag).

4. Your child is grounded until the jobs are completed. You can decide the specifics of what it means to be grounded, but a few guidelines are suggested below:
   a. Attending school and other activities you believe are necessary (e.g., church, organized sport activities)
   b. Completing all required household duties normally part of your child's routine
   c. No television, phone privileges, video games, etc. (Note: Computer access can be allowed for school work purposes but should not be allowed for other purposes.)
   d. No social activities, including having friends visit.
   e. No other nonrequired activities that your child normally enjoys

5. Grounding ends when your child completes his or her job(s) correctly as determined by you (the parent). If the jobs are not completed correctly, you should review the steps with your child and have him or her redo the job. Note that this should not be viewed as a negotiation. It is important to stick to the grounding until the job cards have been completed.

6. The grounding period lasts as long as it takes for the child to correctly complete the jobs. If your child has only one job to complete and does it immediately, the grounding time will be very short. However, if your child has multiple jobs to complete or particularly if he or she stalls in completing the jobs, the grounding time may be quite long. Do not nag or remind your child about the jobs.

Note. Adapted from Job Card Grounding description and handout from Christophersen (1998). Copyright 1998 by Edward Christophersen. Adapted by permission.

FORM 4.7

Using Privileges

Positive Behaviors

_____

_____

_____

_____

_____

Rewards

_____

_____

_____

_____

_____

Daily Chores

_____

_____

_____

_____

Automatic Privileges

_____

_____

_____

_____

_____

House Rules

_____

_____

_____

_____

_____

_____

Providing Privileges for Positive Behaviors

With your child, generate a list of positive behaviors or extra chores that your child can do to earn reinforcers as well as rewards your child can earn. These should be rewards your child does not normally have access to (e.g., later bedtime) or additional time in an activity your child does have access to (e.g., extra playtime with Mom/Dad; extra computer time). Make sure to praise your child when you provide him or her with the reinforcer.

Automatic Privileges

In this part of the program, expected daily chores are tied to privileges children automatically have access to. For example, a child may be allowed to play at a friend's house after school without having to earn this privilege. If the child does not complete one of the daily expected chores listed on the left, give him or her **one** warning and a time frame by which the chore should be started. If he or she fails to **begin** the chore by the specified time, take away one or more privilege. For example, "Rex, you need to feed the dog within the next 5 minutes or you won't be able to use the computer tonight." It is generally best not to take away privileges for more than a day. This way your child starts over with a "clean slate" each morning, and you don't have to worry about running out of privileges to take away.

House Rules

Create a brief number of house rules that must be followed. Whenever your child breaks one of the house rules listed on the left, he or she should immediately lose one or more of the automatic privileges listed on the right. For example, "Anna, you just broke the rule of not talking back. You aren't allowed to watch TV or play video games tonight."

FORM 4.8

Home/School Note

DAILY SCHOOL NOTE FOR: _____

Date: _____

_____ is responsible for presenting this form to his/her teachers at the end of each time period, and he/she is responsible for bringing this form home each evening. Each teacher is responsible for initialing in the appropriate column.

Required for evening privileges: _____

Class time

	Y	N	Y	N	Y	N	Y	N	Y	N	Y	N	Y	N
1.														
2.														
3.														
4.														
5.														
6.														

FORM 4.9

Implementing the Problem-Solving Steps

Tackling Problems

Problems will come your way ... some of them can't be easily solved. But having a plan can help take some of the stress out of the situation.

- **Think ahead.**

Sometimes you can guess when a problem might be coming and prevent it. Of course, *preventing* a crisis is always easier than dealing with one!

- **Take a breath and make a plan.**

When a problem does strike, often you don't have to come up with a solution right away. Take a breath and give yourself a chance to relax and think. We usually make better decisions when we're not mad, scared, or embarrassed.

- **Define the problem.**

Sometimes this is not so obvious in the moment. You have to get to the real problem before you can solve it.

- **Think about solutions.**

Almost always, there will be more than one way to solve a problem. Think about all of the possibilities, even ones that don't seem practical. Write these down or get ideas from someone, so that you can see what all of the choices are.

- **Evaluate your solutions.**

Go through each solution you came up with and think about what would happen (good and bad) if you used that solution. A couple of your options may not seem practical. There will likely be one or two that seem best.

- **Pick the best option and give it a try.**

Of the options that seem best, pick the very best and give it a try.

- **How did it work?**

Were you able to give your best option a genuine try? Are you happy with the way that things turned out? If you are satisfied, congratulate yourself! You faced a difficult situation and handled it well.

If it did not work out ...

- **Decide what went wrong and what else you could try.**

Maybe another option from your list would work better and could be used now or next time you have a similar problem.

5

Interventions for
Internalizing Problems

Although internalizing disorders, such as anxiety and depression, have historically received less attention than externalizing problems in the child treatment literature, these are commonly observed problems in school settings. Epidemiological data suggest that rates of clinically significant anxiety and depression range from 2 to 10% in school-age children and 15 to 20% among adolescents (Angold & Rutter, 1992; Kashani & Orvaschel, 1990). Rates of subclinical internalizing symptoms, which may still interfere with typical functioning, are considerably higher (Kashani & Orvaschel, 1990). Typical manifestations of anxiety include school refusal, somatic complaints (e.g., stomachaches, headaches), and inhibition or excessive shyness. Additionally, children who present primarily with acting-out behavior may also experience significant anxiety. Likewise, although symptoms of depression include sadness, fatigue, and decreased interest in previously enjoyed activities, irritability and anger are also common symptoms of depression in children and adolescents. Internalizing disorders often have a negative effect on children's school performance and functioning in the form of absenteeism, missed assignments, reluctance to participate in class, and impaired social functioning. In contrast to externalizing disorders, internalizing symptoms can be easily overlooked or misunderstood by adults. Whereas children with acting-out behaviors almost always get the attention of teachers and school personnel, those with anxiety or depression may do little to draw attention to themselves, and when they do, it may involve irritable behavior that gets mistaken for an externalizing problem.

Treatments for anxiety and depression have traditionally been child focused and, as discussed later in this chapter, research demonstrating the benefits of family involvement remains somewhat limited (Barmish & Kendall, 2005; Diamond & Josephson, 2005). Despite the need for further research and a more clearly defined role for parent/family-focused intervention, we believe that there are multiple opportunities for home/school intervention and inclusion of parents in the interventions process. Indeed, there are several conditions

110

(e.g., school refusal, separation anxiety) for which it is difficult to imagine treatment *without* such collaboration.

This chapter begins with a clinical vignette describing a child with selective mutism, a relatively common condition considered to have an anxiety component that often challenges and frustrates school personnel and families alike. We then provide a brief overview of the empirical literature on the treatment of internalizing problems. The remainder of the chapter focuses on home/school collaboration in the treatment of internalizing problems that are commonly seen in school settings, such as generalized anxiety, school refusal, selective mutism, and depression. We close with a discussion of collaboration with other professionals and when to refer students for services outside the school setting.

Table 5.1 summarizes the techniques covered in this chapter.

TABLE 5.1. Interventions for Internalizing Problems

Intervention	Description	Developmental level
Emotional education	Helping youth to identify different emotions and linking emotions to physiological, cognitive, and behavioral responses. Parents are involved via education regarding these links and discussions in sessions with child.	All ages; most typically applied with elementary school-age and older children.
Exposure	Helping youth and parents understand how escape or avoidance of unpleasant situation can be maintaining the problem behavior. Setting up exercises to promote exposure to feared stimulus.	All ages, though with younger children emphasis will be on parent education.
Using coping behaviors	Identifying alternative thoughts and behaviors that youth can use when facing a situation in which anxious or depressive feelings result. Examples include cognitive restructuring and relaxation. Parents may be involved by coaching youth (especially younger children) in using these methods outside the intervention setting.	All ages, with cognitive techniques applied more with upper elementary school-age children. Modifications in other techniques may be required for younger children.
Contingency management	Parents (and teachers) reinforce youth for appropriate behavior, including approaching fearful object, speaking in class setting, etc. Children are not provided reinforcement for inappropriate behavior.	All ages.
Problem solving	Identifying alternative solutions to situations in which anxious or depressive feelings often result. Parents can help youth work through problem-solving steps.	Primarily for children ≥ 8 years; may be applied to younger children with some modifications.
Communication skills	Helping parents use effective communication skills such as active listening skills.	All ages.

Clinical Vignette

Corey is a 6-year-old boy whose kindergarten teacher has expressed concern because he "never talks," even though it is well into the school year. Corey resides with his mother, father, and older sister in a middle-class neighborhood. Before kindergarten, he was enrolled in a church-based preschool 3 days per week. In that setting, he was described as extremely shy. His preschool teacher shared that she heard him speak only on one occasion over the course of the year, and that was when he was outside the classroom talking with his older sister. The impression of preschool staff had been that he would begin talking with more exposure to other children. Corey's parents report that he speaks at home and in other familiar settings (e.g., with extended family members) but often "clams up" in social settings. At times, this has been a source of embarrassment for his parents at social gatherings (e.g., with colleagues from work), where Corey's older sister and virtually all of the other children seem very comfortable playing and conversing with one another. Children and even some adults have asked Corey's parents what is "wrong with him" and whether he can talk. In an effort to help him, his parents have coached him before social events, practicing what he might say to others. They have even tried "making deals" to reward him if he speaks in public. If anything, they report that these efforts have backfired and made him even more reluctant. They are now wondering whether his silence is indicative of a power struggle and whether they should "give in" or press him even harder. Corey's developmental and medical histories are unremarkable. His parents do note that his articulation is immature for a child his age, although they are able to understand him without much difficulty.

EVIDENCE-BASED INTERVENTIONS
FOR INTERNALIZING PROBLEMS

Until recently, the evidence base for the treatment of internalizing disorders in children and adolescents was restricted to a few uncontrolled trials and numerous case reports. Research has significantly improved in rigor and quantity over the last 5 to 10 years, although the literature remains limited compared with the volume of studies on childhood externalizing problems. For both anxiety and depression, the best studied contemporary treatments are those utilizing a cognitive-behavioral framework (see discussions later in this chapter related specifically to anxiety and depression). Although a comprehensive discussion of cognitive-behavioral theory and practice is beyond the scope of this chapter (interested readers will find more detailed descriptions in Kendall, 2006), a brief overview is warranted. Cognitive-behavioral therapy (CBT) interventions have evolved from the social learning perspective and encompass a broad array of treatment strategies. In general, treatments using a CBT approach are problem specific and focused on symptom reduction (as opposed to more insight-oriented therapies), utilize a psychoeducational format, and involve ideographic assessment to better understand the thoughts, behaviors, and situational factors that contribute to a particular problem behavior. CBT interventions are generally delivered in individual or group settings, although clinicians providing consultation to parents and teachers may also utilize some of the basic principles of CBT.

As an example, as applied to the treatment of anxiety, CBT focuses on fostering adaptive cognitions (e.g., positive self-talk during stressful or anxiety-provoking situations), using reinforcement to shape a repertoire of adaptive coping behaviors, and implementing behavioral strategies to assist with symptom reduction (e.g., exposure and systematic desensitization). These strategies would be implemented with a combination of psychoeducation, in-session activities (e.g., modeling, practice with therapist feedback), and structured homework assignments that a client would complete between sessions. Similarly, a CBT depression intervention might target thoughts that contribute to feelings of worthlessness and despair and behaviors that limit access to reinforcement (e.g., social withdrawal). We provide details on many of these intervention strategies later in this chapter.

Although CBT methods have been more commonly applied in intervention settings, there have also been several efforts to tailor CBT for use as a preventive intervention by bolstering protective factors and helping to ameliorate risk factors *before* children demonstrate pathology. With regard to internalizing disorders, commonly identified risk and protective factors include child temperament, academic success and connection to school, parent–child attachment, social skills, attributional style, parental history of anxiety/depression, and exposure to traumatic or stressful life events (Barrett & Turner, 2004). Prevention efforts strive to address those factors that are most modifiable to improve functioning in children who would otherwise be vulnerable to anxiety/depression. For example, the Penn Prevention/Penn Resiliency Program is one such prevention program targeted toward students ages 10 to 15. This program is delivered via group format and consists of cognitive and social problem-solving components. As reviewed by David-Ferdon and Kaslow (2008), this program has considerable empirical support and is considered "a probably efficacious treatment in reducing depressive symptoms" (p. 83). In addition, a recent study evaluating the effectiveness of combining the student-focused Penn Resiliency Program with a parent intervention component found positive effects for this combined treatment on symptoms of depression and anxiety (Gillham et al., 2006). In Australia, researchers have been actively investigating the efficacy of universal anxiety and depression prevention programs for the last 10 years (e.g., Barrett & Turner, 2001; Dadds, Spence, Holland, Barrett, & Laurens, 1997), including the FRIENDS program, described in more detail later.

Another development in the CBT research is the emphasis on *modular* treatments consisting of the various components of empirically supported treatments (Chorpita, Daleiden, & Weisz, 2005). This involves dismantling an intervention and using selected components as needed or varying the order of presentation based on clients' individual needs. This approach acknowledges that whereas some children require a full treatment protocol delivered in a specified sequence, others might only need certain elements or may benefit from an alternative ordering of components. For example, a child with depression may be judged to be too young or immature to benefit from a highly cognitive intervention involving challenging irrational beliefs, but may still benefit from behavioral strategies such as pleasant event scheduling or behavioral activation. Research to date has focused on the efficacy of treatment packages rather than these individual components. Thus, it is not entirely clear at this point which elements will prove to be the most critical for successful intervention. Research on the individual components of these packages may help to answer critical questions about what works for whom and help to reduce the gap that often exists between the science of empirically supported treatment and clinical practice.

The importance of family in the development and perpetuation of anxiety and depression has long been recognized (e.g., Birmaher, Arbalaez, & Brent, 2002; Cummings, Davies, & Campbell, 2000; Diamond & Josephson, 2005). Further, there are studies suggesting that family and parent variables can have a significant impact on treatment outcome (e.g., Berman, Weems, Silverman, & Kurtines, 2000; Southam-Gerow, Kendall, & Weersing, 2001). Nonetheless, research on the benefits of including parents in the treatment of internalizing problems is relatively new. Despite the clinical and theoretical justifications for including parents, findings from existing outcome studies have been more variable than one might expect. In a review of the anxiety literature, Barmish and Kendall (2005) found that outcomes from RCTs were mixed, with some studies suggesting robust improvements above and beyond individual child treatment when parents are included and others reporting minimal effects. Similarly, findings with regard to the treatment of depression have been equivocal, with some showing increased efficacy of a combined adolescent–parent treatment (Clarke, Rohde, Lewinsohn, Hops, & Seeley, 1999; Lewinsohn, Clarke, Hops, & Andrews, 1990) and others showing little added benefit (e.g., Brent et al., 1997). It appears likely that parent involvement will prove to be particularly important for some diagnostic categories and populations. For example, Barrett, Dadds, and Rapee (1996) found that in younger children (ages 7–10 years) treatment effects were larger when they received individual CBT plus parent involvement versus individual CBT alone. For older children and adolescents, parent involvement did not confer benefits above and beyond those achieved with individual CBT alone. Further, there are certain diagnoses (e.g., separation anxiety disorder, school refusal) that, by their nature, heavily involve parents, making it difficult to imagine an effective treatment without extensive parent involvement. Finally, consulting with both parents and teachers is most likely to lend itself to a time-limited intervention that would be feasible in school settings.

Evidence-Based Practice in the School

Most of the evidence-based interventions discussed previously can be implemented in a school setting with little adaptation. As discussed in the following sections, several intervention and prevention programs have been developed for and tested in the schools either during or after school hours. For example, Barrett, Duffy, Dadds, and Rapee's (2001) FRIENDS anxiety prevention program was successfully implemented by teachers and other school personnel along with periodic evening sessions for parents. In the depression literature, Clarke and colleagues (1995) have demonstrated success with a group CBT depression prevention program that was delivered by trained school psychologists and school counselors after school. Thus, these interventions can be used in the schools, and for prevention programs in particular, this is really the current state of the art given the access to at-risk youth who may not be able to secure mental health care in the community. Most of these interventions are time limited (e.g., 10–20 sessions) and skills focused, which enhances their feasibility. However, in some settings further abbreviation may be needed. Although an absolute minimum duration has not been identified, interventions of fewer than five sessions have generally not proven as effective (e.g., Clarke, Hawkins, Murphy, & Sheeber, 1993). As an alternative or adjunct to direct intervention, there are at least some data showing that providing parents with written psychoeducational materials offers some benefit, although not to the same degree as in-person intervention (e.g., Rapee, Abbott, & Lyon, 2006). Finally, as discussed in Chapter 1, the inclusion of parents and a successful collaboration often require flexibility in terms of scheduling (e.g., evening sessions to reduce time missed from work) and other accommodations for high-risk families (e.g., assistance with transportation, helping to arrange child care for siblings).

BEHAVIORAL TARGETS AND APPROPRIATE APPLICATIONS

As we have noted throughout this book, successful treatment of symptoms is facilitated by identifying clear behavioral targets for intervention. This can sometimes be more difficult for anxiety and depression, because many of the core symptoms are subjective and not readily observable. Child and adolescent report is, therefore, critical to initial assessment and treatment monitoring. There are a few behavioral rating scales that can be used for this purpose, with repeated assessment to monitor treatment progress (see Chapter 3 for a description). However, tailoring such an assessment to the individual child can often be more helpful, because this can focus more exclusively on the symptoms that the child views as most troubling. For younger children in particular, this may require clinicians to work with the child to develop a common language for the child's symptoms. For example, a 7-year-old child might describe his or her anxiety as a "yucky feeling in my tummy" or "feeling shaky." Whatever the metaphor, it is important to develop a common understanding and to operationally define symptoms to the extent possible. Often the use of visual prompts can be helpful. For example, several evidence-based interventions ask children to rate their level of anxiety on a scale from 0 to 10 (0 = *no worry at all*, 10 = *most worried you can imagine*) using a worry thermometer (see Figure 5.1 on p. 119 and Form 5.1 at the end of the chapter). Others have children draw a picture of their worry/fear or indicate on an outline drawing of a person where they feel it most when they are scared. In addition, parents may be able to provide important input regarding how a child talks about his or her symptoms of anxiety. Ultimately, a goal of treatment will often be to help the child, as well as his or her parents, begin to understand the connection between these subjective symptoms and external events or triggers.

Other targets may be readily observable and may, in fact, be what brought the child to treatment in the first place. For example, teachers may describe an anxious child as exhibiting excessive shyness (e.g., reluctance to participate in class, failure to initiate interactions with peers), poor assertiveness, or recurrent somatic complaints (e.g., stomachaches or headaches). A child with depression may be overly emotional, cry frequently, or be irritable/hostile. It is important to involve both parents and teachers in identifying these behavioral manifestations of internalizing symptoms. Monitoring these symptoms can be accomplished via the use of a standardized rating scale, a rating scale developed for an individual child, or various observational strategies (see Chapter 3).

Most interventions for internalizing symptoms will involve direct work with the child or adolescent, either in an individual or a group format. Group interventions, in particular, are well suited to school-based mental health settings. In most situations, these will be time limited (e.g., 10–20 sessions) and skills focused versus insight oriented. As discussed in detail in the following sections, parents may be involved directly by attending their own group sessions or by attending sessions with their child. Parent-specific interventions might focus on psychoeducation about anxiety, parenting skills training, and suggestions for home activities (e.g., relaxation strategies). Parents may participate in individual sessions with their child and learn skills to directly address their child's symptoms (e.g., reinforcing nonanxious behaviors) or skills they can use at home to assist their child with the application of techniques learned in therapy. Even when parents are not active participants, treatment may be enhanced by providing regular updates on treatment goals and progress. When appropriate, comparable notes may be provided to a child's teacher, who can then help the child practice target skills and provide reinforcement in the classroom. Of course, with older children and adolescents, in particular, clinicians will need to discuss with their client what information will be shared and how that communication will take place.

Some of the symptoms and associated problems encountered by children with internalizing problems may be beyond the scope of practice of certain school-based professionals. In addition, for students requiring more intensive services, resources may not be available within the schools for the mental health professionals to provide, even if they have the requisite training. For example, children with recurrent self-injury or severe suicidal ideation and suicide attempts are likely to require ongoing, intensive treatment that is impractical in a school setting. Similarly, successful treatment of anxiety for some children involves ongoing individual treatment, which may be more extensive than what can be offered in many schools. As discussed later in this chapter, even in these circumstances school-based professionals can lend valuable assistance by helping families to access needed services or by consultation with providers in the community.

INTERVENTIONS FOR GENERALIZED ANXIETY AND RELATED SYMPTOMS

Much of the research on the treatment of anxiety has focused on generalized anxiety and related symptoms, such as inhibition and excessive shyness. The work of Kendall and colleagues (see Kendall, Aschenbrand, & Hudson, 2003, for a review) has been particularly influential, and there are now several widely available treatments that incorporate a comparable CBT approach. Kendall's Coping Cat program involves several CBT strategies, such as psychoeducation about anxiety, identifying cues and symptoms of anxiety, learning relaxation and problem-solving strategies, addressing cognitions that contribute to anxiety, and exposure (see Kendall's 2006, manual for a detailed description and treatment materials). The program has been investigated as an individual and a group treatment with children ages 7 to 14 years. Findings have suggested that the Coping Cat program is effective relative to wait-list and attention control conditions and that results are maintained at follow-up

(Kendall et al., 2003). This program has been modified for use in Australia (e.g., the Coping Koala or FRIENDS program by Barrett and colleagues; e.g., Barrett & Turner, 2001), where these findings have been replicated. A recent large-scale RCT comparing CBT (based on the Coping Cat) and the medication sertraline (Zoloft) demonstrated positive effects for both CBT and medication compared with placebo (Walkup et al., 2008). However, the combination of CBT and medication was the most effective.

In the original Coping Cat, parents were involved in two sessions to review the material being covered with their child/other children in the group. In the Australian adaptation, Barrett et al. (1996) developed a family treatment component as an additive treatment to child-focused CBT alone. This family treatment included training for parents in strategies to help them reduce their children's anxiety (e.g., reinforcement for approaching a feared situation, ignoring to deal with complaints) as well as deal with their own emotions, including problem solving related to anxiety-provoking situations, and communication and problem-solving skills training. As noted earlier in this chapter, although the family treatment component did have a beneficial effect over and above the individual treatment component, this was most pronounced in younger children (ages 7–10).

In addition to evaluating this more parent-focused intervention, Barrett, Farrell, Ollendick, and Dadds (2006) evaluated their CBT-based FRIENDS program, a 10-week universal prevention program targeting internalizing symptoms. In this school-based program, teachers or other school personnel (e.g., school counselors) received training in the implementation of the program as part of their classroom curriculum. Parents attended four evening sessions, including psychoeducation (e.g., information about parenting, typical development of childhood fears and anxiety, risk/protective factors related to anxiety) and a discussion of parenting strategies relevant to internalizing symptoms (e.g., reinforcement of adaptive coping behavior). Separate versions of the FRIENDS program are available for younger children (ages 7–11 years) and older children and adolescents (ages 12–16). Results from several studies suggest that the FRIENDS program results in lower rates of internalizing symptoms, which appear to be maintained over intervals of up to 3 years (Barrett & Turner, 2004; Barrett et al., 2006). These findings have been replicated by an independent research group in the Netherlands (Muris, Meesters, & van Melick, 2002). In another prevention trial, LaFreniere and Capuano (1997) tested a 20-session home-based program that focused primarily on assisting mothers by offering psychoeducation about anxiety and temperamental inhibition, providing social support, and promoting parenting competence. They found short-term increases in children's social competence, increased maternal warmth, and decreased intrusive and overcontrolling parenting. Decreases in children's anxious and withdrawn behavior were also observed, although changes were not statistically significant.

Rapee, Kennedy, Ingram, Edwards, and Sweeney (2005) have also reported on a parent education program that included similar components as a preventive intervention for inhibited preschoolers. Interestingly, although preschoolers in this study continued to demonstrate an inhibited temperament posttreatment, they were less likely to show evidence of anxiety or to meet criteria for an anxiety disorder than those in a no-treatment control group. Strategies presented in Rapee et al.'s treatment manuals (*Treating Anxious Children and Adolescents: An Evidence-Based Approach* [Rapee, Wignall, Hudson, & Schniering, 2000] and *Helping Your Anxious Child: A Step-by-Step Guide for Parents* [Rapee, Spence, Cobham, & Wignall, 2000]) were incorporated in a later study by Rapee, Abbot, and Lyneham (2006). These authors reported that having parents read and implement the strategies described in the parent manual resulted in some improvement in children's anxiety relative to a wait-list condition, but the results were not as robust as for standard group CBT treatment.

Based on this literature, a few of the core skills relevant to collaborative home/school interventions include identifying symptoms of anxiety (e.g., somatic, cognitive, behavioral) and understanding the connection between variations in anxiety and environmental and other events, knowledge of escape/avoidance learning as it relates to anxiety, developing coping behaviors, differential reinforcement of coping versus avoidance, and stress management. We provide a bit more detail about integrating these skills into home/school collaboration in the following sections. Practitioners will also want to review the evidence-based treatments discussed previously for additional details and to access treatment manuals.

Identifying Symptoms of Anxiety

Children and adolescents may not be adept at identifying the various symptoms of anxiety that they experience. For example, a child may report being scared without also noting the physiological changes that often accompany anxiety, such as rapid heartbeat, rapid and shallow breathing, or sweaty or shaky hands. Further, children (and sometimes adults for that matter) often do not understand the connection among thoughts, feelings, and behaviors. Such connections are fundamental to CBT, and most interventions include at least brief psychoeducation in this regard. For children and adolescents, psychoeducation can start by asking, "How do you know when you're anxious?" Follow-up questions include "How does your body feel?," "What do you start thinking about?," and "What do you do?" The intent of these questions is to start developing the notion that anxiety involves thinking, feeling, and doing, which will ultimately be important for establishing their involvement in treatment. This can also help to initiate a conversation about differentiating anxiety from other emotions that involve physiological arousal, such as excitement or anger. This understanding can sometimes help to positively reframe arousal and to understand that it can be a good and desirable response to situations.

The use of visual depictions can often be helpful, particularly for young children. This might include having children draw a picture of themselves when they are anxious or drawing on an outline of a person to show "where" they feel anxious. To elicit thoughts related to anxiety, older children may fill in dialogue balloons for cartoons depicting themselves in anxiety-provoking situations. A visual scale may also be useful to help establish gradations in children's anxiety, which again children may not be aware of initially. Children often view being scared as a yes–no issue rather than as a matter of degree. For example, a child might report being worried all the time, without noting that there are actually many variations in degree of anxiety across different situations. Form 5.1 (at the end of the chapter) contains a 1–10 scale on which children can rate the severity of their anxiety as part of identifying the anxiety and the conditions surrounding it (see Figure 5.1 for a filled-in example).

Anxiety ABCs

A What happened before?	How nervous did you feel?	B What did you do?	C What happened after?
The teacher called on me during reading. I knew the answer, but got a lump in my throat and couldn't answer.	10—Worst possible 9— 8— *Pretty bad ... but could have been worse, I guess* 7— 6— 5—Medium 4— 3— 2— 1— 0—Not at all	*Said I didn't know.*	*Teacher said that I should do the reading next time, and called on someone else.*

FIGURE 5.1. Example of completed Anxiety ABCs with fear ranking.

After these skills are developed, children can start to monitor themselves at home by identifying situations in which they felt nervous and their associated thoughts, feelings, and behaviors. They can also monitor their degree of anxiety in different situations and begin to understand the triggers for their anxiety. A work sheet such as the one presented in Form 5.1 can be used to facilitate this tracking.

When working with parents, a comparable explanation regarding the link among feelings, thoughts, and behaviors along with developmental information about children's ability to make such connections is often helpful. Parents may expect that their children will be able to understand and articulate their responses to anxiety-provoking situations when, in fact, children may not be able to. Further, parents may lack a good understanding of the situational triggers and intensity of their children's anxiety, either under- or overestimating the true level of distress. This may result in their being overly critical and dismissing their children's distress or, conversely, stepping in too soon in an effort to protect them. Further, involving parents in the discussion of thinking, feeling, and doing can help to facilitate conversations between parents and their children and help to form the foundation for further intervention. A handout such as the one in Form 5.2 (at the end of the chapter) may be helpful to review with parents (and children) to illustrate the connection among thoughts, feelings, and behaviors.

Reviewing this information with a child's teachers may also be helpful. Although teachers may not be directly involved in the treatment (unless the anxiety has a school-based component), having a better understanding of a child's anxiety may help teachers respond more effectively and empathetically to a child exhibiting significant symptoms of anxiety.

Understanding and Addressing Escape/Avoidance

A good understanding of escape/avoidance and how these relate to anxiety is helpful for both children and their parents, particularly because interventions will generally involve asking the child to attempt tasks that are going to make him or her uncomfortable (e.g., exposure or systematic desensitization). Understanding the rationale behind such interventions may enhance compliance. Visually depicting the cycle of escape/avoidance (see Form 5.3 at the end of the chapter) helps to provide a more tangible understanding that escape, although it may help alleviate anxiety in the short term, can be counterproductive and even make anxiety worse over time. Another option is to develop a table listing good and bad things about escape/avoidance and good/bad things about more active coping. This approach acknowledges that there are some short-term benefits to avoidance (e.g., short-term anxiety reduction), although in the long term there may be significant costs (e.g., growing restrictions on activities, decreased sense of competence).

Parents are likely to benefit from a comparable introduction to the concept of escape/avoidance. Although this may seem intuitive, parents may not have a good understanding of basic escape/avoidance principles and often have not considered how they might apply to their child's anxiety. For example, parents may not recognize a tantrum as a behavior that allows the child to "escape" an anxiety-provoking situation. In addition, parents may inadvertently encourage escape/avoidance by going out of their way to ensure their child does not come in contact with an anxiety-provoking stimuli (e.g., a parent walking a child with a dog phobia to school may take a circuitous route to avoid dogs). Working through some examples can illuminate these cycles and help parents to think differently about their responses to their child's behavior and avoid inadvertently reinforcing the child's anxiety. Having parents generate a comparable list of the costs and benefits associated with escape/avoidance helps parents appreciate the salient reasons why their child may choose to avoid anxiety-provoking situations. Professionals can also discuss with parents developmental issues related to these concepts, including an explanation that for children and adolescents it can be difficult to weigh the long-term potential benefits against the short-term known benefits. We sometimes also ask parents to generate a list of costs and benefits of their own related to an activity that is anxiety provoking for them (e.g., asking a boss for a raise, confronting an overly "helpful" family member). The hope is to generate increased empathy and understanding for the target child or adolescent while also acknowledging that escaping or avoiding an anxiety-provoking situation rarely leads to long-term benefits. Another, related topic that can be helpful to review with parents is the normal progression of anxiety. Like the discussion of the extinction burst described in Chapter 4, this can be charted visually (e.g., via a line graph showing the typical course of the extinction burst) to help parents understand that their child is going to feel distressed, likely even more so than in the past, as he or she first begins to attempt anxiety-provoking activities. However, the child's anxiety will subside with practice (i.e., exposure). Again, examples that most adults can relate to may be helpful here (e.g., public speaking). This discussion is important for parents who may be inclined to "rescue" their child from anxiety-provoking situations. In order for a child to develop a sense of efficacy about his or her ability to handle the situation and feel confident that the anxiety really will subside, the parents will likely have to convey a similar sense of confidence. Of course, this is easier said than done, because no parent likes to see his or her child experiencing distress. It is important to obtain parental buy-in and acceptance of these strategies before having a child implement exercises that involve exposure.

Developing Coping Behaviors

Clearly, a primary aim for anxiety treatments is to help the child develop alternative coping strategies. Important messages for children to receive are that (1) their anxiety is not going to go away immediately, and in order to produce long-term change, for a while they will need to do some things that make them uncomfortable and (2) there are alternative things they can do to help them cope with their anxiety and get through difficult situations. Our impression is that the first message is often not received by children and that treatment can even be counterproductive in this regard. Youth (and adults for that matter) often reason that they will start doing more things just as soon as their anxiety goes away. They, therefore, may attempt some of the relaxation and distress tolerance activities discussed during treatment in hopes that these will make their anxiety go away entirely. Of course, this almost never happens. The reality is that the anxiety that has been conditioned over years in many cases does not go away easily. When they find that their anxiety has not dissipated, patients can feel disenfranchised or lied to, assume that the relaxation or other coping strategies taught in treatment do not work, or drop out of treatment altogether. Discussing this up front with both children and their parents provides a realistic expectation and can bring about a degree of acceptance that, somewhat paradoxically, can contribute to anxiety reduction.

Coping strategies might include both cognitive and behavioral approaches. When discussing cognitive approaches with children, Rapee and colleagues (Rapee, Wignall, et al., 2000; Rapee, Spence, et al., 2000) suggest using a "detective" metaphor. Specifically, when they notice themselves feeling worried, children are coached to examine the evidence by (1) identifying the thought contributing to their anxiety, (2) looking for evidence supporting/refuting the thought based on past experience, alternative possibilities, and general knowledge; (3) evaluating the validity of the thought; (4) examining the consequences of the feared event (i.e., what is the worst-case scenario, and is that really so bad?); and (5) generating an alternative, calming thought. Of course, younger children and youth with developmental delays are likely to need more coaching and may need a simplified version of this approach, although our experience has been that even early school-age children can understand the principle of generating alternative thoughts.

A discussion of cognitive restructuring is also appropriate when collaborating with parents. Skillful parents can embed some elements of cognitive restructuring in their conversations with their child, gently challenging unrealistic and anxiety-provoking thoughts and offering more adaptive alternatives. However, before pursuing this course of action, it is important that the clinician, parent, and child are on the same page in terms of the parent's role. Upon learning about cognitive strategies, it is easy for well-intentioned parents to go overboard with their challenges and for parent–child interactions to dissolve into an all-out argument. This puts the child or adolescent in the position of working hard to convince his or her parents that the anxiety is valid, which makes treatment very difficult. Most parents can identify with the frustration of expressing fear or anxiety, only to have their significant other explain all of the reasons why they are being irrational. Clinicians will, therefore, need to make a judgment about whether parents will be able to coach their children effectively with these strategies or whether they are better off emphasizing empathy and supporting other approaches to coping. The parent may initially be encouraged to experiment with taking the child's perspective and offering a brief empathic response, without any attempt to "correct" the child's thinking. For example, rather than saying anything to challenge an exaggerated and anxiety-provoking thought, the parent may respond by saying, "I'm sorry. I can tell that you are really worried." A next step might be for the parent to start with the empathic response and provide some coaching to use cognitive strategies that the child is working on in individual therapy. The parent might be encouraged to say something like "I know that you're really feeling anxious about this. Can we try using the homework that the school psychologist gave you last week?"

Behavioral coping strategies include various forms of relaxation and distress tolerance. Progressive muscle relaxation, deep breathing, imagery, and meditation have all been used successfully with children and adolescents. Before attempting to implement one of these strategies, it is important to provide some rationale and again talk about realistic expectations. The rationale for relaxation can be tied to the physiological changes associated with anxiety. When people feel anxious, their bodies (sympathetic nervous system) tell them that they need to breathe more quickly, their heart needs to beat faster, and their muscles need to tense up so that they are ready for "fight or flight." Of course, these can all be very adaptive responses. However, for people with significant anxiety, their bodies send this message even when they really do not need to fight or flee. Using relaxation strategies helps them to regain control over this physiological process. Often clients' expectation for treatment is that they will come to the psychologist's office and learn a relaxation strategy that they can then easily use whenever they feel nervous. Unfortunately, it is generally not that simple. Learning to control one's breathing, heart rate, and muscle tension requires practice, and this is much easier when a person is not already in the midst of an anxiety-provoking situation. Therefore, it is important to emphasize that, although these strategies are eventually going to be helpful in anxiety-producing situations, it is going to take a fair amount of practice (i.e., daily).

A variety of scripts and specific strategies are available for presenting relaxation techniques to children and adolescents (e.g., Merrell, 2008; see Form 5.4 at the end of the chapter for one example). To our knowledge, there are no data to suggest superiority of one strategy over the others. It is most important to select a strategy that the child will actually use, and this will depend on the individual's symptoms and strengths. For example, an adolescent who describes prominent shortness of breath may be easier to engage if the strategy addresses this issue. A child with a vivid imagination may be particularly well suited for imagery. As one would expect, strategies will need to be fairly brief and concrete for younger children and may be more detailed for adolescents. Parents can be involved by learning relaxation strategies and practicing these with their child at home and modeling their use. Although it can be helpful to have parents prompt their child to practice relaxation, this can also become counterproductive (i.e., few adolescents will appreciate being told to "go relax" when they are upset). Sometimes the clinician can help prevent problems by asking the child or teenager for "permission" to have a parent to prompt him or her at home. For example, the clinician might say, "Is it going to be OK with you if your mom or dad reminds you to practice this week?" If the adolescent says "No" (as adolescents often do), the therapist can help to negotiate a deal, saying something like "OK, so I'll let your mom and dad know that there should be no prompting this week. But that means that when I see you next time, you will have practiced on your own at least four times." Younger children, however, may be more open to one-on-one time with their parents and may be eager to practice relaxation skills with their mother or father if the parent is also engaging in the relaxation steps.

The use of problem-solving skills (as discussed in Chapter 4) may also be a helpful coping strategy for children who have anxiety. Children who find themselves in an anxiety-provoking situation (or who know they will soon face one) can be encouraged to work through these steps, and the support of parents may be helpful. Solutions generated may include a combination of behavioral and cognitive techniques. For example, an adolescent who is worried about giving a speech in class may decide to go ahead and attend class (rather than skip class, one potential option that may be generated) and remind him- or herself to use deep breathing and coping statements (e.g., "I practiced my speech and if I did at home, I can do it in school") to help decrease the anxiety related to giving the speech. As when these skills are used with externalizing problems, parents can be part of this intervention by encouraging children to use these steps when faced with a situation that may lead to anxiety.

Differential Reinforcement of Coping Behaviors

Perhaps the single most important thing that parents can do to support the treatment of their child with anxiety is to examine their own parenting behaviors and to think about how they might be accidentally reinforcing their child's anxious behaviors. Parents of children with generalized anxiety, some of whom will be prone to anxiety themselves, may have a low tolerance level for their child's distress. This can result in very different responses, ranging from efforts to dismiss their child's emotions (i.e., minimizing the significance of the child's experience) or jumping in to "rescue" the child, thereby preventing him or her from tackling fear-producing situations independently. The ideal response is somewhere in the middle, acknowledging that the situation is difficult while also conveying a sense of confidence that the child can handle things on his or her own.

As discussed in Chapter 4, parents often benefit from the use of handouts and examples to help illustrate differential reinforcement. Having parents note and track the antecedents and consequences of anxious behavior can be helpful. We generally take a particular example of when a child exhibits anxious behavior, and carefully go through the details of the situation to identify potential antecedents and consequences for the child's behavior. Often when doing this, the payoffs (reinforcers) for anxious behavior become obvious. For example, a clinician might observe, "So when you drop your child off at school [antecedent], she refuses to get out of the car and starts to cry and even scream sometimes [behavior]. Then you spend some extra time reassuring her that everything is OK and, at least some of the time, you take her back home [consequence]." This can be contrasted with the payoffs for coping behavior: "Let's see ... if she didn't start crying and refuse to get out of the car, she doesn't get the same warm reassurance and she doesn't get to stay home for the day. I know which one I would choose!" Parents can then be coached about providing reinforcement contingent on the child's demonstration of coping behaviors. This can be tied to a fear hierarchy developed with the child, starting with lower order fears where the child is likely to be successful and moving toward more anxiety-provoking situations. Reinforcers might include parental praise or small tangible rewards, contingent on the child's use of adaptive coping skills. For example, a parent and child might develop a set of adaptive coping goals for the week, such as the child raising his or her hand in class or asking the teacher a question, and talk about potential reinforcers for successful completion (e.g., extra computer time, a small toy, getting to choose what is for dinner one night). Often this might necessarily involve collaboration with others when the adaptive coping is most likely to be demonstrated in the classroom or other school setting, and access to the reinforcer might be contingent on a report from the child's teacher (e.g., in the form of a home/school note; see Chapter 4).

SCHOOL REFUSAL

School refusal is a relatively common reason for referral to school-based mental health providers and is closely related to other forms of anxiety, such as separation anxiety or generalized anxiety. Interested readers are encouraged to consult Kearney's (2001) book, *School Refusal Behavior in Youth: A Functional Approach to Assessment and Treatment*, for a full discussion of the history, etiology, and treatment of these behaviors and Kearney and Albano's (2007) treatment manual and parent workbook describing their cognitive-behavioral approach to treatment.

The term "school refusal" encompasses a variety of related behaviors, with severity ranging from attending school under duress, actively resisting but nonetheless attending school (e.g., arguing with caregivers about attending, behaviors to stall getting ready), partial refusal (e.g., tardiness); to full refusal (e.g., failing to attend school for several weeks, months or longer). In the literature, distinctions are also made depending on the chronicity of the behavior. For example, Kearney and Silverman (1996) differentiate types of school refusal: (1) self-corrective (i.e., remitting spontaneously within 2 weeks), (2) acute (i.e., lasting between 2 weeks and a calendar year), and (3) chronic (lasting more than a calendar year). It is also important to distinguish between the many reasons that school absenteeism may occur. Although school *refusal* often has an anxiety component, we acknowledge that anxiety is only one of the potential contributors to school absenteeism. Comparable absenteeism can also be observed in youth with conduct disorders, who may skip school to engage in antisocial behaviors in the community; children who are maltreated or neglected, whose parents may not facilitate their school attendance or actively dissuade them from attending; and youth who are homeless or move frequently. Of course, the interventions deemed appropriate will be very different for these diverse presentations. Thus, it is important to understand the larger context in which absenteeism is occurring prior to designing a treatment program.

Interventions for school refusal will depend largely on the hypothesized functions of the behavior. Kearney (2001) describes four potential functions of school refusal: (1) avoidance of stimuli that produce negative affect (i.e., anxiety, depression, somatic complaints), (2) escape from unpleasant social or evaluative situations, (3) obtaining caregivers' attention, and (4) accessing reinforcers outside of the school setting. These functions should not be considered mutually exclusive, and in fact a combination of one or more of these functions is the rule rather than the exception. A common thread across all of these manifestations of school refusal is the need for a quick return to school. Often parents and even teachers who appreciate a child's discomfort with school attendance will suggest a partial return or an initial period of treatment with anxiety reduction interventions. To some extent, this mirrors the notion that individuals will engage in an anxiety-provoking situation *just as soon as their anxiety goes away*. Although it may sometimes be necessary to use these types of strategies, in general, the recommendation is to get children who refuse school back in the school setting as soon as possible and to the greatest extent possible. Next, we discuss collaborative home/school intervention strategies using the functions hypothesized by Kearney (2001).

Escape/Avoidance

For children who refuse to attend school to avoid stimuli that produce negative affect or to escape from unpleasant social or evaluative situations, the interventions discussed for generalized anxiety are all quite relevant. CBT-based interventions typically include psychoeducation about anxiety and school refusal, reestablishing a daily schedule, discussion of coping strategies, exposure, and differential reinforcement of coping behavior. Efforts to reestablish a schedule are important for both the child and his or her parents, because youth who are out of school for a prolonged period of time may have developed a daily routine that is difficult to interrupt (e.g., sleeping late, watching morning television). There can be several secondary gains associated with this altered schedule for both children and their parents. Thus, even before a child's actual return to school, making changes in these aspects of the morning routine are likely to be helpful. For example, before the child returns to school, parents may be encouraged to set the expectation that the child will be out of bed, dressed, and ready for school at the regular time. This may also mean a change in the parents' schedule, so that they are able to ensure the child's compliance.

Coaching in the use of various coping strategies (e.g., cognitive restructuring, relaxation) is much like what we discussed earlier in this chapter. An additional aspect of this treatment that deserves special attention is the development of a fear hierarchy (see Form 5.5 at the end of the chapter) and use of imaginal and *in vivo* exposure. For example, a child might be asked to rate his or her level of distress associated with getting ready for school, riding the bus or being dropped off, entering the classroom, recess or lunch, etc. (see Figure 5.2). These can then be used to develop an intervention using desensitization. This may be done using imaginal or *in vivo* procedures. With imaginal procedures, the child will be asked to think about the anxiety-provoking situations from his or her hierarchy. This might be aided with photos or other stimuli that remind the child of the situation. Before these exposures, the clinician and the child may need to develop a system for the child to provide feedback about his or her level of distress, for example, a number system (0 = *no distress at all*, 10 = *worst distress possible*) or a visual system (e.g., a distress thermometer). During the exposure, the child would then be able to use this system to provide information about his or her level of distress and would be coached to use relaxation strategies when he or she became uncomfortable. *In vivo* exposure involves actual exposure to anxiety-provoking situations. Again, this would proceed along a gradient based on the child's fear hierarchy. For example, *in vivo* exposures might include a child getting dressed and ready for school and riding with her parent to the school building, entering the classroom without other children present, or staying at school for increasingly longer periods without calling to check in with a parent. The child would be coached to use relaxation strategies and would be able to signal the therapist or caregiver if the level of distress became too great and he or she needed to temporarily stop the exercise and use some of these coping strategies. It is key that the exposures be set up so that they are tolerable and the child is likely to be successful to avoid further conditioning of an avoidance/escape response.

All of these procedures will require the buy-in of parents and extensive collaboration. A discussion of potential secondary gains associated with school absenteeism for both parent and child is an important part of this process. Although parents will generally acknowledge that their child should be in school and should get there on time, there may be several benefits associated with having the child home. As has been discussed, a child's negative affect can be very difficult for parents to tolerate, and keeping the child home for the day may help a parent to avoid dealing with the child's distress. Other secondary gains for a parent might include being able to sleep later, feeling important and close to his or her child, having the child around to assist with chores or child care during the day, or having the child home for company during the day. Although these might not be the reasons why a child initially misses school or the primary function of the behavior, they might make it difficult for a parent to intervene. Although challenging, an open discussion of these possibilities is an important first step in establishing a treatment.

Parents will also need to have a good understanding of anxiety and the rationale for the strategies used. Exposure procedures, in particular, can feel like cruel and unusual punishment to a parent. Because many exposure exercises will be undertaken between sessions, the parent needs to have a very good understanding of the goals of this treatment and why it is expected to work. Parents should also be asked about the level of child distress that they will be able to tolerate. Perhaps the worst outcome of this type of intervention comes when the child exhibits distress and the parent discontinues the exposure exercise (or, worse still, stops treatment altogether) instead of pausing and coaching the child to use relaxation strategies. This can, in fact, produce further conditioning of a fear response.

School-based mental health professionals can also serve as a liaison between parents and school staff. Occasionally, teachers and other school personnel blame the parent for the child's absence and take a punitive approach. Even when there is some reality to such perceptions, this often becomes counterproductive and might even contribute to further avoidance of the school setting. A parent may dread taking her child back to the classroom and enduring the accusing looks or comments that she receives (or at least perceives). Teachers might also engage in misguided efforts with the child, such as dismissing comments regarding his or her anxiety or an overly protective approach. Thus, school staff will need to be informed of the interventions being used and the rationale for any modifications suggested to their normal classroom routine. Collaboration and ongoing communication between

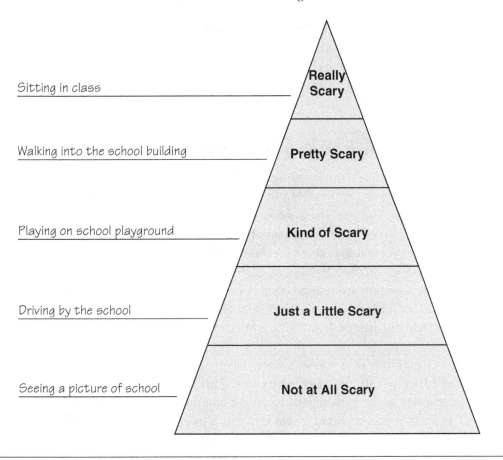

Sitting in class

Walking into the school building

Playing on school playground

Driving by the school

Seeing a picture of school

Really Scary

Pretty Scary

Kind of Scary

Just a Little Scary

Not at All Scary

FIGURE 5.2. Example of a completed Fear Hierarchy.

school personnel and parents can also be helpful if the child tries to get out of school once he or she is there. For example, a child may claim to be sick in attempt to get sent home for the day. If school personnel and parents can come to an agreement on what criteria need to be met for the child to actually get sent home for being sick (e.g., vomiting, high temperature), there is less of a chance the child will be sent home when he or she is simply using this as a means of attempting to escape from school and the associated anxiety.

In addition, school staff can serve as valuable partners with parents in other aspects of the intervention plan. It can often be helpful for a parent to drop his or her child off at school and leave quickly, even if the child is crying and begging to stay with the parent. Having a teacher, psychologist, counselor, or any other school professional present who is willing to greet the child (in the parking lot, school lobby, or classroom depending on the drop-off procedures), help engage the child in school activities, and ensure the child's safety can be helpful for the parent, allowing him or her to leave the situation more quickly. As an example, take the situation of a 6-year-old girl seen in one of our clinics recently who was exhibiting school refusal. Her mother typically drove her to school and then walked her into the classroom but had difficulties separating from her daughter once there: the child would cling, cry, whine, and so on. Her mother was reluctant to drop her daughter off outside the school building (as many parents did) because when she had done this in the past her daughter had attempted to leave the school grounds and follow the mother home. In this case, the school principal agreed to meet the mother and child every morning in the parking lot. The principal guided the child inside the school building, helped reinforce the child for nonanxious behavior (e.g., engaging in morning activities), and ensured that the child was safe and in the school.

Obtaining Parent Attention/Reinforcers Outside of School

Dawdling and taking one's time getting ready, engaging in prolonged arguments about school, and making phone calls asking to come home because of somatic complaints are all powerful attention getters. Even when it is not a primary function of school refusal, the behavior often serves to engage a parent in one way or another. Interventions for this function are very comparable to those for the disruptive behavior disorders. In general, the approach is to provide ample attention for desirable behaviors (e.g., through child-directed play), reduce the attention given to problem behaviors (e.g., selective ignoring), and provide structure and accommodations to facilitate success. Most of these strategies have been discussed extensively in Chapter 4, although a few details specific to school refusal are worth mentioning.

Parents of children who refuse school, particularly those who are chronically late, often report difficulty with the morning routine. This can be addressed with interventions to increase parents' skills with regard to giving commands and providing natural consequences. As an example, a parent might develop a morning schedule in which the child is able to obtain a reward (e.g., extra one-on-one time with the parent, access to desired activities) if the child takes age-appropriate steps to get ready for school. In these cases, our experience has also been that it is also worth asking about the child's nighttime and sleep routine. Although it seems obvious, sometimes parents will report that their child or adolescent is routinely up late watching television or playing video games and likely getting inadequate sleep. This can easily become a vicious cycle, with sleep deprivation adding to the youth's reluctance to get up and ready for school. Punishments might also be added if the child fails to take specified steps toward getting ready or refuses to attend school (e.g., loss of a privilege). During the school day, parents can take steps to limit the amount of attention and reinforcement the child gets by staying away from school. For example, if the child is kept home, this would include limiting access to television, video games, and other activities. The child might also be required to complete nonpreferred activities, such as independent schoolwork. For a parent who is home with the child, attention should be limited during school hours to the extent possible. At the same time, differential enforcement might be used to reward the child for getting ready for and attending school. By definition, if the function of school refusal is to obtain parent attention, parent attention ought to be a salient motivator. Rewards for school attendance might, therefore, include things like one-on-one time spent with the child at the end of the school day.

For the child who skips school to engage in other reinforcing activities (e.g., hanging out with peers, drug/alcohol use), intervention will seek to make school more reinforcing and making those outside reinforcers less available. Kearny (2001) recommends family contracting as a starting point. Often this will not mean an immediate return to school. Rather, the youth might agree to comply with a morning routine and perhaps limited school attendance. Assuming this is successful, full attendance is then required as soon as possible thereafter. The youth may negotiate with his or her parents for rewards contingent on school attendance, such as after-school privileges or tangible rewards. Along with contracting, other steps might be necessary to limit the child's access to outside reinforcers. For example, a parent may need to find a way to escort the youth to school in the morning, and accommodations may be needed so that the adolescent is escorted between classes during the day. Punishers should be implemented for school absence (i.e., loss of privileges).

Parents clearly play an important role in the effective treatment of school refusal. By engaging parents at the beginning of the treatment process, school-based mental health clinicians will often be able quickly resolve the school refusal. It is very important that intervention, in collaboration with parents, begin as soon as a problem is noted. The longer a child is out of school the more difficult it can become to have him or her easily return to school.

SELECTIVE MUTISM

Selective mutism is a disorder of its own (listed in the "other disorders of childhood" section in DSM-IV), not subsumed under the anxiety or depression diagnoses in the DSM. However, selective mutism is often considered to have a significant anxiety component (e.g., Freeman, Garcia, Miller, Dow, & Leonard, 2004). The hallmark of selective mutism is the lack of verbal communication in specific settings. Children with selective mutism can and do talk in certain settings (typically at home) but not at all in other settings (typically school). Because this disorder is often manifest in the school setting, school-based mental health professionals are in a perfect position to intervene. Most treatments for selective mutism involve behavioral approaches (Anstendig, 1998; Cohan, Chavira, & Stein, 2006; Freeman et al., 2004; Stone, Kratochwill, Sladezcek, & Serlin, 2002) in which speech is reinforced and slowly shaped while nonverbal communication is put on extinction (i.e., ignored). Techniques such as these have been successful in school settings (e.g., Cohan et al., 2006). It is worth noting that treatment outcome data are limited, however, and most of the published studies have used a single-subject design or have involved case reports. We are not aware of larger randomized studies including a control sample (Cohan et al., 2006).

When using a reinforcement and shaping program to increase speech within the school setting, teachers can begin by reinforcing the child for any attempts at speech. Reinforcement can include verbal praise, allowing access to desired activities for speaking, allowing escape from aversive activities or situations (e.g., group projects) for speaking, and providing tangible reinforcers (e.g., small edibles) or tokens that can later be exchanged for tangible reinforcers or access to desired activities. As always, it is important to help teachers and other caregivers think about what will be reinforcing to the individual child (e.g., calling attention to the child with verbal praise may be experienced as quite aversive). At the same time the teacher is reinforcing speech, he or she can also begin to slowly withdraw reinforcement to the child for using nonverbal means of communicating. For example, if the child "asks" to sharpen a pencil by pulling at the teacher's arm and pointing toward the pencil sharpener, the teacher can gradually increase the vocalization demands on the child by first requiring that the child say one simple word to the teacher (e.g., "pencil") before the student is allowed to sharpen the pencil and then proceeding from there (e.g., next a two-word sequence like "sharpen pencil" might be required).

In terms of shaping communication with other students in the school setting, often treatment begins by having the child speak in the classroom setting with one other person with whom the child is comfortable and speaks with outside the home. This might be a peer from the neighborhood or a sibling or a parent. In sessions held after school or at other times when class is not in session, the child can be encouraged (and rewarded) for talking with this "safe" person. As the child increases vocalizations with this person, other individuals, including peers from the classroom and the child's teacher, can then be added gradually to the conversation. If the parent (or sibling) was initially present in these conversations, as the child increases in his or her verbalizations with others present, the parent can be faded from the conversation mix.

In addition to speech being reinforced in school, parents can also be encouraged to reinforce the child's speech in a variety of situations. For example, if the child only speaks within the home, parents can be encouraged to provide reinforcement if the child speaks while, for example, at his grandparents' house or in a store. As with school-based reinforcement programs, home-based reinforcement programs may include the use of points or tokens that the child can accumulate and exchange for tangible reinforcers or access to a preferred activities (e.g., extra story with Dad at bedtime, lunch out with parents) at a later point in time. It is also important that parents be discouraged from punishing or making fun of their child for not talking (e.g., Kearney & Vecchio, 2007). Many parents experience frustration that their child is not talking, but negative comments such as "Why don't you talk? All your siblings do" or "Don't be so shy. Don't you know it is rude to not say 'Hi' to someone you see in the store?" are unlikely to do anything to increase the child's verbal behavior and may, in fact, impede the process. However, parents can encourage their children to use verbal methods of communication and, as in school, gradually withdraw reinforcement for nonverbal methods of communication.

In addition to reinforcement and shaping, researchers have also noted that systematic desensitization may be helpful for some children with selective mutism (Cohan et al., 2006; Kearney & Vecchio, 2007). Systematic desensitization was discussed earlier in this chapter, and the same methods described previously would be applicable to children with selective mutism. In this type of treatment, parents may need to be involved initially to provide information to the mental health professional to start the process of exposure to increasingly greater anxiety-provoking situations.

For children with selective mutism, it may also be important to consult with other professionals in the school, most notably the speech–language pathologist. Although not all children with selective mutism have speech difficulties—and the number with such difficulties is not clear (Freeman et al., 2004)—it is important that language delays be ruled in or out so that a comprehensive treatment plan can address these difficulties if they are present.

Regardless of how treatment proceeds for children with selective mutism, it is important to have parent buy-in to the treatment process. Because children with selective mutism typically do speak with no difficulties in the home setting, some parents may not realize the difficulties their child is having in school. Ensuring that parents understand why treatment is being recommended, how it will proceed, and the benefits of treatment will be important for school-based mental health professionals to communicate.

CHILD/ADOLESCENT DEPRESSION

As with the treatments for anxiety disorders, the primary treatments for school-age children with depression consist of CBT. In a review of psychosocial treatments for depression, David-Ferdon and Kaslow (2008) conclude that CBT for children and adolescents and interpersonal therapy (IPT) for adolescents have the most empirical support at this time. In addition, the authors note that adding a parent component to the treatment package often had positive effects. In addition to the CBT and IPT treatment modalities, the authors indicate that other treatment modalities have shown promise. For example, Trowell et al. (2007) evaluated the use of individual and family psychodynamic therapy for children and adolescents ages 9 to 15. Results indicate positive changes, with the majority of youth no longer meeting criteria for a depressive disorder at the end of treatment. However, studies on modalities other than CBT and IPT are limited. Because of the support for CBT and the ability to implement CBT in a school setting in collaboration with parents, we focus on this treatment modality here.

CBT interventions usually include psychoeducation about the nature of depression, identification of feelings, behavioral activation (increasing involvement in pleasurable activities), and problem solving. In the following sections, we draw from the existing literature to illustrate how parents can be involved in various aspects of CBT programs for depression. First, however, we summarize some of the empirical support for comprehensive interventions for depression that utilize family-based treatment components.

One of the more recent empirical evaluations of a comprehensive treatment program for depression is the National Institute of Mental Health-funded Treatment of Adolescents with Depression Study (TADS; TADS Team, 2004, 2007). This RCT compared the efficacy of CBT alone, fluoxetine (Prozac) alone, and the combination of the two treatments in a sample of adolescents (ages 12–17) with a diagnosis of major depressive disorder. A placebo control group (provided with typical clinical management) was utilized in evaluating the short-term outcomes of the interventions. The CBT program involved 12 weeks of treatment, covering basic CBT skills such as psychoeducation, goal setting, problem solving, and cognitive restructuring. Two parent sessions were required and other joint adolescent–parent sessions were held if needed (TADS Team, 2004). Parent–youth activities that were included as modules within the TADS study included problem-solving skills, family communication, family contingency management, high expectations and positive reinforcement, and family attachment and commitment (used in families in which the parent and child have become disengaged; Wells & Albano, 2005). For readers interested in more in-depth information on these family-focused activities, the TADS study CBT treatment manual can be accessed online (*trialweb.dcri.duke.edu/tads/manuals.html*). Results from this study indicate that the combination treatment (Prozac plus CBT) was the most effective at reducing symptoms of depression immediately after treatment. The combined treatment was more effective than either treatment alone. Prozac alone was more effective than CBT alone or a placebo; however CBT alone was not more effective than the placebo treatment (TADS Team, 2004). The authors note that it is somewhat surprising that CBT alone was not more effective than a placebo and that this may have to do with the severity of depressive symptoms in the adolescents in this sample. In a follow-up study (TADS Team, 2007) evaluating results to 36 weeks from baseline, the researchers noted continued improvements for all three treatment groups (the placebo condition was discontinued and youth obtained treatment immediately postintervention), with response rates fairly similar at 36 weeks (86% for combined treatment; 81% for Prozac alone and for CBT alone). Taking into account risks (e.g., increased suicidal events) the TADS Team concluded that the combined treatment appears to be superior to either treatment alone. They noted that both medication and CBT should be made available to youth with depression.

Stark et al. (2006, 2008) also make use of parent-directed interventions in their ACTION treatment program, a CBT intervention for depression targeted toward adolescent girls. Parent-focused components of the ACTION program include training in problem-solving skills, behavioral management, training in active listening skills, and conflict resolution. On the basis of preliminary results, Stark et al. (2006) report a significant reduction in depressive symptoms for the adolescents who took part in this program. A unique aspect of the ACTION program is that it was developed to be implemented in the schools with groups of girls (rather than individually, as is more typical). Thus, in addition to the youth-focused and the parent-focused sessions, teacher consultation is also built into this program. This teacher consultation is less formal than the youth and parent sessions and is intended to let teachers know the skills that are being taught in sessions so that they can prompt and provide opportunities for the use of the skills in the classroom.

Other evaluations of CBT programs for depression have also included parent components with positive outcomes. For example, in an evaluation of a telemedicine CBT program, Nelson, Barnard, and Cain (2006) included parent-focused treatment components such as behavior management skills, problem solving, and anger management. Results from this study indicated that children who received face-to-face intervention as well as those who received the intervention via interactive video had a reduction in depressive symptoms.

Other programs targeting depression in youth have included more limited family involvement. For example, Asarnow, Scott, and Mintz (2002) noted positive outcomes from a group CBT intervention for children with depression that included a family education session in which the skills taught to children were discussed and demonstrated to parents.

Although there are a variety of positive outcomes from comprehensive treatment programs that do involve parents, as noted earlier in this chapter, it is not clear whether parent treatment components lead to increased benefits above and beyond those seen from child/adolescent-focused treatment. Whether to actively involve parents in the treatment of a child or adolescent with depression may depend on a number of factors, including the state of the parent–child relationship, comorbid problems the child is experiencing, and parental willingness to be involved in the treatment process.

Parent Involvement in Problem Solving

As noted, problem solving is a common component of CBT interventions for depression, and this is one area in which parent involvement can be beneficial. Although specific intervention studies have used slightly different problem-solving steps, problem solving for youth with depression is generally approached in a similar manner as problem solving for children with externalizing behavior problems (outlined in Chapter 4). As Wells and Albano (2005) note, the rationale for using family problem solving is that youth with depression often experience family conflict and have negative exchanges that family members are unable to resolve in a positive manner. Thus, incorporating problem-solving skills can reduce this overt conflict and ideally lead to more positive family interactions.

Several outcome studies have involved parents in problem-solving sessions as part of CBT programs. For example, in the TADS project, family problem solving (involving the child and parent in a joint sessions) was included as an optional session within the study's modular framework. Both parents and youth in this study were taught a problem-solving paradigm separately, and the optional session allowed the parents and youth to work through a conflictual family issue using this same paradigm in a joint manner (Wells & Albano, 2005). Problem-solving interventions were also a treatment component in a telemedicine CBT program (Nelson et al., 2006) and in Stark's ACTION treatment program (Stark et al., 2006, 2008).

In Chapter 4 we provided an overview of problem solving utilized in collaboration with parents who have a child exhibiting externalizing behavior problems. These same problem-solving steps ("What is the problem?" "What are possible solutions to the problem?," "Evaluate the solutions," "Choose a solution," and "Evaluate the outcome.") can be taught to parents and children together to help increase healthy problem solving within the family. Parents and children can be instructed on how to use these steps individually to solve their own problems as well as jointly to solve parent–child conflicts. When used jointly, parents and youth each engage in the steps, but the evaluation of solutions is typically a collaborative effort, with both parties providing feedback on the pros and cons of solutions. Ultimately, the parent and child need to agree on a solution to implement.

Contingency Management/Positive Reinforcement

Contingency management methods have also been used as part of comprehensive treatment programs for children with depression. Positive reinforcement, either as a treatment component in its own right or as part of a contingency management protocol, has been a targeted skill in several intervention studies. In many studies, including the TADS study, basic contingency management methods are used to help address comorbid externalizing problems as well as increase motivation in youth related to aspects of depression (Wells & Albano, 2005). In addition, positive reinforcement may be used to help parents increase their rate of reinforcement of their children and decrease excessively high expectations, which may be seen in parents of children with depression (Wells & Albano, 2005). Within the ACTION program (Stark et al., 2006, 2008), behavioral management is also a part of the parent-focused sessions. Specifically, parents are taught to increase their use of positive reinforcement, including use of privileges. Parents are also instructed on how to decrease the use of punishment. Nelson et al. (2006) also utilized training in behavior management skills as one of their parent-focused treatment components.

As described in Chapter 4, contingency management consists of establishing target behaviors and utilizing some type of system (e.g., points, privileges) to reinforce appropriate/desired behavior and punish inappropriate behavior (e.g., through loss of points, privileges). However, reinforcement is typically stressed as the first part of a comprehensive contingency management program, with the thought being that if behaviors can be modified with more positive methods, there will be less of a need to utilize punitive interventions.

Effective Communication Skills

Successful treatment programs that involve parents in the treatment process (e.g., TADS, ACTION) have also often included a component of treatment that addresses the use of effective communication skills. For example, with the TADS study, a family communication module covers ways in which parents can more effectively communicate with their children, including using active listening skills such as summarizing and reflecting. Wells and Albano (2005) note that this type of instruction may need to occur before family problem solving to help facilitate good communication within the problem-solving process. Stark et al. (2006, 2008) also include a treatment component directed toward the use of active listening skills, including empathetic listening.

PREVENTION OF INTERNALIZING PROBLEMS

Many of the strategies discussed in this chapter can be adapted for use in preventive interventions. Because most children will have some experience with anxiety-provoking or stressful situations, information about relaxation, identification of anxiety symptoms, problem solving, and pitfalls of avoidance can all be used proactively. In addition, psychoeducation regarding emotions is a common element of evidence-based treatments and prevention programs for internalizing disorders. The rationale for these efforts is that an understanding of emotions will help children and adolescents to communicate and manage their feelings more effectively. Various classroom curricula are available for children from preschool through high school, and these have become part of an integrated health education program in many schools (see discussion of social and emotional learning programs in Chapter 2 as well as *www.casel.org*). Here, we highlight a few social–emotional education strategies that have been effectively used with parents or that can easily be adapted and used in collaboration with parents to help prevent internalizing problems.

Identifying and Labeling Emotions

Several intervention programs for internalizing disorders include components designed to help children to label emotions and develop an "emotional vocabulary." These types of activities can be used in a preventive manner to help children learn to recognize and express emotions in adaptive ways. In addition, many of these activities can easily be adapted for use by parents, and they are especially applicable for young children. For example, in his group treatment for depression, Stark (1990) includes several affective education activities. In one activity that uses playing cards labeled with various emotions (positive as well as negative), players choose a card and describe the emotion and a time when they experienced the emotion, discuss what a person experiencing the emotion might be thinking and feeling, or act out the emotion for others to guess. Although these activities have been designed for use in group interventions, they are easily adapted for use by parents in the home. Indeed, for some families these activities can be a useful way of prompting more open discussion of emotions in the home. When implementing the strategy at home, it is important to provide at least brief consultation for parents to ensure that they have an adequate understanding of the goals and buy in to the strategy.

Emotion Coaching

In an elegant line of developmental research, John Gottman and colleagues (e.g., Hooven, Gottman, & Katz, 1995) examined various parenting strategies or styles that parents displayed in response to their child's emotions. Interested readers are encouraged to read *The Heart of Parenting: Raising an Emotionally Intelligent Child* by Gottman and DeClaire (1997). There are also some useful resources available through the Talaris Institute, a nonprofit organization focused on child development and parenting (*www.talaris.org*). These include a DVD on emotion coaching, online materials, and various parent-friendly print materials. Treatment development research on an emotion-coaching intervention for families with a history of domestic violence is also underway by Lynn Fainsilber Katz and colleagues at the University of Washington (personal communication, January 26, 2009). We are not aware of work directly applying these principles to the treatment or prevention of internalizing problems, although it is not difficult to see how they might apply. Children often display strong emotions; having a strategy for addressing these emotions can be extremely valuable for parents.

On the basis of their research, Gottman and colleagues categorized parents' styles as dismissive, disapproving, laissez-faire, and emotion coaching. Although their work was with parents, similar styles may also apply to teachers and other care providers. As the name implies, dismissive parents tended to downplay their child's emotions and either overtly or implicitly encouraged them to "just get over it." These parents tended to be uncomfortable with emotional displays and viewed negative emotions as undesirable, and they focused on minimizing the situation or helping their child by distracting him or her. Disapproving parents viewed negative emotional displays as unacceptable and actively communicated to their children that their emotions needed to be suppressed. Laissez-faire parents had a generally accepting view of strong emotional displays, but they provided little or no guidance to assist the child with understanding and regulating his or her emotions. Finally, emotion-coaching parents tended to empathize with their child and engage in active communication about emotions. These parents were accepting of emotional displays, and they were able to engage in conversations about emotional-laden topics, set limits when appropriate, and help children to problem solve. For example, in contrast to a parent characterized as laissez-faire, an emotion-coaching parent might say, "I can see that you were really upset with your brother, but it just wasn't OK to hit him. What else could you have done?" Not surprisingly, these very different styles were associated with different outcomes for children. Children whose parents used an emotion-coaching style tended to have the best outcomes with regard to social competence, behavior problems, and academic functioning (Hooven et al., 1995). Interestingly, they were also more resilient in the context of parents' marital discord and tended to have fewer infectious illnesses (Hooven et al., 1995).

Gottman and DeClaire (1997) suggest five basic steps to successful emotion coaching: (1) emotional awareness, (2) recognizing emotions as an opportunity for intimacy and teaching, (3) listening empathetically and validating the child's feelings, (4) labeling emotions, and (5) setting limits while helping the child problem solve. The first step involves parents becoming more self-aware of their own emotions and looking for clues into the child's emotional experience. Often the child's emotions are obvious (e.g., as in the midst of a tantrum), but sometimes they are more subtle and come out in the context of play or conversations. Clinicians may encourage this by asking parents to observe their child's emotions over the course of a week. Sometimes a conversation about how the child felt and encouraging a parent to assume the child's perspective can be useful in this regard. Recognizing emotions as an opportunity for intimacy is more difficult for some parents (e.g., parents who tend to be more dismissive or disapproving). However, even in these cases, a parent almost always has the child's best interests in mind. Often such parents are responsive to the notion that the child's strong emotions are likely not going to go away, and that talking with their child about his or her emotions may help to bring them closer together and help the child to learn skills that are going to be important in the long term as he or she manages difficult emotions in relationships with peers, significant others, coworkers, and employers. Listening empathetically is a strategy familiar to most mental health professionals, although not always easily applied in parent–child relationships. This involves trying to understand the child's perspective without automatically trying to "fix" something or make the difficult emotion go away. School-based clinicians, who spend their careers working with children and adolescents, have the advantage of experience in this regard and can help parents to understand how different the child's perspective might be. For example, adults tend to forget what it feels like to be a young child always looking up at others in an adult-sized world or how difficult it is to be an adolescent breaking up with a significant other and how utterly unreassuring it is to hear that "there are more fish in the sea." We have sometimes found it useful to practice empathizing with parents in session, as they engage with their child in a difficult conversation. As a homework assignment, parents may be asked to practice responding first with empathy before trying to fix something or intervene. Labeling emotions fits nicely with this, and parents are usually responsive to the notion that the child needs to learn a vocabulary for discussing emotions. For young children, this can facilitate efforts to express emotions adaptively with words rather than behavioral outbursts.

Finally, setting limits and helping children problem solve are comparable to some of the strategies discussed in Chapter 4 (e.g., like those used in the CPS model). The keys here are helping parents to understand that acknowledging their child's emotional experience does not have to mean avoiding limit setting. Rather, the message ought to be that even when we have very powerful emotions, we are still responsible for our behavior and still have to find ways to function effectively. For example, a parent can completely empathize and under-stand a child's fear about going to school after being teased by a peer, while also setting the expectation that the child is going to return and helping him or her to think through some of the things that he or she might do to get through the day.

In combination with other interventions, we have found these strategies to be effective with families. Use of these strategies with children who are prone to anxiety is supported by data suggesting that, relative to parents of nonanxious children, parents of children with anxiety disorders tend to respond to their child's negative emotions (e.g., anger, fear) with criticism, arguing, and intrusive strategies (Hudson, Comer, & Kendall, 2008). The direc-tionality of this association is unclear (i.e., whether this parenting style leads to the devel-opment of anxiety or whether highly anxious child behavior shapes this parenting style over time). Nonetheless, strategies to encourage adaptive parenting responses to emotion are likely to be helpful for parents struggling to manage the "typical" expressions of child emotions in a constructive manner and potentially prevent the development of internalizing problems. Generally, the concepts make sense to parents intuitively, and often they realize that they have not responded effectively to their child's emotions. It is worth noting that there are times when these strategies may be counterproductive. For example, parents who become extremely frustrated and emotionally dysregulated themselves are unlikely to be effective emotion coaches until they gain better self-control. Additionally, it can be difficult for parents to determine when to emotion coach and when to set a limit or use another behavioral strategy (e.g., selective ignoring in the context of a tantrum).

COLLABORATING WITH OTHER PROFESSIONALS

As when treating externalizing disorders, there are a variety of professionals with whom the school-based mental health professional may consult or collaborate when treating children with internalizing problems. Medications, most notably the selective serotonin reuptake inhibitors, are increasingly being used to treat both anxiety and depression in children and adolescents. Although only a few of these medications are approved by the U.S. Food and Drug Administration (FDA) specifically for use with children or adolescents, many physi-cians will use these medications "off label." For depression, Prozac is FDA approved to treat children ages 7 to 17. However, this is the only medication FDA approved to treat depres-sion. In terms of anxiety disorders, there are several medications that have FDA approval to treat obsessive–compulsive disorder (Prozac, Zoloft, Luvox, and Anafranil). However, although there is some support of the use of medications for other anxiety disorders, there are no FDA-approved medications for them. It should be noted that the FDA currently requires most antidepressants to carry a "black-box" warning on the label indicating that these medications may increase the risk of suicidal thoughts/behaviors. Although such a response is rare, it is important that youth who are prescribed antidepressants be monitored to ensure that there are no adverse responses. If school mental health professionals note adverse changes in children on medication, especially those who have recently started tak-ing medication, it is important that these observations be communicated to the parent as well as the prescribing physician, if there is an appropriate release of information.

In addition to collaborating with medical professionals for children who are taking medications, school professionals are also likely to collaborate with community-based mental health providers in the treatment of children and adolescents with internalizing problems. Often children may receive services for such problems outside the school setting. However, because anxiety and depression can impact a child's school performance, it can be important for school personnel to have some information on treatment targets and treatment progress from the treating mental health professional and for the treating professional to receive feedback from school personnel on the child's progress. For example, is the child engaging more with peers or showing a reduced amount of anxiety in social situations? Regardless of who the primary mental health provider is, collaboration and communication between all involved will ultimately lead to better services for the child.

CHAPTER SUMMARY

Although internalizing disorders are often thought of as disorders that are best addressed by individual treatment, it is clear that there is a role for parental involvement in the treatment process for most children experiencing these difficulties. For some disorders (such as school refusal), parents are likely to play a key role in the treatment process. For other disorders (such as depression), parental involvement may vary based on the presence or absence of comorbid disorders as well as child–parent conflict. Regardless of how actively involved parents are in the treatment process, it is important for school-based mental health professionals to consider parental involvement and how it can be used to facilitate a positive outcome for the child.

Anxiety ABCs

A What happened before?	How nervous did you feel?	B What did you do?	C What happened after?
	10—Worst possible 9— 8— 7— 6— 5—Medium 4— 3— 2— 1— 0—Not at all		
	10—Worst possible 9— 8— 7— 6— 5—Medium 4— 3— 2— 1— 0—Not at all		

FORM 5.2

The Thinking–Feeling–Doing Connection

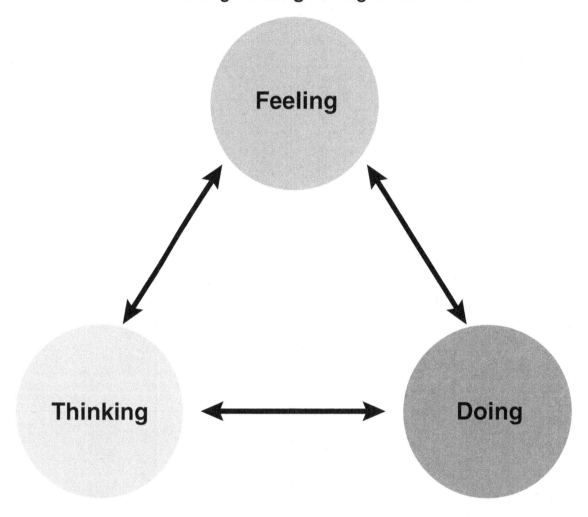

Thinking, feeling, and doing (behavior) are all closely related: A change in any one is likely to affect all of the others. For example, avoidance behavior and catastrophic thinking are common reactions to the physiological responses associated with anxiety (heart beating fast, sweaty palms, shaking). Often we assume that the feeling has to change before all of the other things can change. For example, a common statement is something along the lines of "I'll raise my hand and start asking more questions in class ... after I feel more comfortable with the teacher." But the reverse is also true (e.g., "You'll feel more comfortable after you start participating in class").

The Fear–Avoidance Connection

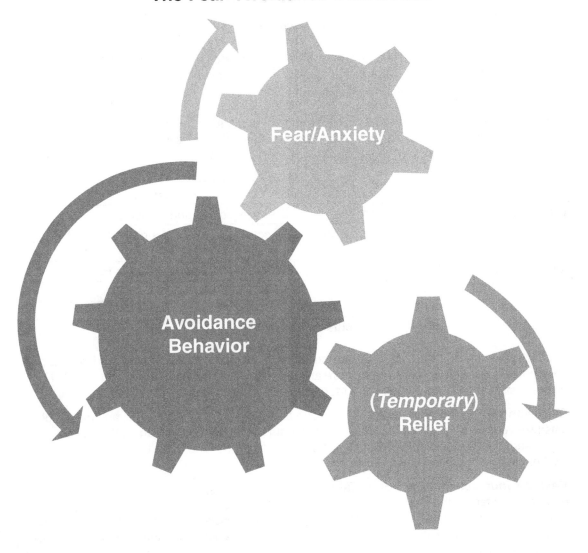

Avoidance is a normal response to fear or anxiety. In fact, it's often necessary and very adaptive —for example, avoiding a real danger. But sometimes people end up avoiding things that don't really pose a danger and might be important, like going to school, talking to other kids, or participating in class. This gives a temporary relief from fear, and makes it more likely that the person will use the same avoidance behavior the next time he or she gets that scared feeling. It is easy for this to get out of hand, and people can end up avoiding many different situations.

FORM 5.4

Relaxation Script

Relaxation

These are several things that you can do to calm down when you are feeling anxious, upset, or tense. You might find one of these that you like the best or (when you get really good) you might decide to use more than one at the same time.

When we're nervous, our bodies have a natural "fight or flight" response. Of course, this can be a good thing (e.g., preparing for action); but sometimes this kicks in when it's not needed. Relaxation strategies can help regain control over this process.

Relaxed	Nervous
Breathing is regular, slow, and deep.	Breathing is fast and shallow.
Muscles are floppy (like a loose rubberband).	Muscles are tight (like a rubberband stretched tight).
Mind is calm and focused.	Mind is racing, and it's hard to focus.
Heartbeat is regular and slow.	Heartbeat is fast.

Muscle Relaxation

This helps you notice tension in your muscles and relax your body. Practice should take about 10 minutes. Find a quiet place where there aren't a whole lot of other things going on (no TV, brothers/sisters to bug you). Get comfortable and close your eyes.

Start with your hands and arms. Take a deep breath, stretch out your arms, and make tight fists (like you're trying to squeeze all of the water out of a sponge). Hold on ... then let go and breathe out. Let all of the tension leave your arms, hands, and fingertips. Say to yourself, "Relax," and let your arms lay down at your side.

Next, do your face and shoulders. Take a deep breath, shrug your shoulders up to your ears, and tighten up the muscles of your face so that you look very wrinkly. (Yes, you will look funny ... just pay attention to how it feels when all of the muscles are tight.) Hold on and count to 5, then let go and breathe out. Completely relax your face, let your shoulders drop, and say to yourself, "Relax."

Now try your tummy. Take a deep breath, and pull in the muscles of your stomach as far as you can. Hold it ... then breathe out and let your tummy relax all the way. Let your whole body sink into the chair or floor, completely relaxed.

This last one is for your legs. Breathe in and stretch out your legs really straight. Squeeze all of the muscles in your legs, all the way from your bottom to the tips of your toes. Count to 5, then let go and breathe out. Let your legs go all floppy, like they are made of jelly.

Now let your whole body relax, like a jellyfish. Notice how good it feels to be so calm and relaxed. Take a few minutes if you want, then slowly open your eyes and when you're ready stand up.

(cont.)

Deep Breathing

When we get nervous, we generally start to breathe faster (which can actually make us even more nervous). Deep breathing helps you to slow down your breathing and relax. This is a good one because it's easy to do in lots of situations.

Take in a deep, slow breath through your nose. Hold it for just a second, then slowly breathe out through your mouth. Imagine trying to blow a really big bubble ... you don't want to breathe out too fast, or it will pop. Say to yourself, "Relax" or "Calm." Try again ... do this about 5 or 10 times, and notice how your breathing gets slower and more relaxed each time.

Imagination

Sometimes when we get nervous, our minds get focused on things that make us even more scared. Using imagination can help a lot and (like breathing) is easy to do in lots of situations.

Close your eyes and imagine a place where you feel very comfortable (e.g., in your backyard, a favorite chair or spot in your house). Try to picture just what it looks like, smells like, and feels like to be there. Other thoughts might pop into your mind, and that's OK. Just let them come and go, and return back to the place where you're most comfortable.

Fear Hierarchy

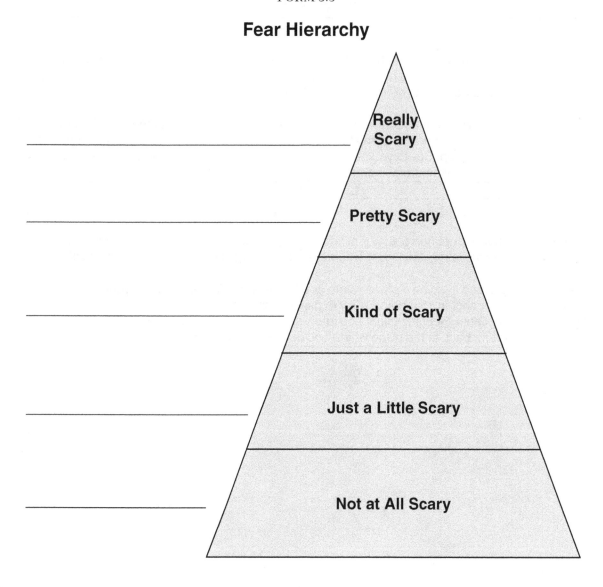

6

Interventions for
Academic Problems

with Donna Gilbertson

Academic problems are some of the most common reasons parents seek assistance for their children, especially within the schools. Given the primary goals of the education system (i.e., advancing students' knowledge and skills in the areas of reading, math, language, and so on), it should not be surprising that academic concerns are so common. Reading, in particular, has emerged as an important academic skill domain in terms of long-term outcomes. Children who lack adequate reading skills are at risk for other academic problems as well as behavioral problems (e.g., Halonen, Aunola, Ahonen, & Nurmi, 2006). As noted in Chapter 2, a large percentage of students experience significant difficulties in this and other academic areas. Thus, addressing important academic domains can be critical in promoting successful life outcomes.

Academic problems vary widely in severity and impact on the child. At the severe end of the spectrum are "specific learning disabilities," which significantly impact a child's ability to learn in the regular classroom environment. However, even children who do not have a diagnosed learning disability may struggle with academic tasks. Some children may lack motivation for academic tasks, whereas others might have the basic abilities and motivation to perform but lack fluency (i.e., the ability to apply academic skills in an accurate and quick manner), making even routine assignments laborious. These skill and/or motivation difficulties are often present not just in the school setting but also at home when students are expected to complete homework tasks. Homework time is particularly challenging for parents who want to encourage and assist their children but are unsure of how to best do this. As schools attempt to implement higher academic standards to comply with federal

Donna Gilbertson, PhD, is Associate Professor in school psychology at Utah State University. Her research focuses on service delivery models and strategies that help educators respond effectively to learning and behavior problems, with an emphasis on culturally diverse students.

laws such as No Child Left Behind, there has been an increase in the amount of homework children are given. As parents will attest, even kindergarteners and first graders are now receiving homework assignments. As a result, parent–child battles over homework can begin early in the child's educational experience. In this chapter, we cover interventions for some of the common academic problems children may face. Given that the focus of this book is on home/school collaboration, our emphasis is on interventions that parents can implement with their children at home. Before covering specific interventions, we first discuss issues in involving parents in the assessment and intervention process as well as assessment of the function of academic problems.

Table 6.1 provides a summary of the techniques covered in this chapter.

Case Vignette

Sam is a third-grade student whose teacher and parents are concerned about his academic progress. Sam has received low grades in reading throughout school, and he is performing below his peers on standardized reading tests. Because of his low reading scores, Sam receives small group support for 30 minutes a day with a reading specialist. Sam's parents would like to help facilitate his progress, but they have been hesitant to do anything extra at home for fear that they will stifle his interest in school by adding to his current workload. According to Sam's parents, he is already reluctant to read and gets upset when asked to do so.

A reading CBM consisting of having Sam read three 1-minute reading passages reveals that Sam's score falls within the "at-risk" range because of slow reading pace and reading errors such as word omissions and mispronunciations. On the three 1-minute reading probes, Sam read 28 words correctly with 16 errors compared with the average of 80 words per minute read by his classmates. On the basis of these scores, the school psychologist developed several working hypotheses regarding Sam's performance. For example, the low reading rate and high error rate suggest that Sam may need additional support to increase reading accuracy and fluency on grade-level materials or may be working on reading materials that are too difficult for him to make adequate progress. Sam's frustration with reading also suggested that he may need some motivational support to practice reading with his mother.

INVOLVING PARENTS
IN THE ASSESSMENT/INTERVENTION PROCESS

As mandated in IDEIA, parents must have some involvement in the assessment process when students are being evaluated for possible special education services, including learning disabilities. However, too often parents are involved only at a minimum level: providing consent for the initial testing to occur and being present at the IEP meeting to provide consent for services (assuming their child qualifies for services). In our discussions with parents in the schools and in clinical settings, it appears that many parents have a limited understanding of the services that their children are receiving. Frequently, parents are even unsure of whether their child is actually receiving special education services. This is unfortunate because, for parents to be true collaborative partners in their children's education, they must be actively involved in the process from the initial stages. Many parents

TABLE 6.1. Interventions for Academic Problems

Intervention	Description	Developmental level[a]
Interventions to increase academic motivation		
Contingency management	Provide rewards to child for engaging in academic work for a certain period of time or for completing a certain amount of work. The mystery motivator is one example of this type of intervention. This intervention can be applied at school (with reinforcers given at school and/or at home) and at home for homework.	All ages.
Self-monitoring	Student (with assistance of teacher and/or parent) is taught to self-monitor work completion. Rewards are provided for reaching a certain goal.	All ages.
Reading interventions		
Repeated readings	Students reread a brief passage three to four times to increase fluency. Parent/teacher may provide feedback when student makes an error.	All ages, although most research is with elementary and middle school-age children.
Listening preview	Parent or teacher first reads passage to child while child follows along before child reads passage him- or herself. Can be combined with repeated readings.	All ages, although most research is with elementary school-age children.
Phrase drill error correction	As child reads aloud from passage, parent/teacher follows along on written copy of passage and underlines errors. Parent/teacher models correct pronunciation where child made errors and child rereads sections in which errors were made to increase reading accuracy.	All ages, although most research is with elementary school-age children.
Asking key questions	Intervention to address reading comprehension. Students are informed of key questions they will be asked before reading passage (e.g., Who is the story about? What happened in the story?). After reading the story, children answer these questions.	All ages, although most research is with elementary school-age children.
Story mapping	Similar to asking key questions, but "story map" containing boxes with key components is presented to child and child fills in boxes.	All ages, although most research is with elementary and middle school-age children.
Math interventions		
Cover, copy, and compare	Students are provided math problems with correct answers. Students look at problem and answer, then cover problem and answer, and rewrite problem and then provide answer (or answer on identical work sheet without answers). They then uncover problem with answer and compare correct answer to their own answer.	All ages, although most research is with elementary and middle school-age children.

(cont.)

147

TABLE 6.1. *(cont.)*

Intervention	Description	Developmental level[a]
Math interventions *(cont.)*		
Explicit timing	Students are provided with a math work sheet and told to complete as many problems as possible in a specific time interval. Often combined with goal setting.	All ages, although most research is with elementary and middle school-age children.
Flashcards	Students are presented with flash cards containing math problems. If unable to answer quickly, answer is provided and then same card is re-presented to student.	All ages.
Written language interventions		
Flow sheets	Students use flow sheet/story map to guide writing process and ensure all key parts of writing assignment are included.	All ages.
Revising checklists	Students use checklist to ensure story has all needed parts. Checklists can also be used to help spot mechanical errors in writing.	All ages.
Story starters	Students are provided with an idea for a story and then instructed to think about story idea and then write for a specific period of time.	All ages.
Homework interventions		
Homework routines	Parent and teacher are involved in setting a specific routine for homework completion in school and home setting.	All ages.
Homework checklists and contracts	Written checklists and/or contracts are used to specify what student needs to do with regard to homework (including bringing homework home). Rewards are typically provided contingent on performance on identified aspects of homework.	All ages.
Self-monitoring	Students are taught to self-monitor implementation of homework routines. Parents provide rewards for self-monitoring and meeting goals.	All ages.
Timing for on-task behavior	In collaboration with teacher, parent determines how much time student should be spending on homework. A timer is set for this amount of time. If child works consistently during this time, he/she earns access to a reinforcer.	All ages.

[a] "All ages" refers to all children of school age who have started working on a certain academic skill.

enter their discussion with school staff prepared for an adversarial process. Occasionally, this stems from "horror stories" handed down by other parents or from fairly subtle cues in the process. For example, we had a discussion with a group of parents whose children were receiving special education services. One set of parents noted that when they attended an IEP meeting, the tables were prearranged to have an "us" versus "them" feel, with the parents at the head of a semicircular table and the school professionals grouped around the arch of the table. The parents noted that they felt "surrounded," although they did not believe that this was intentional on the part of the school personnel. Nonetheless, it is these little things—as well as the bigger things, such as soliciting information from parents and involving parents in the decision-making process—that help contribute to a true partnership.

Other difficulties parents have noted involve being able to access school personnel to discuss their concerns regarding their children and to request an evaluation to determine whether their child has learning problems. We frequently have conversations with parents who have significant concerns regarding their child's educational progress but do not know that they can request school personnel to conduct an evaluation. Other parents have attempted to contact school personnel to request an evaluation but either have met with resistance (e.g., "We don't evaluate children before age 8") or have been unable to talk to someone who is knowledgeable about the assessment process and mechanisms for requesting evaluation.

Barriers to parent involvement do not end once the assessment process is complete, even if everyone agrees that the child is struggling and needs additional service. Because teachers and other educators are seen as the experts in remediating academic problems, parent involvement in this process may not even be considered, and parents may not know to ask about how they can become involved. Clearly, we believe that parents can play a key role in the intervention process and the evidence bears this out. Although much of the literature on academic interventions is geared toward teachers and the classroom settings, there is a growing body of literature on parent involvement, particularly related to reading. In addition, many of the interventions originally geared toward teachers can be adapted so that parents can also be involved in the intervention process.

Within the context of reading, the development of early literacy skills and later language skills has been linked to parent involvement with reading at home, including exposing children to books and reading to them (Senechal & LeFevre, 2002; Weinberger, 1996). Likewise, in an investigation of parent involvement with children in Title I programs, greater parent involvement was associated with increased reading and math achievement (Shaver & Walls, 1998). Although parent involvement in children's reading is linked to positive outcomes, there are fewer studies that examine specifically what parents can do or how school personnel can help parents in assisting their children with reading skills. In a review of parent involvement in interventions designed to address children's academic achievement and behavior, Fishel and Ramirez (2005) conclude that, although findings are mixed and existing studies have methodological problems, parent home tutoring for academic problems shows promise. We next summarize results from several studies in which parents have effectively been involved as tutors.

In Persampieri, Gortmaker, Daly, Sheridan, and McCurdy's (2006) parent-guided intervention, parents were instructed in the use of a packaged reading intervention, including repeated readings, error correction with sentence repeat, and rewards for improvement in performance. Parents had children read aloud from a passage, noted errors while the child was reading, correctly pronounced any mispronounced words, and had the child repeat the word and reread the sentence containing the word. Children then reread the whole passage. Parents provided stickers to children, which could be used toward rewards the researchers provided. The researchers also provided rewards for children meeting individualized goals (based on words read correctly per minute and errors made). In two experiments, with slightly different training methods, parents were able to effectively implement these strategies and children demonstrated an increase in words read correctly per minute.

In a similar study, Resetar, Noell, and Pellegrin (2006) taught parents to implement a home-tutoring program in which the parent began by reading a passage to the child (modeling) and then had the child read the passage to the parent, with the parent correcting mistakes the child made. The parents received training in phonics and used these skills to assist the child. Children were also provided with positive reinforcement (praise) for increasing the number of words read correctly per minute on a reading probe. After the fluency portion of each training session, a comprehension portion occurred. During this, the parent had the child read a passage silently, after which the parent asked the child three questions about the passage. Praise was provided for correct answers and corrective feedback was provided for incorrect answers. Across the five children with whom this intervention was implemented, all demonstrated an increase in words read correctly during the tutoring session. However, these effects carried over into the school setting for only three of the children, although the authors hypothesize that with a longer intervention (the current one was only 3 weeks) more generalization to the school setting might have been seen.

Using a procedure similar to those described previously (repeated readings with performance feedback), Hook and DuPaul (1999) demonstrated that such interventions increase the reading fluency of children with ADHD. Although some improvement in reading fluency was noted in the classroom, the intervention had the largest impact in the home (tutoring session) setting. At a 1-month follow-up, there was some decline in students' performance from the intervention phase but students continued to perform better than during the baseline phase.

With the increasing number of students from linguistically and culturally diverse backgrounds, an important consideration in designing effective interventions is to develop feasible ways to involve parents who are assisting English language learners. Lopez and Cole (1999) trained five Puerto Rican parents on a simple academic intervention to help their kindergarten children learn the letters of the alphabet. Parents were trained on a drill technique to help their child practice a mix of known and unknown letters by showing the child flash cards, modeling letter naming, and using the letter in an English or Spanish word. Results from weekly progress-monitoring sessions showed that the parents, with various levels of English proficiency levels, were able to implement the intervention and increased their child's letter naming toward acceptable levels.

Based on these studies, it seems clear that parents can be effectively included in implementing interventions for children who struggle with academic problems. School personnel will need to do some of the up-front work in terms of evaluating the problem, determining the functions and the best way to address the problem, choosing appropriate skill work sheets to use for the interventions, and training parents in the implementation of the interventions. In addition, school personnel will likely need to be involved in progress monitoring and decision making regarding when to move on to harder skill sheets and change or terminate interventions. However, parents can implement much of the actual intervention component in the home setting, and this has the potential to increase the intensity of intervention in a cost-effective manner.

EVALUATING THE FUNCTION OF ACADEMIC PROBLEMS

Before designing and implementing interventions to address academic problems, it is important to have a good understanding of why such problems are occurring. Functional assessment methods, which have been used extensively to obtain information on students' behavioral problems and how to address them, can also be applied to problems of an academic nature. Daly, Witt, Martens, and Dool (1997) provide a framework for using functional assessment methods for academic problems. As they outlined, there are five common reasons (functions) for poor academic performance: (1) The student does not want to do the work; (2) the student has not spent enough time doing the work; (3) the student has not received enough help to do the work; (4) the student has not had to previously do the work in the manner requested; and (5) the work is too hard for the student. Daly et al. go on to describe each of these possible hypotheses. Next, we summarize assessment and intervention procedures from their work. Although the determination of the function of academic problems will likely fall to school personnel (rather than parents), school psychologists will be able to utilize this information to work with parents to develop the most effective intervention for an individual child's difficulties.

One of the first areas to investigate when a student is struggling academically is whether he or she truly cannot perform the skill (a "can't do" problem) or has the ability to perform a skill but does not want to (a "won't do" problem). With a "can't do" problem, the child does not possess the ability or background knowledge to complete work at the expected level; this is referred to as a skill deficit. Interventions for such problems involve more intensive practice in an area, remedial work, teaching of foundation skills, and so on. With a "won't do" (or performance-deficit) problem, the child possesses the ability, skills, and background knowledge to complete a task but is hindered from performing as expected because of a lack of motivation or attention to the task. Typically, "won't do" problems can be effectively addressed with behaviorally based interventions that increase children's attention and motivation, allowing them to complete the tasks. To help determine whether the problem is of a "can't do" or "won't do" nature, the student can be asked to complete academic material (using curriculum-based probes) initially without reinforcement and a second time with reinforcement for completing more work correctly. If it is a "won't do" problem, continued incentives can be provided for the student to engage in higher levels of the academic work. Additional interventions suggested by Daly et al. (1997) include providing students with a choice on the work to be performed (e.g., choices on what material to read for a reading assignment) or on the order in which the work is completed.

A second reason a child may have difficulties with work is that he or she has not spent enough time doing the work. If this seems to be the function of a student's academic problems, Daly et al. (1997) recommend utilizing strategies to increase the student's responding. This may be as simple as providing more time for the child to engage with his or her work. Other options include providing more structure in the tasks the child is to do and providing immediate feedback to the student.

A potentially related problem is that students may not have received enough help to accomplish the academic tasks. Providing increased feedback to a student can improve engagement time as well as overall academic achievement. Providing feedback can be quite simple and easily utilized by parents. For example, if a child is going over multiplication facts at home, an interaction with feedback might look something like this:

PARENT: What is 2 × 4?

CHILD: 8

PARENT: Right! 2 × 4 = 8

PARENT: What is 3 × 4?

CHILD: 9.

PARENT: No. The correct answer to 3 × 4 is 12.

Daly et al. (1997) point out that, for some children, simply increasing the amount of feedback they receive may not be enough to improve their performance. In these cases, one must pay more attention to the child's skill level to develop appropriate interventions. For example, when first learning a skill, modeling and prompting are important. Later, when the child is working to become more fluent with the skill, practice with reinforcement can increase fluency.

A fourth function Daly et al. (1997) discuss is that students have not had to do the work in the way being asked before. This problem relates to the instructional materials being used and the fact that such materials may not be helping the student practice his or her use of the skill being taught. As one example, Daly et al. suggest that having children circle spelling words in word puzzles does not adequately prepare them for spelling words on their own on a written spelling test.

The final function Daly et al. (1997) mention—the work being too hard—also relates to the instructional material. As Daly et al. indicate, students perform best when work is at their instructional level (i.e., when they work on material that is neither too easy nor too hard). Obviously, the solution to this problem is to have the teacher modify students' instructional materials. However, Daly et al. indicate, this may be difficult for teachers to do when working with children of various instructional levels. Parents likely have little control over the instructional level of the material their children are asked to complete. However, if parents believe that the work their child is asked to complete is too difficult, this should be evaluated in collaboration with school personnel to determine whether some modifications to instructional level would be appropriate.

As a way of evaluating these different hypotheses to determine the function of any individual child's academic problems, Daly et al. (1997) suggest implementing a multielement brief experimental analysis design in which, following a baseline evaluation of a student's skills (via CBM probes), different interventions are implemented to determine their effect on the child's performance. Since Daly et al.'s overview of these functional hypotheses and methods, researchers have increasingly applied brief experimental analysis (BEA) to the selection of academic interventions in an attempt to choose the most efficacious treatment for each individual child. Interventions with empirical support are chosen for evaluation and are compared with the child's performance in a baseline (no intervention) condition. In BEA procedures, curriculum-based probes are first conducted with a child under a baseline/no treatment condition. Following this, different interventions are implemented one by one followed by a curriculum-based probe to assess the effects of intervention on academic performance.

For example, in the case of Sam presented earlier, the school psychologist might conduct a few brief assessments to test interventions that may address the potential reasons for Sam's reading difficulties. The school psychologist might start by administering a brief intervention, Listening Preview, to determine whether Sam could improve his reading accuracy and fluency with modeling, practice, and error correction. This intervention might be implemented using a passage at Sam's instructional level as well as one at a lower grade level to help determine whether Sam may need assistance on less difficult material. Sam could also complete this task with the opportunity to earn a reward for increased reading performance to determine the effects of a motivational strategy.

A visual inspection of the data can determine under what treatment condition the child evidences the greatest improvements in performance. This intervention is then selected and data continue to be collected to validate that this intervention is having the intended impact on the targeted skills. Using this method, the most effective intervention for an individual child can be developed. Thus, the studies supporting the BEA procedures use different interventions to determine what functionally works best for a child. In studies conducted, different interventions are noted to have different effects for the individual child participants. Because the experimental phase is brief, this is an easy way to individualize interventions in a relatively brief period of time. A variety of studies have supported the use of these techniques in identifying effective interventions for students across academic areas, although the majority of studies have focused on reading (e.g., Daly, Martens, Dool, & Hintze, 1998; Daly, Murdoch, Lillenstein, Webber, & Lentz, 2002; Daly, Persampieri, McCurdy, & Gortmaker, 2005). More details on conducting these brief functional assessments can be found in a comprehensive guide by Witt, Daly, and Noell (2000).

In the following sections, we outline interventions, by academic area, that are commonly used when intervening with academic problems. It should be stressed, however, that using a BEA approach to evaluate interventions before choosing one to implement is likely the best way to proceed. In these sections, we have focused on interventions that are most likely able to be implemented by parents in the home setting with some guidance and support from school personnel.

EVIDENCE-BASED INTERVENTIONS FOR ACADEMIC PROBLEMS

Not surprisingly, much of the literature on effective instruction and interventions to address academic problems focuses on what can be done in the classroom by teachers. Rathvon (2008) discussed numerous intervention methods that can be used to address academic problems. These include interventions focused on behavioral issues (e.g., teaching classroom rules, providing contingent praise) as well as interventions that focus on increasing academic productivity (e.g., peer tutoring, performance feedback). Although much of the original empirical support for academic interventions is based on evaluations of these techniques in the classroom, many of these methods can be easily used by parents at home, with some assistance from school personnel. In the following sections, we review some of the more commonly used intervention techniques and note some of the evidence for these as well as how parents can be involved in implementing such interventions. For each section, we have included parent handouts that outline the steps involved in the interventions. However, many of these interventions make use of academic probes and skill sheets that will need to be created by school personnel and then provided to parents.

Interventions Designed to Increase Academic Motivation

As noted, inadequate motivation (a "won't do" problem) is a common reason for academic underperformance. Motivation problems can be addressed in similar fashion across a variety of academic subjects and are, therefore, discussed here as one set of interventions.

One way to address motivational issues is to simply provide a reward to the child for engaging in academic work for a certain period of time. The provision of rewards can occur in a variety of ways. One method is to use a grab bag method, in which rewards a child wishes to earn are written on slips of paper and placed in a container. If the child stays on task for a certain period of time or completes a certain number of problems correctly, he or she is allowed to draw from the grab bag and earn the reward drawn. Variations on this method can include the student earning points, which can be redeemed for various reinforcers, or working toward a specific reinforcer.

One intervention that is frequently cited as an effective way to increase motivation is the mystery motivator. First, a menu of rewards the child would like to earn is created. Then a mystery motivator chart is created. The chart can be created through a picture or a chart with squares or any other graphic. Using an invisible ink marker, code letters or numbers are written in each square of the chart. When the child has performed as expected, he or she is allowed to use a revealer marker to color in one square. When this marker is used the code number written in invisible ink is revealed. If the code number revealed is the reward code, then the child is allowed to choose a reward from the reward menu. If the code revealed is not the one associated with being able to choose a reward, the child does not get to select a reward in that instance. If an invisible ink marker is not available, then a spinner or a lotto jar with papers with written earned rewards can be used to determine rewards earned. Several studies have supported the use of the mystery motivator procedure to increase homework completion and accuracy rates (Madaus, Kehle, Madaus, & Bray, 2003; Moore, Waguespack, Wickstrom, Witt, & Gaydos, 1994).

Self-monitoring procedures, in which students are trained to track their own behaviors, can also be used as part of a treatment program to address "won't do" difficulties. Students who pay attention to their own study behaviors often react by changing their behaviors to meet a goal such as improved academic performance (Mace, Belfiore, & Hutchinson, 2001). When parents are involved in this process, it is likely that academic study behaviors and performance will increase (Kahle & Kelley, 1994; Miller & Kelley, 1991; Olympia, Sheridan, & Jenson, 1994a; Rhoades & Kratochwill, 1998). When setting up a self-monitoring program, school psychologists and parents should keep in mind some factors that have been shown to influence a student's responsiveness to self-monitoring. For example, students are more likely to change their behavior when just a few behaviors are monitored (Mace et al., 2001). Thus, parents can help in the selection of the most salient behaviors to record initially. Also, recording increases in desired behaviors rather than decreases in undesired behaviors is preferable because attention to decreasing negative behavior does not always result in students using more appropriate behaviors (Skinner & Smith, 1992). In addition, it is important to keep in mind a student's ability to perform the academic tasks with minimum support because the effectiveness of the self-monitoring procedures is dependent on students performing tasks without additional instructional support (Reid, 1996). Finally, it is important to keep in mind that the exact function of self-monitoring effects may vary for each student (Reid, Gonzalez, Nordness, Trout, & Epstein, 2004). Self-monitoring might work because (1) the procedures serve as a cue to manage behavior, (2) the student learns what strategies effectively meet a goal with minimal time and effort, (3) the student becomes motivated by the recorded progress toward a goal, and (4) the student gains adult praise for an increase in performance. Although self-management interventions are designed to teach students to control their own behavior, parents can cue their child on when and how to observe important behaviors and praise increases in their child's awareness of his or her own behaviors to maintain gains in independent performance. Given that the mechanism of self-monitoring is still unknown, it is difficult to determine which child will respond to this intervention and why. Thus, it is important to closely monitor the effects of the intervention on individual performance.

Reading Interventions

Because of the importance of reading, a significant amount of research has been conducted on interventions designed to increase children's ability to read. Although there is certainly research on basic principles of teaching reading skills (e.g., as noted in the *Report of the National Reading Panel* [National Institute of Child Health and Human Development, 2000], phonics instruction is particularly helpful in teaching children to read), one area that has received significant attention more recently is reading fluency. As indicated in the *Report of the National Reading Panel*, "Fluent readers are able to read orally with speed, accuracy, and proper expression. Fluency is one of several critical factors necessary for reading comprehension. Despite its importance ... fluency is often neglected in the classroom" (p. 11). Interventions related to reading fluency are relatively simple to implement, and with some assistance, parents can easily implement such interventions in the home setting.

Repeated readings is probably the most common method that has been designed to increase children's fluency with reading and has a significant amount of empirical support. In this method, students reread brief passages until a certain level of fluency is obtained. This method can be used both with and without models, and models can be peers or adults (e.g., parents). When used with a model, the model provides feedback to the child on how to correctly pronounce words that are missed when the student initially reads the passage. Thus, this procedure also includes an error correction component, which can lead to a quicker reduction in the amount of errors a child makes. Incorporating an overcorrection procedure (e.g., having the child repeat the correct pronunciation of a word initially mispronounced) can also help reduce errors and increase fluency. In the review of studies on repeated readings included in the *Report of the National Reading Panel* (National Institute of Child Health and Human Development, 2000), significant support for this method in increasing reading fluency was noted. Chard, Vaughn, and Tyler (2002) summarized the existing literature on reading fluency interventions for children with learning disabilities and noted that repeated reading interventions were effective in improving students' fluency. Furthermore, they concluded that repeated readings with a model were more effective than repeated readings without a model. Although the vast majority of research on repeated readings has been with younger (elementary school) students (e.g., Chafouleas, Martens, Dobson, Weinstein, & Gardner, 2004; Daly et al., 2002; Nelson, Alber, & Gordy, 2004), some studies have suggested that it can also be implemented effectively with middle school- (Mercer, Campbell, Miller, Mercer, & Lane, 2000) and high school-age (Valleley & Shriver, 2003) children. Form 6.1 (at the end if this chapter) contains a repeated readings intervention outline that parents could use with their children at home after some initial guidance and support from school personnel. In particular, school personnel would need to assist parents in locating reading passages that are at the student's instructional level.

Listening preview is another reading technique with empirical support that provides modeling in addition to fluency practice with feedback. When using this method, an individual (e.g., parent) reads the passage to the child, while the child follows along, before the child attempts to read the passage him- or herself (see Form 6.2 at the end of the chapter). Listening preview can be combined with repeated readings so that a child has the passage modeled first (via listening preview) and then procedures related to repeated readings are followed. A variety of researchers have evaluated and noted empirical support for listening preview, both as a stand-alone intervention and in combination with other readings interventions (e.g., Begeny & Silber, 2006; Eckert, Ardoin, Daly, & Martens, 2002; Skinner, Cooper, & Cole, 1997).

Phrase drill error correction is another reading intervention technique with empirical support that can be effective for students who are making a number of reading errors (i.e., mispronunciations or word omissions). In this intervention, the child reads aloud from a passage. The teacher or parent listens and follows along on a written copy of the passage, underlining errors that are made. The teacher/parent models the correct pronunciation and the child then rereads the section that contains the places in which he or she made the errors initially (see Form 6.3 at the end of the chapter). This method has been shown to be effective in comparison to other error correction methods (O'Shea, Munson, & O'Shea,

1984) and has also been used as a supported intervention in studies making use of BEA techniques (e.g., Daly et al., 1998, 2002).

Tracking children's progress on these reading interventions is a key part of their implementation. It is important to determine whether the intervention is having the desired impact and, if not, to make changes so that parents are making the best use of their time. Form 6.4 (at the end of the chapter) is a tracking sheet for parents and school psychologists to record and evaluate student progress on the number of words read correctly on reading passages practiced with the repeated readings, listening preview, or phrase drill intervention.

Although interventions aimed primarily at reading fluency can also increase reading comprehension (Chard et al., 2002), specifically addressing comprehension may provide additional benefits to the student. One method of increasing comprehension involves *asking key questions* about a passage (e.g., Short & Ryan, 1984), for example: Who is the main character in the story? Who is the story about? What is the main idea of the story? What happened in the story? Where did the story take place? When did the story take place? What do you think will happen next? Students are informed of these questions before reading the story, then they read the story, and attempt to answer these questions. See Form 6.5 (at the end of the chapter) for a parent handout describing this intervention technique and Form 6.6 (at the end of the chapter) for a tracking sheet to record student progress. *Story mapping* is a similar technique in which a pictorial outline is presented to the students before they read the passage. For example, a story map might contain boxes for the setting, the problem, the goal, the action, and the outcome (Idol, 1987). These types of megacognitive strategies have been demonstrated to improve reading comprehension in students (e.g., Boulineau, Fore, Hagan-Burke, & Burke, 2004; Idol, 1987; Short & Ryan, 1984; Taylor, Alber, & Walker, 2002). When using these types of comprehension aids, parents can provide corrective feedback to the child. If the child has difficulties answering the question, the parent can assist the child in finding the section of the story in which the question is addressed.

To illustrate the use of reading interventions with parents, let's return to our case example of Sam. Following a BEA in which the school psychologist identified Listening Preview with a reward for performance, as likely the most effective intervention for Sam, the school psychologist could then meet with Sam's parents to train them on the Listening Preview intervention. During training, Sam's parents would be provided with written instructions and materials to conduct the intervention. Sam's parents would then conduct the intervention for 10 minutes a day, administering a 1-minute reading probe and graphing Sam's progress to evaluate whether he was meeting a daily goal (i.e., beating his prior best score). The school psychologist would review the data with the parents to determine whether the intervention was having the intended effect.

Mathematics Interventions

By far, the most research on academic intervention techniques is related to reading interventions. However, there are data on interventions related to improving mathematical skills and many of these interventions can also be implemented in collaboration with parents.

As with reading interventions, math interventions have targeted accuracy with basic skills as well as fluency with math skills. In a meta-analytic review, Kroesbergen and Van Luit (2003) concluded that direct instruction in math facts was most effective in remediating basic skill math-related difficulties. However, they concluded that self-instruction methods were also effective, particularly in relation to increasing mathematical problem-solving skills.

The *cover, copy, and compare* method is a recommended math skills intervention that makes use of self-instructional methods, and a number of studies support the use of this technique. In this procedure, students are presented with a sheet of math problems with the correct answer provided. Students look at the problem with the correct answer and then cover the problem and answer, rewrite the problem and answer the math problem (or write the answer to the problem on an identical work sheet without the answers provided), and then uncover the problem and correct answer and compare this with the student-generated answer. This procedure allows a student to practice his or her math skills while receiving immediate feedback. Because the child can compare his or her answer to the correct answer on his or her own, the use of adult time and resources is limited. This procedure has been used in group and individual settings within the school setting with positive results (e.g., Lee & Tingstrom, 1994; Skinner, McLaughlin, & Logan, 1997). Parents can easily be taught to help their children implement this technique in the home setting (see Form 6.7 at the end of the chapter).

Explicit timing is another easy-to-implement intervention for increasing math fluency (Van Houten & Thompson, 1976). In this intervention, children are provided with a math work sheet and are instructed to complete as many problems as possible during a brief, specified time interval (e.g., 2 minutes). After the specified time interval, children score their responses by comparing them with an answer key or consulting with an adult (see Form 6.8 at the end of the chapter). As part of this intervention, children can be encouraged to beat their previous best score and earn rewards for doing so. In a variety of studies, researchers have demonstrated positive outcomes with this technique (e.g., Rhymer, Henington, Skinner, & Looby, 1999; Rhymer et al., 2002).

The use of *math flash cards* can also be incorporated easily in home-based interventions for math difficulties (McCallum, Skinner, Turner, & Saecker, 2006). When implementing such an intervention, flash cards with basic math facts to be mastered are created. The math problem is on one side of the card (e.g., 2×3) and the answer on the other side (e.g., 6). The parent presents the flash card to the child, who then provides an answer. If the child produces the correct answer, the parent praises the child (e.g., "That's right, 2×3 is 6"). If the child is unable to answer after 3 to 5 seconds or provides a wrong answer, the parent shows the child the correct answer on the card. The same card is then re-presented to the child. Form 6.9 (at the end of the chapter) contains a handout outlining the steps in this type of intervention.

As with reading interventions, it is important that parents have a quick method of tracking progress with these math interventions to ensure the intervention is having the desired effect. Form 6.10 (at the end of the chapter) provides a tracking sheet for parents and school psychologists to record and evaluate student progress with the flash card, explicit timing, or cover, copy, and compare interventions.

Written Language Interventions

Although the process of writing is complex, there are three key writing stages in which parents can provide support to their children in improving their skills: prewriting activities to plan and organize before writing a draft, revising the draft, and editing the final revisions (Graham, Harris, MacArthur, & Schwartz, 1991). For the first writing stage, *flow sheets* have been effectively used as a structural framework to guide the student's prewriting planning or organization (Englert & Mariage, 1991; Troia & Graham, 2003). Form 6.11 (at the end of the chapter) shows how parents can use such a structured tool, which can be completed with the student to outline or brainstorm key concepts and organize conceptual categories to facilitate writing flow. Parents and their children can begin practicing prewriting planning by selecting a topic or reading about a topic from a textbook. After selecting a topic, the student completes a flow chart that guides his or her organization. For example, a student can complete an outline by first writing three main ideas followed by three details about each main idea (see Form 6.12 at the end of the chapter). The story map flow sheet (Form 6.13 at the end of the chapter) can also be used in this manner to write a narrative story. Initially, parents and the student can work together to complete a sheet while the student learns to independently use the strategy. After a sheet is complete, the student writes about the topic in a brief, timed writing session. Parents and teachers can monitor the student's progress by assessing the number of words written and determine the number of key ideas written in the order presented in the flow chart.

Parents can also be involved in the process of assisting students with revising the content of a writing draft. Graham, MacArthur, and Schwartz (1995), for example, showed improvement in the quality of writing samples by simply directing students to add three things to improve their writing after a timed writing session. The additional use of a revising guide also produced greater improvements in the quality of the revision, although students tend to focus more on editing words than changing sentence structure. Form 6.14 (at the end of the chapter) illustrates a *revising checklist protocol* that parents and students can follow.

A student may write a planned story quickly but make many mechanical errors. Grammar can be addressed immediately after the student has completed a writing sample by providing a key to help him or her look for grammatical errors (e.g., focus on capitalization). Parents then check the student's work after he or she has attempted to identify errors (Graham, Harris, & Larsen, 2001). Form 6.15 (at the end of the chapter) illustrates a *revising checklist for mechanical errors* in which common proofreading elements are listed. Some students may be able to edit all common errors on the checklist, whereas others may not recognize any errors. The goal is to increase accurate student editing with minimal parent editing. Starting with a few common types of errors and adding a new proofing skill each week allows the student to become fluent on a few highlighted errors at a time instead of working on a heavily marked edited paper (Bos & Vaughn, 2002).

Interventions targeting written language have been designed to also target writing quantity for those students who struggle to get words written. The simplest option to increase quantity of writing is to have children engage in brief, daily writing exercises. Children can be provided with *story starters*, which they are instructed to think about for 1 to 2 minutes. They are then instructed to free-write for several minutes based on the story starter provided. In order for the student to monitor his or her progress, the student can count the number of words written after the end of the writing time and graph this on a chart. Form 6.16 (at the end of the chapter) is a handout outlining this type of intervention, with a tracking sheet in Form 6.17 (at the end of the chapter). Moxley, Lutz, Ahlborn, Boley, and Armstrong (1995) evaluated the effectiveness of having students engage in free-writing for a certain period of time and recording word counts after completing their writing. Students were also provided with reinforcers for meeting certain goals. In this study, elementary schoolchildren improved in terms of both the number of words they wrote and the detail and complexity of their sentences.

Because students benefit from frequent practice and guided feedback, interventions that parents can reasonably implement in a consistent manner will lead to the greatest writing gains. Using flow sheets and revision guides for the three writing stages to support student writing can be implemented to increase student skill proficiency with brief 15-minute daily writing sessions before students write more complex drafts. Parents can also add goal-setting strategies to motivate students (Graham et al., 2001). For example, Page-Voth and Graham (1999) examined the effects of goal setting on the essays of middle school students with learning disabilities in writing. Students who set goals to increase either the number of reasons supporting a paper's premise or the number of counterarguments refuted by the writer wrote essays of greater quality and length with more supporting reasons than essays written by students who did not set goals.

HOMEWORK INTERVENTIONS

Problems surrounding homework are likely the area in which parents can be the most involved in collaborating with school professionals to help their children succeed more academically. Homework problems occur frequently and because they, by definition, involve a home component, parental involvement is often key to intervention. Although there has been, and likely will continue to be, some debate regarding whether homework is positively related to academic success, the available literature suggests that homework is important in increasing academic achievement, particularly for middle school and high school students (Keith & Keith, 2006).

Although many children are not spending significant amounts of time on homework (e.g., Keith, Diamond-Hallam, & Fine, 2004, reported that high school students spend more hours per week watching television than they do completing homework), it is not uncommon for parents to report that their children have "too much" homework and that they are spending hours each night helping their child complete homework. Although there are no established guidelines for the ideal quantity of homework, a summary by Keith and Keith (2006) of previous recommendations suggests that homework activities in early elementary school grades should take less than 1 hour per day, whereas in the high school years several hours of homework a day may be appropriate. However, given that there is a great deal of variability in terms of homework expectations, it can be important for parents to talk to their child's teacher regarding expectations. Understanding how much time the teacher expects the child to spend on homework can be helpful in allowing parents to gauge whether there is a problem in terms of time the child is spending on homework and how much of a problem there is. For example, if the teacher indicates that homework is expected to take 45 minutes to an hour each night and a child is spending 3 hours, then clearly something is amiss. School psychologists can help facilitate this discussion between parents and teachers regarding homework issues (e.g., amount of homework, expectations for parent involvement).

Some comprehensive parent training programs have addressed homework-related issues. For example, Rhoades and Kratochwill (1998) implemented a 5-week training program with parents of children who were having difficulties completing homework. Components of this program included developing a study time, ongoing collaboration between parents and teachers, and training in developing reinforcement/incentive programs. Outcome data suggest that this program was effective in increasing the amount of homework students completed. Others have reported some preliminary support for parent training-based homework programs but more often have described programs without providing outcome data (e.g., Jenson, Sheridan, Olympia, & Andrews, 1994). Thus, more research is needed on these comprehensive programs to determine their efficacy in promoting homework completion and accuracy. In the following discussion, we present some specific techniques that may be helpful to address children's problems with homework.

Similar to the academic interventions discussed previously, homework success depends on the match between the homework problem and the intervention addressing the variables controlling the problem (Olympia, Sheridan, & Jenson, 1994b). After a student learns how to initially perform a skill with accuracy in the classroom, homework is given to provide practice opportunities to enhance skill competency. One type of problem resulting in poor homework performance is that a student may not have acquired the skills to the degree that is necessary to perform the task (i.e., a skill deficit). The academic interventions discussed previously are more suitable for students who need to enhance prerequisite skills required to complete typical homework tasks. For those students who are able to do the work but choose not to (i.e., a performance deficit), several homework interventions can be effective, as discussed next.

Parent supervision is a key factor in homework completion. Simply having a monitoring system that requires parents to sign completed work has the strongest relationship with time spent on homework (Holmes & Croll, 1989). Setting up a homework routine is a process parents can use to maintain consistent supervision and support (Patton, 1994). A *daily homework routine* consists of scheduling a homework time when parent supervision is available in a distraction-free study area with all the needed resources (e.g., pencils, dictionary, paper). Routines may also include common tasks such as (1) completing homework independently, (2) showing completed work to the parent for review, (3) spending 10 minutes correcting work, (4) earning parent praise or rewards for the completion of homework requirements, and (5) organizing materials to bring back to school (Toney, Kelley, & Lanclos, 2003).

Even with an established homework routine, a common problem reported by parents is the tracking of daily homework requirements and materials needed to complete the work. Students wishing to "escape" from homework time will often deny that homework was assigned or will fail to bring homework materials home. One method that has been used to increase homework completion and submission is the home/school note method, discussed previously in Chapter 4. This method has the benefit that it requires minimal "hands-on" time from the parent or teacher but still fosters ongoing home/school collaboration to benefit the child. In addition, this method addresses the potential issue that parents may not be aware of their children's homework and thus be in no position to implement a program to assist with homework completion. In one method, a note is simply sent home informing parents of the percentage of homework the child has submitted. Parents are requested to sign and return the note. In another method, a school–home note routine is established requiring the student to (1) write down homework assignments in a homework notebook, (2) have teachers sign the notebook, and (3) bring the notebook and homework materials home. The notebook can contain daily or weekly notes that are divided into time periods or academic subjects, much like the note system described in Chapter 4. When signing the notebook, the teacher also rates how much of the homework is complete and correct for each time/class period. Thus, this system provides parents with the information that the student successfully turned in the completed homework and received timely feedback from the teacher on progress. Form 6.18 (at the end of the chapter) presents a daily homework checklist that is to be completed by a teacher, parent, and student. Form 6.19 (at the end of the chapter) provides a procedure that parents can follow when adhering to the steps needed to complete the daily homework checklist and supporting a student as he or she completes homework assignments.

As with the home/school note system described in Chapter 4, parents could provide reinforcers at home dependent on a student's performance if the school homework checklist is ineffective without a motivation strategy. A common problem encountered is that the homework checklist or needed homework materials are not brought home by the student. Such a difficulty is often successfully addressed by incorporating a reward system. A child may simply earn rewards for various aspects of the intervention program. For example, a student can earn 1 point for bringing home a list of written homework assignments with teacher signatures, 1 point for each completed assignment, and 2 points for turning in assignments with 80% or more accuracy. The student will be able to get a reward after earning a predetermined number of points.

A student *homework contract* may be used as part of this system whereby the student and parent agree on what the student needs to do in order to earn reinforcers (see Form 6.20 at the end of the chapter). Establishment of an effective contract involves clearly defined student, parent, and teacher behaviors and a system to assess progress of all three participants in adherence to the contract.

An additional homework intervention is student *self-monitoring of homework progress* using the intervention steps in Form 6.21 (at the end of the chapter). This combined intervention links behaviors that parents and students take at each homework step to promote parent support leading to student independent functioning. Teaching students to self-monitor their implementation of homework routine steps can be an effective strategy to help them self-regulate their study behaviors with minimal parent prompting. Parent monitoring of homework is effective, but Toney et al. (2003) found that student self-monitoring was equally as effective for reducing parent-reported homework problems. The advantage of student self-monitoring is the minimal degree of parent involvement and student responsibility for his or her own homework behavior. A critical role of the parent is to assist the student with goal setting (Kahle & Kelley, 1994) or to pair praise or rewards with successful self-monitoring behaviors (Nelson, Smith, Young, & Dodd, 1991).

A second common homework problem is student off-task behaviors that extend a homework routine to hours rather than the allotted minutes intended by a teacher. To increase time on task, parents can use a *timing intervention* adapted from a classroom-based intervention for work completion. In this method, the parent (in collaboration with the child's teacher) determines how much time the child should be spending on homework each night. At the designated homework time, the parent sets a timer for this amount of time (e.g., 30 minutes) and informs the child that if he or she works consistently on his or her homework during this time, the child can gain access to a certain privilege or activity (e.g., extra time on the computer, time to play outside). If the child gets off-task during the homework time, the timer is stopped and not reset until the child once again begins attending to the task. A handout on this intervention is provided in Form 6.22 (at the end of the chapter). Specific goals can also be put into place when using this intervention to help solve other common problems. For students who refuse to do acceptable work unless someone works with him or her, a goal is set to independently complete a portion of the work at 80% or more accuracy before the timer rings.

CHAPTER SUMMARY

Individual students experience academic difficulties for a variety of reasons, but a few common problems explain the majority of deficiencies in academic performance: low motivation, inaccurate work, unmastered proficiency level, difficulty of task, and difficulty generalizing or adapting a recently learned skill to novel tasks. There are well-supported instructional strategies that have been shown to effectively address each of the common factors that affect student performance in the classroom. The greatest difficulty is to find the time and resources to initiate interventions. Parents can be an important resource to help implement interventions if the intervention can be reasonably conducted in the home setting. The procedures described in this chapter provide some simple, time-efficient strategies that parents can use. However, it is imperative that the parents' time and effort are valued by closely monitoring intervention outcomes. When the intervention produces positive growth, parents will be reassured that their time and effort are producing meaningful results for their child. If the intervention does not produce the intended results, modifying parents' efforts is warranted. Because of individual differences, intervention adjustments are frequently needed to lead to successful outcomes as educators gain a more complete understanding of the problem. When parents' efforts are adequately supported, parent assistance with the academic interventions presented in this chapter can be an important resource to provide children with additional instructional support.

FORM 6.1

Repeated Reading Intervention

Materials Needed

Two copies of a reading passage (200–400 words)

Stopwatch

Pencil

Tracking sheet

Procedures

1. Practice: Place one reading passage in front of the child and say, "Here is a story that I want you to read to me. To get better at reading, I am going to have you read this story three times. Each time I will tell you how fast you read the story and how many words you read. Read the story out loud. If you come to a word you do not know, I will tell you."

2. Say "Begin" and start the stopwatch when the child says the first word.

3. Error correction: When the child hesitates on a word for more than 3 seconds, mispronounces a word, or omits a word, say the word to the child and have him/her repeat the word correctly before continuing to read.

4. Stop the stopwatch when the child says the last word. Tell the child how long it took him or her to read the passage.

5. Have the student read the passage three times with error correction.

6. Independent practice: Have the child reread the passage for 1 minute.

Progress Monitoring

Record how many words the child reads correctly in 1 minute during the independent practice.

Listening Preview Intervention

Materials Needed

Two copies of a reading passage

Stopwatch

Pencil

Tracking sheet

Procedures

1. Take out the child's copy of the reading passage.

2. Model: Read the passage aloud to the child. Read somewhat slower than you normally would so that the child can easily follow along.

3. Practice: Have the child read the passage aloud to you.

4. Error correction: If the child gets stuck on a word for 3 seconds or mispronounces a word, tell the child the word and have the child repeat the word correctly.

5. Independent practice: Have the child reread the passage for 1 minute.

Progress Monitoring

Record how many words the child reads correctly in 1 minute during the independent practice.

Phrase Drill Error Correction

Materials Needed

Reading passages of approximately 200 words

Stopwatch

Pencil

Tracking sheet

Procedures

1. Practice: Ask the child to read a passage out loud.

2. Error correction: Stop the child whenever a word is omitted, substituted, or mispronounced or if the child cannot read the word. Tell the child the missed word. Ask the child to say the missed word correctly five times.

3. Feedback: Praise the child by saying, "That's right! That word is _____" if the child says the word correctly.

4. Tell the child to continue reading the passage, starting with the sentence containing the missed word.

5. Continue to correct the child if he or she misses a word: Ask the child to say the word five times, and repeat the sentence containing the missed word as the child continues to read the passage.

6. Independent practice: Have the child reread the passage for 1 minute.

Progress Monitoring

Record how many words the child reads correctly in 1 minute during the independent practice.

Tracking Sheet: Words Read Correctly

Date	Words read correctly	Number of errors

Reading Comprehension via Asking Key Questions

Materials Needed

Five instructional-level reading passages

List of key questions

Tracking sheet

Procedures

1. Pick a passage to read with the child.

2. Tell the child that he/she will be answering questions following the story. These questions include:

   a. Who is the main character in the story? Who is the story about?

   b. What is the main idea of the story? What happened in the story?

   c. Where did the story take place?

   d. When did the story take place?

   e. What do you think will happen next?

3. Tell the child to read the story out loud.

4. After the child has read the story, ask the child each of the questions about the story and have the child answer without looking back at the story.

5. Provide corrective feedback to the child if needed and assist the child in finding the section of the story that helps answer the questions missed.

Progress Monitoring

Record the child's number of correct answers.

Tracking Sheet: Reading Comprehension via Asking Key Questions

Mark in each box whether the child correctly answered the question.

	Monday	Tuesday	Wednesday	Thursday	Friday
Who is the story about?					
What happened in the story?					
Where did the story take place?					
When did the story take place?					
What do you think will happen next?					
Total correct					

Cover, Copy, and Compare Math Procedure

Materials Needed

A math assignment without answers

The same assignment with answers to the problems

Pencil

Tracking sheet

Stopwatch

Procedures

1. Give the child a math assignment and a copy with answers.

2. Tell the child to do the problems following these five steps.
   a. Look at the solution of the problem.
   b. Cover the correct answer.
   c. Do the problems on your own paper.
   d. Uncover the correct answer.
   e. Compare your answer with the correct answer.

3. Once the child has finished, have the child do a similar work sheet without using the cover, copy, and compare procedure.

4. If the student is unable to do the problems correctly, help the student with the problem and then have the student redo problem using the cover, copy, and compare method.

Progress Monitoring

Using 2-minute timings, calculate the number of digits the child completed correctly on both the problems given after the cover, copy, and compare procedure and any independent homework given to the child using the same math skill.

Using Explicit Timing to Teach Math Facts

Materials Needed

Math work sheets

Stopwatch

Pencil

Tracking sheet

Procedures

1. Get out materials.

2. Set the timer for 2 minutes.

3. Instruct the child to complete as many problems as possible within 2 minutes.

4. When the timer rings, have the child stop working.

5. Count the number of problems completed correctly.

6. Provide a reward to the child for completing more problems correctly than he or she did last time.

Progress Monitoring

Record the number of digits the child correctly completes during each timing session.

Using Flash Cards to Teach Math Facts

Materials Needed

A set of flash cards for math facts (e.g., multiplication by 3s)

A work sheet with the same facts randomly arranged

Stopwatch

Tracking sheet

Procedures

1. Present each flash card to the child while verbally prompting the child with the question (e.g., "What is 3×3?").

2. Praise the child for correct responses given within 3 seconds of the prompt.

3. If no response or an incorrect response is given:
   a. Provide the child with the correct answer.
   b. Redeliver the verbal prompt.
   c. Move on to next problem after second presentation.

Progress Monitoring

Give the student a work sheet with problems presented in flash cards and give the child 2 minutes to complete as many problems as possible. Count the number of digits the child completed correctly.

FORM 6.10

Math Tracking Sheet: Digits Correct

Date	Number of digits correct	Number of digits incorrect

Note. In calculating digits correct take into account each digit in the answer. For example, 2 × 6 = 12 is 2 digits correct; 2 × 6 = 11 is 1 digit correct.

Working on the Writing Process: Planning

Materials Needed

Topic idea or passage from student's textbook

Flow sheet

Paper and pencil or computer

Timer

Procedures

Prewriting planning and organization:

1. Develop a topic for writing or write about a topic just read in a school textbook.

2. Select a flow sheet that will help identify key ideas and develop a written plan.

3. Give the student 10 to 15 minutes to brainstorm ideas for the writing sample and write down the ideas on the flow sheet.

4. Prompt or ask questions to expand on/clarify plan for writing.

5. Develop a list of vocabulary or key words that you could use that are related to the topic.

Writing the draft:

1. Place the flow sheet in front of the student with writing materials.

2. Set the timer for 5 to 15 minutes.

3. Tell the student to write a story using the flow sheet and vocabulary words.

Progress Monitoring

Record the number of words written per minute.

Student may also earn up to 5 points for including the following features:

_____ Topic sentence.

_____ Related details fit.

_____ Information is logically sequenced.

_____ Transitional or signal words present.

_____ No intrusive (unrelated) material.

Outline Planning Flow Sheet

Main topic/purpose of paper:

_____

_____

_____

First idea about main topic

Topic sentence: _____

_____

List details, reasons, or details about idea.

1. _____

_____

2. _____

_____

3. _____

_____

Important vocabulary words to use:

Second idea about main topic

Topic sentence: _____

_____

List details, reasons, or details about idea.

1. _____

_____

2. _____

_____

3. _____

_____

Important vocabulary words to use:

(cont.)

Third idea about main topic

Topic sentence: _____

_____

List details, reasons, or details about idea.

1. _____

_____

2. _____

_____

3. _____

_____

Important vocabulary words to use:

CONCLUSION

Summarize.

1. _____

_____

2. _____

_____

3. _____

_____

Story Map Flow Sheet

SETTING

Place: _____

Characters: _____

_____

PROBLEM AND GOAL

_____

_____

_____

_____

ACTION

_____

_____

_____

_____

OUTCOME

_____

_____

_____

Working on the Writing Process: Revising Drafts

Materials Needed

A draft of a paper written by the student (see *Working on the Writing Process: Planning*).
Pencil

Procedures for Revising Content and Organization

1. Read the draft.
2. Provide praise for specific efforts such clear points, sentences, or word choices.
3. Have the student write three questions and determine whether the questions can be answered by reading his or her draft.
4. Read the draft out loud and follow the checklist to determine what revisions are needed.

Checklist

_____ Introduction states purpose/why the paper is written and how topics will be organized.

_____ Key words or concepts used in the introduction.

_____ Each paragraph has a topic sentence containing the main idea of the paragraph.

_____ Each paragraph makes at least one point about the topic.

_____ Each major point is stated clearly.

_____ The ideas flow smoothly with an order that makes sense.

_____ All details fit topic.

_____ Enough details are written to make readers understand the main point.

_____ Terms and words that readers might not know are defined.

_____ A conclusion that summarizes points in the paper is included.

Progress Monitoring

Rate each skill on a scale such as 1 = *not present*; 2 = *some errors*; 3 = *accurate/present*.
Track progress on total score or scores on selected target skills.

Working on the Writing Process: Editing Mechanical Errors

Some students will need to review mechanical writing errors that they will be identifying and correcting using a grammar text. If this is the case, begin by reviewing one to two skills per day. Students can then edit by circling correct and underlining incorrect skills to determine whether they understand the skill. Below are common mechanical errors to edit beginning with the simpler skills that are frequently taught in early grades.

_____ Check for punctuation.

_____ Check for capitalization after every period.

_____ Check spelling. Start at the end of your story and check each word to the beginning. Underline any words that don't look right to you. Look up the underlined words in the dictionary to check spelling.

_____ Check whether all present tense words are used correctly.

_____ Check whether all past tense words are used correctly.

_____ Check commas.

_____ Check apostrophe errors (e.g., *Dan's bike or all students' work, "it's" = "it is"*).

_____ Check informal wording or slang that needs to be changed.

_____ Read each sentence or word order and make sure it makes sense if read by itself.

_____ Check that sentences contain a noun and a verb.

_____ Check whether all words are needed in each sentence.

_____ Vary sentence length and structure.

_____ Check use of connecting words such as "and," "but," "however," and "therefore."

Progress Monitoring

Rate each skill on a scale, such as 1 = *not present incorrect*; 2 = *some errors*; 3 = *accurate*.

Track progress on total score or scores on selected target skills if child is making numerous errors.

Story Starter Writing Intervention

Materials Needed

Written Expression story starter work sheet (e.g., One day I woke up and I was small ... ;
We went slowly into the deep dark woods ... ; The kind man gave me a magic ring. The magic
ring ...)

Stopwatch

Pencil

Tracking sheet

Procedures

1. Give the child a paper with the story starter at the top. Place the paper face down in front of
   the child, instructing him/her not to turn it over until told to do so.

2. Instruct the child: "This is a writing assignment. Turn your paper over and you will see a story
   starter at the top of the page. You will be writing a story using this starter. You will have 1
   minute to think about what you would like to write. Do not begin writing until I say, 'Begin.' Are
   there any questions?"

3. Set the timer for 1 minute. Tell the child, "This is your think time." Begin the timer.

4. After think time is over, explain to the child that he/she needs to work as quickly as possible
   but should also be very careful not to make spelling and capitalization errors.

5. Set the timer for 3 minutes. Tell the student, "Begin."

6. When the timer rings, say, "Stop. Put your pencil down."

7. Read the paragraph together with the child. Edit the paragraph and ask the child to make
   corrections on the paper.

Progress Monitoring

Count the number of words written and errors made during the writing time.

Tracking Sheet: Words Written

Date	Number of words written correctly	Number of errors made

Daily Homework Checklist

Date: _____

Subject	Teacher's signature for turning in assignments due today	New assignment to complete (including no homework)	Materials needed for assignment	Teacher's signature for writing correct assignment	Parent's signature for viewing completed assignment
Math					
Reading					
English					
History					
Science					

Daily Homework Checklist: Parent Procedures

Materials Needed

Homework binder

Daily Homework Checklists

Procedures

1. Place *Daily Homework Checklists* in a homework binder.

2. At the beginning of a school day, remind the student to complete the checklist.

3. At a set homework time, review the checklist and praise the student's accurate completion of this requirement. Check to see whether all homework materials were brought home.

4. Prompt the student to begin homework at the set homework time and place or praise if the student is already working.

5. After 10 minutes of work time, check for on-task behavior.

6. Assist the student with homework tasks if needed and appropriate.

7. At the end of homework time, sign in the "parent's signature" column on the Daily Homework Checklist for each assignment that is completed.

8. If using a self-monitoring component, have the student rate his or her behavior for each of the behaviors on the monitoring sheet.

9. If using a reinforcement system, provide points as predetermined. Points are turned in for selected rewards.

10. Prompt the student to organize homework materials to bring to school the next day.

Academic Homework Contract

I, _____ [student's name], agree to be responsible for the
following three steps:

1. Writing down the homework assignment in a homework notebook for the following subjects
    each day and getting teacher signatures **even when there is no homework.**

2. Asking teachers to write notes such as "HW complete," "Classwork completed," "Great day!"

3. Completing and turning in the homework on Monday through Thursday for the following
    subjects (circle):

Social Studies

Science

Language Arts

Reading

Math

Other _____

I understand that if I follow these three steps, then my parents will give:

1. **1** point for every **signature.**
2. **1** point for every **homework assignment** that they **see** completed.
3. **1** point for every **good note.**

If I earn a total of _____ points by Friday, then I will earn one reward from the following for the
weekend.

1.   4.

2.   5.

3.   6.

_____   _____

Student   Date

_____   _____

Parent   Date

_____

Daily Homework Checklist: Student Self-Monitoring Procedures

Step	What to do	Rate if step completed	Parent check (if accurate)
1	Homework and homework binder was brought to school.	YES or NO	
2	Completed the *Daily Homework Checklist* by 1. Having teachers check off that homework due today was turned in. 2. Writing down the new homework assignments. 3. Getting my teachers' signatures for correctly written assignments.	YES or NO	
3	Brought home materials needed to complete the homework.	YES or NO	
4	Worked on homework during the set homework time at the set quiet place.	YES or NO	
5	Completed all homework assignments, staying on task for 90% of the time.	YES or NO	
6	Asked for help when needed.	YES or NO	
7	Had parent check and sign all work and immediately completed any parent-suggested changes.	YES or NO	
8	Completed self-monitoring checklist.	YES or NO	
9	Determined points earned with parent.	YES or NO	
10	Organized homework materials to bring back to school in the morning.	YES or NO	

Time for Homework

This procedure is designed to maintain the time allotted for homework. Parents set up a specific amount of time for students to complete homework and then provide reinforcement/free time for consistent work during that time.

Procedures

1. Determine the amount of time the child should spend on homework tasks.

2. Give the child any needed directions.

3. Tell the child the amount of time he/she is required to spend doing homework.

4. Explain to the child that you will set the timer for that amount of time and stop the timer whenever he/she is not working or following directions.

5. Set the timer and tell child to begin.

6. If the child is off task, stop the timer.

7. Tell the child what he/she should be doing.

8. If the child does not comply, warn the child that the timer is stopped and free time is being lost.

9. When the child begins work again, restart the timer.

10. To make this intervention work, make sure that the child is allowed free time/access to a desired activity as planned.

References

Achenbach, T. M., & Rescorla, L. A. (2000). *Manual for the ASEBA preschool forms and profiles.* Burlington: University of Vermont, Research Center for Children, Youth, & Families.

Achenbach, T. M., & Rescorla, L. A. (2001). *Manual for the ASEBA school-age forms and profiles.* Burlington: University of Vermont, Research Center for Children, Youth, & Families.

Altarac, M., & Saroha, E. (2007). Lifetime prevalence of learning disability among U.S. children. *Pediatrics, 119,* S77–S83.

American Psychiatric Association. (1994). *Diagnostic and statistical manual of mental disorders* (4th ed.). Washington, DC: Author.

American Psychological Association. (2002). *Ethical principles of psychologists and code of conduct.* Washington, DC: Author. Retrieved February 29, 2008, from *www.apa.org/ethics/code2002. pdf.*

American Psychological Association Presidential Task Force on Evidence-Based Practice. (2006). Evidence-based practice in psychology. *American Psychologist, 61,* 271–285.

Angold, A., Erkanli, A., Farmer, E. M. Z., Fairbank, J. A., Burns, B. J., Keeler, G., et al. (2002). Psychiatric disorder, impairment, and service use in rural African-American and White youth. *Archives of General Psychiatry, 59,* 893–901.

Angold, A., & Rutter, M. (1992). Effects of age and pubertal status on depression in a large clinical sample. *Development and Psychopathology, 4,* 5–28.

Anstendig, K. (1998). Selective mutism: A review of the treatment literature by modality from 1980–1996. *Psychotherapy, 35,* 381–391.

Asarnow, J. R., Scott, C. V., & Mintz, J. (2002). A combined cognitive-behavioral family education intervention for depression in children: A treatment development study. *Cognitive Therapy and Research, 26,* 221–229.

Bagner, D., & Eyberg, S. (2003). Father involvement in parent training: When does it matter? *Journal of Clinical Child and Adolescent Psychology, 32,* 599–605.

Barkley, R. A. (1997). *Defiant children: A clinician's manual for assessment and parent training* (2nd ed.). New York: Guilford Press.

Barkley, R. A., Edwards, G. H., & Robin, A. L. (1999). *Defiant teens: A clinician's manual for assessment and family intervention.* New York: Guilford Press.

Barmish, A. J., & Kendall, P. C. (2005). Should parents be co-clients in cognitive-behavioral therapy for anxious youth? *Journal of Clinical Child and Adolescent Psychology, 34,* 569–581.

Barrett, P. M., Dadds, M. R., & Rapee, R. M. (1996). Family treatment of childhood anxiety: A controlled trial. *Journal of Consulting and Clinical Psychology, 64,* 333–342.

Barrett, P. M., Duffy, A. L., Dadds, M. R., & Rapee, R. M. (2001). Cognitive-behavioral treatment of anxiety disorders in children: Long-term (6–year) follow-up. *Journal of Consulting and Clinical Psychology, 69,* 135–141.

Barrett, P. M., Farrell, L. J., Ollendick, T. H., & Dadds, M. (2006). Long-term outcomes of an Australian universal prevention trial of anxiety and depression symptoms in children and youth: An evaluation of the FRIENDS program. *Journal of Clinical Child and Adolescent Psychology, 35,* 403–411.

Barrett, P. M., & Turner, C. M. (2001). Prevention of anxiety symptoms in primary school children: Preliminary results from a universal school-based trial. *British Journal of Clinical Psychology, 40,* 399–410.

Barrett, P. M., & Turner, C. M. (2004). Prevention of childhood anxiety and depression. In P. M. Barrett & T. H. Ollendick (Eds.), *Handbook of interventions that work with children and adolescents: Prevention and treatment* (pp. 429–474). New York: Wiley.

Begeny, J., & Silber, J. (2006). An examination of group-based treatment packages for increasing elementary-aged students' reading fluency. *Psychology in the Schools, 43,* 183–195.

Berman, S. L., Weems, C. F., Silverman, W. K., & Kurtines, W. M. (2000). Predictors of outcome in exposure-based cognitive and behavioral treatments for phobic and anxiety disorders in children. *Behavior Therapy, 31,* 713–731.

Birmaher, B., Arbalaez, C., & Brent, D. (2002). Course and outcome of child and adolescent major depressive disorder. *Child and Adolescent Psychiatric Clinics of North America, 11,* 619–637.

Bos, C. S., & Vaughn, S. (2002). *Strategies for teaching students with learning and behavior problems.* Boston: Allyn & Bacon.

Boulineau, T., Fore, C., Hagan-Burke, S., & Burke, M. D. (2004). Use of story-mapping to increase the story-grammar text comprehension of elementary students with learning disabilities. *Learning Disability Quarterly, 27,* 105–121.

Brent, D. A., Holder, D., Kolko, D., Birmaher, B., Baugher, M., Roth, C., et al. (1997). A clinical psychotherapy trial for adolescent depression comparing cognitive, family, and supportive therapy. *Archives of General Psychiatry, 54,* 877–885.

Briggs-Gowan, M. J., Horwitz, S. M., Schwab-Stone, M. E., Leventhal, J. M., & Leaf, P. J. (2000). Mental health in pediatric settings: Distribution of disorders and factors related to service use. *Journal of the Academy of Child and Adolescent Psychiatry, 39,* 841–849.

Brinkmeyer, M. Y., & Eyberg, S. M. (2003). Parent–child interaction therapy for oppositional children. In A. E. Kazdin & J. R. Weisz (Eds.), *Evidence-based psychotherapies for children and adolescents* (pp. 204–223). New York: Guilford Press.

Chafouleas, S. M., Martens, B. K., Dobson, R. L., Weinstein, K. S., & Gardner, K. B. (2004). Fluent reading as the improvement of stimulus control: Additive effects of performance-based interventions to repeated readings on students' reading and error rates. *Journal of Behavioral Education, 13,* 67–81.

Chambless, D. L., Baker, M. J., Baucom, D. H., Beutler, L. E., Calhoun, K. S., Crits-Christoph, P., et al. (1998). Update on empirically validated therapies II. *The Clinical Psychologist, 51*(1), 3–16.

Chard, D. J., Vaughn, S., & Tyler, B.-J. (2002). A synthesis of research on effective interventions for building reading fluency with elementary students with learning disabilities. *Journal of Learning Disabilities, 35,* 386–406.

Chorpita, B. F., Daleiden, E. L., & Weisz, J. R. (2005). Identifying and selecting the common elements of evidence based interventions: A distillation and matching model. *Mental Health Services Research, 7,* 5–20.

Christenson, S. L. (2004). The family–school partnership: An opportunity to promote the learning competence of all students. *School Psychology Review, 33,* 83–104.

Christenson, S. L., & Sheridan, S. M. (2001). *Schools and families: Creating essential connections for learning.* New York: Guilford Press.

Christophersen, E. R. (1998). *Little people: Guidelines for common sense child rearing* (4th ed.). Overland Park, KS: Overland Press.

Clarke, G. N., Hawkins, W., Murphy, M., & Sheeber, L. (1993). School-based primary prevention of depressive symptomatology in adolescents: Findings from two studies. *Journal of Adolescent Research, 8,* 183–204.

Clarke, G. N., Hawkins, W., Murphy, M., Sheeber, L., Lewinsohn, P. M., & Seeley, J. R. (1995). Targeted prevention of unipolar depressive disorder in an at-risk sample of high school adolescents: A randomized trial of a group cognitive intervention. *Journal of the American Academy of Child and Adolescent Psychiatry, 34,* 312–321.

Clarke, G. N., Rohde, P., Lewinsohn, P. M., Hops, H., & Seeley, J. R. (1999). Cognitive-behavioral treatment of adolescent depression: Efficacy of acute group treatment and booster sessions. *Journal of the American Academy of Child and Adolescent Psychiatry, 38,* 272–279.

Cohan, S. L., Chavira, D. A., & Stein, M. B. (2006). Practitioner review: Psychosocial interventions for children with selective mutism: A critical evaluation of the literature from 1990–2005. *Journal of Child Psychology and Psychiatry, 47,* 1085–1097.

Collaborative for Academic, Social, and Emotional Learning. (2003). *Safe and sound: An educational leader's guide to evidence-based social and emotional learning (SEL) programs.* Chicago: Author.

Collaborative for Academic, Social, and Emotional Learning. (2008). *Social and emotional learning and student benefits: Implications for the Safe School/Health Students core element.* Washington, DC: National Center for Mental Health Promotion and Youth Violence Prevention.

Collett, B. R., Scott, S., Rockhill, C., Speltz, M., & McClellan, J. (2008). Oppositional defiant disorder and conduct disorders. In P. Tyrer & K. R. Silk (Eds.), *The Cambridge textbook of effective treatments in psychiatry* (pp. 796–807). New York: Cambridge University Press.

Connell, A., Dishion, T., Yasui, M., & Kavanagh, K. (2007). An adaptive approach to family intervention: Linking engagement in family-centered intervention to reductions in adolescent problem behavior. *Journal of Consulting and Clinical Psychology, 75,* 568–579.

Conners, C. K. (1997). *Conners' Rating Scales—Revised.* North Tonawanda, NY: Multi-Health Systems.

Conners, C. K. (2008a). *Conners* (3rd ed.). North Tonawanda, NY: Multi-Health Systems.

Conners, C. K. (2008b). *Conners Comprehensive Behavior Rating Scale.* North Tonawanda, NY: Multi-Health Systems.

Connolly, A. J. (1988). *Keymath—Revised.* Circle Pines, MN: American Guidance Service.

Connor, D., Barkley, R., & Davis, H. (2000). A pilot study of methylphenidate, clonidine, or the combination in ADHD comorbid with aggressive oppositional defiant or conduct disorder. *Clinical Pediatrics, 39,* 15–25.

Costello, E. J., Mustillo, S., Erkanli, A., Keeler, G., & Angold, A. (2003). Prevalence and development of psychiatric disorders in childhood and adolescence. *Archives of General Psychiatry, 60,* 837–844.

Cummings, E. M., Davies, P. T., & Campbell, S. B. (2000). *Developmental psychopathology and family process: Theory, research, and clinical implications.* New York: Guilford Press.

Dadds, M., Spence, S., Holland, D., Barrett, P., & Laurens, K. (1997). Prevention and early intervention for anxiety disorders: A controlled trial. *Journal of Consulting and Clinical Psychology, 65*, 627–635.

Daly, E. J., Martens, B. K., Dool, E., & Hintze, J. M. (1998). Using brief functional analysis to select interventions for oral reading. *Journal of Behavioral Education, 8*, 203–218.

Daly, E. J., Murdoch, A., Lillenstein, L., Webber, L., & Lentz, F. (2002). An examination of methods for testing treatments: Conducting brief experimental analyses of the effects of instructional components on oral reading fluency. *Education and Treatment of Children, 25*, 288–316.

Daly, E. J., Persampieri, M., McCurdy, M., & Gortmaker, V. (2005). Generating reading intervention through experimental analysis of academic skills: Demonstration and empirical evaluation. *School Psychology Review, 34*, 395–414.

Daly, E. J., Witt, J. C., Martens, B. K., & Dool, E. J. (1997). A model for conducting functional analysis of academic performance. *School Psychology Review, 26*, 554–574.

David-Ferdon, C., & Kaslow, N. J. (2008). Evidence-based psychosocial treatments for child and adolescent depression. *Journal of Clinical Child and Adolescent Psychology, 37*, 62–104.

Deno, S. L. (2002). Problem solving as "best practice." In A. Thomas & J. Grimes (Eds.), *Best practices in school psychology–IV* (pp. 37–55). Bethesda, MD: National Association of School Psychologists.

Diamond, G., & Josephson, A. (2005). Family-based treatment research: A 10-year update. *Journal of the American Academy of Child and Adolescent Psychiatry, 44*, 872–887.

Dishion, T., & Kavanagh, K. (2003). *Intervening in adolescent problem behavior: A family-centered approach.* New York: Guilford Press.

Dishion, T., Kavanagh, K., Schneiger, A., Nelson, S., & Kaufman, N. (2002). Preventing early adolescent substance use: A family-centered strategy for the public middle school. *Prevention Science, 3*, 191–201.

Dishion, T., Nelson, S., & Kavanagh, K. (2003). The family check-up with high-risk young adolescents: Preventing early-onset substance use by parent monitoring. *Behavior Therapy, 34*, 553–571.

Drugli, M. B., & Larsson, B. (2006). Children aged 4–8 treated with parenting training and child therapy because of conduct problems: Generalisation effects to day-care and school settings. *European Child and Adolescent Psychiatry, 15*, 392–399.

DuPaul, G. J., & Carlson, J. S. (2005). Child psychopharmacology: How school psychologists can contribute to effective outcomes. *School Psychology Quarterly, 20*, 206–221.

DuPaul, G. J., & Eckert, T. L. (1997). The effects of school-based interventions for attention-deficit hyperactivity disorder: A meta-analysis. *School Psychology Review, 26*, 5–27.

DuPaul, G. J., Power, T. J., Anastopoulos, A. D., & Reid, R. (1998). *ADHD Rating Scale–IV: Checklists, norms, and clinical interpretation.* New York: Guilford Press.

Eckert, T., Ardoin, S., Daly, E., & Martens, B. (2002). Improving oral reading fluency: A brief experimental analysis of combining an antecedent intervention with consequences. *Journal of Applied Behavior Analysis, 35*, 271–281.

Eisenstadt, T. H., Eyberg, S., McNeil, C. B., Newcomb, K., & Funderbunk, B. (1993). Parent–child interaction therapy with behavior problem children: Relative effectiveness of two stages and overall treatment outcome. *Journal of Clinical Child Psychology, 22*, 42–51.

Elster, A., Jarosik, J., VanGeest, C. J., & Fleming, M. (2003). Racial and ethnic disparities in health care for adolescents: A systematic review of the literature. *Archives of Pediatric and Adolescent Medicine, 157*, 867–874.

Englert, C. S., & Mariage, T. V. (1991). Shared understandings: Structuring the writing experience through dialogue. *Journal of Learning Disabilities, 24,* 330–342.

Esler, A. N., Godber, Y., & Christenson, S. L. (2008). Best practices in supporting school–family partnerships. In A. Thomas & J. Grimes (Eds.), *Best practices in school psychology: V* (pp. 917–936). Bethesda, MD: National Association of School Psychologists.

Eyberg, S. (1993). Consumer satisfaction measures for assessing parent training programs. In L. VandeCreek, S. Knapp, & T. L. Jackson (Eds.), *Innovations in clinical practice: A source book* (Vol. 12, pp. 377–382). Sarasota, FL: Professional Resource Press.

Eyberg, S. M., Nelson, M. M., & Boggs, S. R. (2008). Evidence-based psychosocial treatments for children and adolescents with disruptive behavior. *Journal of Clinical Child and Adolescent Psychology, 37,* 215–237.

Eyberg, S. M., & Pincus, D (1999). *Eyberg Child Behavior Inventory and Sutter–Eyberg Student Behavior Inventory—Revised: Professional manual.* Odessa, FL: Psychological Assessment Resources.

Farmer, E. M. Z., Burns, B. J., Phillips, S. D., Angold, A., & Costello, E. J. (2003). Pathways into and through mental health services for children and adolescents. *Psychiatric Services, 54,* 60–66.

Fishel, M., & Ramirez, L. (2005). Evidence-based parent involvement interventions with school-aged children. *School Psychology Quarterly, 20,* 371–402.

Fletcher, J. M., Francis, D. J., Morris, R. D., & Lyon, G. R. (2005). Evidence-based assessment of learning disabilities in children and adolescents. *Journal of Clinical Child and Adolescent Psychology, 34,* 506–522.

Forgatch, M. S., Bullock, B. M., & Patterson, G. R. (2004). From theory to practice: Increasing effective parenting through role-play. In H. Steiner (Ed.), *Handbook of mental health interventions in children and adolescents: An integrated developmental approach* (pp. 782–813). San Francisco: Jossey-Bass.

Freeman, J. B., Garcia, A. M., Miller, L. M., Dow, S. P., & Leonard, H. L. (2004). Selective mutism. In T. L. Morris & J. S. March (Eds.), *Anxiety disorders in children and adolescents* (2nd ed., pp. 280–301). New York: Guilford Press.

Gadow, K. D., & Sprafkin, J. (1997a). *Adolescent Symptom Inventory–4 screening manual.* Stony Brook, NY: Checkmate Plus.

Gadow, K. D., & Sprafkin, J. (1997b). *Early Childhood Inventory–4 norms manual.* Stony Brook, NY: Checkmate Plus.

Gadow, K. D., & Sprafkin, J. (1998). *Adolescent Symptom Inventory–4 norms manual.* Stony Brook, NY: Checkmate Plus.

Gadow, K. D., & Sprafkin, J. (2000). *Early Childhood Inventory–4 screening manual.* Stony Brook, NY: Checkmate Plus.

Gadow, K. D., & Sprafkin, J. (2002). *Childhood Symptom Inventory–4 screening and norms manual.* Stony Brook, NY: Checkmate Plus.

Gillham, J. E., Reivich, K. J., Freres, D. R., Lascher, M., Litzinger, S., Shatte, A., et al. (2006). School-based prevention of depression and anxiety symptoms in early adolescents: A pilot of a parent intervention component. *School Psychology Quarterly, 21,* 323–348.

Gilliam, W., & Zigler, E. (2000). A critical meta-analysis of all evaluations of state-funded preschool from 1977 to 1998: Implications for policy, service delivery and program evaluation. *Early Childhood Research Quarterly, 15,* 441–473.

Gottman, J. M., & DeClaire, J. (1997). *The heart of parenting: Raising an emotionally intelligent child.* New York: Simon & Schuster.

Graham, S., Harris, K. A., & Larsen, L. (2001). Prevention and intervention of writing difficulties for students with learning disabilities. *Learning Disabilities Research and Practice, 16*(2), 74–84.

Graham, S., Harris, K. R., MacArthur, C. A., & Schwartz, S. (1991). Writing and writing instruction for students with learning disabilities: Review of a research program. *Learning Disability Quarterly, 14*(2), 89–114.

Graham, S., MacArthur, C., & Schwartz, S. (1995). Effects of goal setting and procedural facilitation on the revising behavior and writing performance of students with writing and learning problems. *Journal of Educational Psychology, 87*, 230–240.

Greenberg, M. T., Domitrovich, C., & Bumbarger, B. (2001). The prevention of mental disorders in school-aged children: Current state of the field. *Prevention and Treatment, 4*(1), 1a.

Greenberg, M. T., Weissberg, R. P., O'Brien, M. U., Zins, J. E., Fredericks, L., Resnik, H., et al. (2003). Enhancing school-based prevention and youth development through coordinated social, emotional, and academic learning. *American Psychologist, 58*, 466–474.

Greene, R. W., & Ablon, J. S. (2006). *Treating explosive kids.* New York: Guilford Press.

Greene, R. W., Ablon, J. S., Monuteaux, N. C., Goring, J. C., Henin, A., Raezer-Blakely, L., et al. (2004). Effectiveness of collaborative problem solving in affectively dysregulated children with oppositional-defiant disorder: Initial findings. *Journal of Consulting and Clinical Psychology, 72*, 1157–1164.

Gresham, F. M., & Elliott, S. N. (1990). *The Social Skills Rating System.* Circle Pines, MN: American Guidance Service.

Gresham, F. M., & Elliott, S. N. (2008). *Social Skills Improvement System Rating Scales.* Bloomington, MN: Pearson Assessments.

Gureasko-Moore, D. P., DuPaul, G. J., & Power, T. J. (2005). Stimulant treatment for attention-deficit/hyperactivity disorder: Medication monitoring practices of school psychologists. *School Psychology Review, 34*, 232–245.

HaileMariam, A., Bradley-Johnson, S., & Johnson, C. M. (2002). Pediatricians' preferences for ADHD information from schools. *School Psychology Review, 31*, 94–105.

Halonen, A., Aunola, K., Ahonen, T., & Nurmi, J.-E. (2006). The role of learning to read in the development of problem behaviour: A cross-lagged longitudinal study. *British Journal of Educational Psychology, 76*, 517–534.

Hammill, D. D., & Larsen, S. C. (1996). *Test of written language* (3rd ed.). Austin, TX: PRO-ED.

Hanf, C. (1969). *A two-stage program for modifying maternal controlling during mother–child (M-C) interaction.* Paper presented at the meeting of the Western Psychological Association, Vancouver, British Columbia, Canada.

Harrison, P. L., & Oakland, T. (2003). *Adaptive Behavior Assessment System* (2nd ed.). San Antonio, TX: Psychological Corporation.

Henggeler, S. W., & Lee, T. (2003). Multisystemic treatment of serious conduct problems. In A. E. Kazdin & J. R. Weisz (Eds.), *Evidence-based psychotherapies for children and adolescents* (pp. 301–322). New York: Guilford Press.

Holland, M. L., Gimpel, G. A., & Merrell, K. W. (2001). *The ADHD Symptoms Rating Scale.* Wilmington, DE: Wide Range.

Holmes, M., & Croll, P. (1989). Time spent on homework and academic achievement. *Educational Research, 31*, 36–45.

Hood, K. K., & Eyberg, S. M. (2003). Outcomes of parent–child interaction therapy: Mothers' reports of maintenance three to six years after treatment. *Journal of Child Clinical and Adolescent Psychology, 32*, 419–429.

Hook, C. L., & DuPaul, G. J. (1999). Parent tutoring for students with attention-deficit/hyperactivity disorder: Effects on reading performance at home and school. *School Psychology Review, 28,* 60–75.

Hooven, C., Gottman, J. M., & Katz, L. F. (1995). Parental meta-emotion structure predicts family and child outcomes. *Cognition and Emotion, 9,* 229–264.

Hudson, J. L., Comer, J. S., & Kendall, P. C. (2008). Parental responses to positive and negative emotions in anxious and nonanxious children. *Journal of Clinical Child and Adolescent Psychology, 37,* 303–313.

Idol, L. (1987). Group story mapping: A comprehension strategy for both skilled and unskilled readers. *Journal of Learning Disabilities, 20,* 196–205.

Jacob, S., & Hartshorne, T. (2007). *Ethics and law for school psychologists* (5th ed.). New York: Wiley.

Jenson, W. R., Sheridan, S. M., Olympia, D., & Andrews, D. (1994). Homework and students with learning disabilities and behavior disorders: A practical, parent-based approach. *Journal of Learning Disabilities, 27,* 538–548.

Jurbergs, N., Palcic, J., & Kelley, M. L. (2007). School-home notes with and without response cost: Increasing attention and academic performance in low-income children with attention-deficit/ hyperactivity disorder. *School Psychology Quarterly, 22,* 358–379.

Kahle, A. L., & Kelley, M. L. (1994). Children's homework problems: A comparison of goal setting and parent training. *Behavior Therapy, 25,* 275–290.

Kashani, J. H., & Orvaschel, H. (1990). A community study of anxiety in children and adolescents. *American Journal of Psychiatry, 147,* 313–318.

Kataoka, S. H., Zhang, L., & Wells, K. B. (2002). Unmet need for mental health care among US Children: Variation by ethnicity and insurance status. *American Journal of Psychiatry, 159,* 1548–1555.

Kazdin, A. E. (1995). Child, parent, and family dysfunction as predictors of outcome in cognitive-behavioral treatment of antisocial children. *Behaviour Research and Therapy, 33,* 271–281.

Kazdin, A. E. (1996). Dropping out of child therapy: Issues for research and implications for practice. *Clinical Child Psychology and Psychiatry, 1,* 133–156.

Kazdin, A. E. (2003). Problem-solving skills training and parent management training for conduct disorder. In A. E. Kazdin & J. R. Weisz (Eds.), *Evidence-based psychotherapies for children and adolescents* (pp. 241–262). New York: Guilford Press.

Kazdin, A. E. (2004). Psychotherapy for children and adolescents. In M. J. Lambert (Ed.), *Bergin and Garfield's handbook of psychotherapy and behavior change* (5th ed., pp. 543–589). New York: Wiley.

Kazdin, A. E., Bass, D., Siegel, T., & Thomas, C. (1989). Cognitive behavioral therapy and relationship therapy in the treatment of children referred for antisocial behavior. *Journal of Consulting and Clinical Psychology, 57,* 522–535.

Kazdin, A. E., Esveldt-Dawson, K., French, N. H., & Unis, A. S. (1987a). Effects of parent management training and problem-solving skills training combined in the treatment of antisocial child behavior. *Journal of the American Academy and Child and Adolescent Psychiatry, 26,* 416–424.

Kazdin, A. E., Esveldt-Dawson, K., French, N. H, & Unis, A. (1987b). Problem-solving skills training and relationship therapy in the treatment of antisocial child behavior. *Journal of Consulting and Clinical Psychology, 55,* 76–85.

Kazdin, A. E., Holland, L., & Crowley, M. (1997). Family experience of barriers to treatment and premature termination from child therapy. *Journal of Consulting and Clinical Psychology, 65,* 453–463.

Kazdin, A. E., Siegel, T. C., & Bass, D. (1992). Cognitive problem-solving skills training and parent management training in the treatment of antisocial behavior in children. *Journal of Consulting and Clinical Psychology, 60,* 733–747.

Kazdin, A. E., & Wassell, G. (1999). Barriers to effective treatment participation and therapeutic change among children referred for conduct disorder. *Journal of Child Clinical Psychology, 28,* 160–172.

Kazdin, A., & Whitley, M. (2003). Treatment of parental stress to enhance therapeutic change among children referred for aggressive and antisocial behavior. *Journal of Consulting and Clinical Psychology, 71,* 504–515.

Kearney, C. A. (2001). *School refusal behavior in youth: A functional approach to assessment and treatment.* Washington, DC: American Psychological Association.

Kearney, C. A., & Albano, A. M. (2007). *When children refuse school: A cognitive-behavioral therapy approach—Therapist guide* (2nd ed.). New York: Oxford University Press.

Kearney, C. A., & Silverman, W. K. (1996). The evolution and reconciliation of taxonomic strategies for school refusal behavior. *Clinical Psychology: Science and Practice, 3,* 339–354.

Kearney, C. A., & Vecchio, J. L. (2007). When a child won't speak. *Journal of Family Practice, 56,* 917–921.

Keith, T. Z., Diamond-Hallam, C., & Fine, J. G. (2004). Longitudinal effects of in-school and out-of-school homework on high school grades. *School Psychology Quarterly, 19,* 187–211.

Keith, T. Z., & Keith, P. B. (2006). Homework. In G. G. Bear & K. M. Minke (Eds.), *Children's needs: III. Development, prevention, and intervention* (pp. 615–629). Bethesda, MD: National Association of School Psychologists.

Kelley, M. L. (1990). *School–home notes: Promoting children's classroom success.* New York: Guilford Press.

Kelley, M. L., & McCain, A. P. (1995). Promoting academic performance in inattentive children: The relatively efficacy of school-home notes with and without response cost. *Behavior Modification, 19,* 357–375.

Kendall, P. C. (Ed.). (2006). *Child and adolescent therapy: Cognitive-behavioral procedures* (3rd ed.). New York: Guilford Press.

Kendall, P. C., Aschenbrand, S. G., & Hudson, J. L. (2003). Child-focused treatment of anxiety. In A. E. Kazdin & J. R. Weisz (Eds.), *Evidence-based psychotherapies for children and adolescents* (pp. 81–100). New York: Guilford Press.

Kendall, P. C., & Braswell, L. (1985). *Cognitive-behavioral self-control therapy for impulsive children.* New York: Guilford Press.

Kessler, R. C., Berglund, P., Demler, O., Jin, R., Merikangas, K. R., & Walters, E. E. (2005). Lifetime prevalence and age-of-onset distributions of DSM-IV disorders in the National Comorbidity Survey replication. *Archives of General Psychiatry, 62,* 593–768.

Klotz, M. B., & Nealis, L. (2005). The new IDEA: A summary of significant reforms. Retrieved June 20, 2006, from *www.nasponline.org/advocacy/IDEAfinalsummary.pdf.*

Kovacs, M. (1992). *Children's Depression Inventory.* North Tonawanda, NY: Multi-Health Systems.

Kroesbergen, E. H., & Van Luit, J. E. H. (2003). Mathematics interventions for children with special educational needs: A meta-analysis. *Remedial and Special Education, 24,* 97–114.

LaFreniere, P. J., & Capuano, F. (1997). Preventive intervention as a means of clarifying direction of effects in socialization: Anxious-withdrawn preschoolers case. *Development and Psychopathology, 9,* 551–564.

Lee, M., & Tingstrom, D. (1994). A group math intervention: The modification of cover, copy, and compare for group application. *Psychology in the Schools, 31,* 133–145.

Lewinsohn, P. M., Clarke, G. N., Hops, H., & Andrews, J. A. (1990). Cognitive-behavioral treatment for depressed adolescents. *Behavior Therapy, 21,* 385–401.

Loeber, R., Burke, J. D., Lahey, B. B., Winters, A., & Zera, M. (2000). Oppositional defiant and conduct disorder: A review of the past 10 years. Part I. *Journal of the American Academy of Child and Adolescent Psychiatry, 39,* 1468–1484.

Lopez, A., & Cole, C. L. (1999). Effects of a parent-implemented intervention on the academic readiness skills of five Puerto Rican kindergarten students in an urban school. *School Psychology Review, 28,* 439–447.

Mace, F. C., Belfiore, P. J., & Hutchinson, J. M. (2001). Operant theory and research on self-regulation. In B. J. Zimmerman & D. H. Schunk (Eds.), *Self-regulated learning and academic achievement: Theoretical perspectives* (2nd ed., pp. 39–65). Mahwah, NJ: Erlbaum.

Madaus, M. M. R., Kehle, T. J., Madaus, J., & Bray, M. A. (2003). Mystery motivator as an intervention to promote homework completion and accuracy. *School Psychology International, 24,* 369–377.

March, J. S. (1997). *Multidimensional Anxiety Scale for Children.* North Tonawanda, NY: Multi-Health Systems.

Maughan, D. R., Christiansen, E., Jenson, W. R., Olympia, D., & Clark, E. (2005). Behavioral parent training as a treatment for externalizing behaviors and disruptive behavior disorders: A meta-analysis. *School Psychology Review, 34,* 267–286.

Mayes, S. D., & Calhoun, S. L. (2006). Frequency of reading, math, and writing disabilities in children with clinical disorders. *Learning and Individual Differences, 16,* 145–157.

McCallum, E., Skinner, C. H., Turner, H., & Saecker, L. (2006). The taped-problems intervention: Increasing multiplication fact fluency using a low-tech, classwide, time-delay intervention. *School Psychology Review, 35,* 419–434.

McCarney, S. B. (1995a). *The Attention Deficit Disorder Evaluation Scale—Home version* (2nd ed.). Columbia, MO: Hawthorne.

McCarney, S. B. (1995b). *The Attention Deficit Disorder Evaluation Scale—School version* (2nd ed.). Columbia, MO: Hawthorne.

McConaughy, S. H. (2005). *Clinical interview for children and adolescents: Assessment to intervention.* New York: Guilford Press.

McMahon, R. J., & Forehand, R. L. (2005). *Helping the noncompliant child: Family-based treatment for oppositional behavior* (2nd ed.). New York: Guilford Press.

Mercer, C. D., Campbell, K. U., Miller, D. M., Mercer, K. D., & Lane, H. B. (2000). Effects of a reading fluency intervention for middle schoolers with specific learning disabilities. *Learning Disabilities Research and Practice, 15,* 178–189.

Merrell, K. W. (2002a). *Home and Community Social Behavior Scales.* Baltimore, MD: Brookes.

Merrell, K. W. (2002b). *School Social Behavior Scales* (2nd ed.). Baltimore, MD: Brookes.

Merrell, K. W. (2008). *Helping students overcome depression and anxiety: A practical guide* (2nd ed.). New York: Guilford Press.

Miller, D. L., & Kelley, M. L. (1991). Interventions for improving homework: A critical review. *School Psychology Quarterly, 6,* 174–185.

Miller, R. W., & Rollnick, S. (2002). *Motivational interviewing: Preparing people for change* (2nd ed). New York: Guilford Press.

Moore, L. A., Waguespack, A. M., Wickstrom, K. F., Witt J. C., & Gaydos, G. R. (1994). Mystery motivator: An effective and time efficient intervention. *School Psychology Review, 23,* 106–118.

Moxley, R. A., Lutz, P. A., Ahlborn, P., Boley, N., & Armstrong, L. (1995). Self-recorded word counts of freewriting in grades 1–4. *Education and Treatment of Children, 18,* 138–157.

MTA Cooperative Group. (1999). A 14-month randomized clinical trial of treatment strategies for attention-deficit/hyperactivity disorder. *Archives of General Psychiatry, 56,* 1073–1086.

Muris, P., Meesters, C., & van Melick, M. (2002). Treatment of childhood anxiety disorders: A preliminary comparison between cognitive-behavioral group therapy and a psychological placebo intervention. *Journal of Behavior Therapy and Experimental Psychiatry, 33,* 143–158.

Myers, K., & Winters, N. C. (2002). Ten-year review of rating scales: II. Scales for internalizing disorders. *Journal of the American Academy of Child and Adolescent Psychiatry, 41,* 634–659.

National Assessment of Educational Progress. (2007a). *The nation's report card: 12th-grade reading and mathematics 2005.* Washington, DC: National Center for Educational Statistics, U.S. Department of Education. Retrieved July 19, 2007, from *nces.ed.gov/nationsreportcard/pdf/main2005/2007468.pdf.*

National Assessment of Educational Progress. (2007b). The nation's report card: Mathematics 2007. Washington, DC: National Center for Educational Statistics, U.S. Department of Education. Retrieved April 26, 2009, from *nces.ed.gov/nationsreportcard/pdf/main2007/2007494.pdf.*

National Assessment of Educational Progress. (2007c). *The nation's report card: Reading 2007.* Washington, DC: National Center for Educational Statistics, U.S. Department of Education. Retrieved April 26, 2009, from *nces.ed.gov/nationsreportcard/pdf/main2007/2007449.pdf.*

National Assessment of Educational Progress. (2008). *The nation's report card: Writing 2007.* Washington, DC: National Center for Educational Statistics, U.S. Department of Education. Retrieved April 26, 2009, from *nces.ed.gov/nationsreportcard/pdf/main2007/2008468.pdf.*

National Association of School Psychologists. (2000). *Professional conduct manual: Principles for professional ethics—Guidelines for the provision of school psychological services.* Bethesda, MD: Author. Retrieved February 29, 2008, from *www.nasponline.org/standards/Professional-Cond.pdf.*

National Institute of Child Health and Human Development. (2000). *Report of the National Reading Panel: Teaching children to read. An evidence-based assessment of the scientific research literature on reading and its implications for reading instruction.* Retrieved February 19, 2007, from *www.nichd.nih.gov/publications/nrp/upload/smallbook_pdf.pdf.*

Nelson, E.-L., Barnard, M., & Cain, S. (2006). Feasibility of telemedicine intervention for childhood depression. *Counselling and Psychotherapy Research, 6,* 191–195.

Nelson, J. S., Alber, S. R., & Gordy, A. (2004). Effects of systematic error correction and repeated readings on the reading accuracy and proficiency of second graders with disabilities. *Education and Treatment of Children, 27,* 186–198.

Nelson, J. R., Smith, D. J., Young, R. K., & Dodd, J. M. (1991). A review of self-management outcome research conducted with students who exhibit behavioral disorders. *Behavioral Disorders, 16,* 169–179.

Niles, M. D., Reynolds, A. J., & Roe-Sepowitz, D. (2008). Early childhood intervention and early adolescent social and emotional competence: Second generation evaluation evidence from the Chicago Longitudinal Study. *Educational Research, 50,* 55–73.

Nixon, R. D. V., Sweeney, L., Erickson, D. B., & Touyz, S. W. (2003). Parent–child interaction therapy: A comparison of standard and abbreviated treatments for oppositional defiant disorder. *Journal of Consulting and Clinical Psychology, 71,* 251–260.

Nock, M. K., & Kazdin, A. E. (2005). Randomized controlled trial of a brief intervention for increasing participation in parent management training. *Journal of Consulting and Clinical Psychology, 73,* 872–879.

Ollendick, T. H. (2005). Evidence-based parent and family interventions in school psychology: A commentary. *School Psychology Quarterly, 20,* 512–517.

Olympia, D. E., Sheridan, S. M., & Jenson, W. R. (1994a). Homework: A natural means of home-school collaboration. *School Psychology Quarterly, 9,* 60–80.

Olympia, D. E., Sheridan, S. M., & Jenson, W. R. (1994b). Using student-managed interventions to increase homework completion and accuracy. *Journal of Applied Behavior Analysis, 27,* 85–99.

O'Shea, L. J., Munson, S. M., & O'Shea, D. J. (1984). Error correction in oral reading: Evaluating the effectiveness of three procedures. *Education and Treatment of Children, 7,* 203–214.

Ou, S.-R., & Reynolds, A. J. (2006). Early childhood intervention and educational attainment: Age 22 findings from the Chicago Longitudinal Study. *Journal of Education for Students Placed at Risk, 11,* 175–198.

Page-Voth, V., & Graham, S. (1999). Effects of goal setting and strategy use on the writing performance and self-efficacy of students with writing and learning problems. *Journal of Educational Psychology, 91,* 230–240.

Pappadopulos, E., Woolston, S., Chait, A., Perkins, M., Connor, D., & Jensen, P. (2006). Pharmacotherapy of aggression in children and adolescents: Efficacy and effect size. *Journal of the Canadian Academy of Child and Adolescent Psychiatry, 15,* 27–39.

Patrikakou, E. N., & Weissberg, R. P. (2007). School-family partnerships to enhance children's social, emotional, and academic learning. In R. Bar-On, J. G. Maree, & M. J. Elias (Eds.), *Educating people to be emotionally intelligent* (pp. 49–61). Westport, CT: Praeger.

Patton, J. R. (1994). Practical recommendations for using homework with students with learning disabilities. *Journal of Learning Disabilities, 27,* 570–578.

Persampieri, M., Gortmaker, V., Daly, E. J., Sheridan, S. M., & McCurdy, M. (2006). Promoting parent use of empirically supported reading interventions: Two experimental investigations of child outcomes. *Behavioral Interventions, 21,* 31–57.

Prochaska, J. O., & DiClemente, C. C. (1982). Transtheoretical therapy: Toward a more integrative model of change. *Psychotherapy: Theory, Research, and Practice, 19,* 276–288.

Prochaska, J. O., & DiClemente, C. C. (2005). The transtheoretical approach. In J. C. Norcross & M. R. Goldfried (Eds.), *Handbook of psychotherapy integration* (2nd ed., pp. 147–171). New York: Oxford University Press.

Rapee, R. M., Abbott, M. J., & Lyneham, H. J. (2006). Bibliotherapy for children with anxiety disorders using written materials for parents: A randomized controlled trial. *Journal of Consulting and Clinical Psychology, 74,* 436–444.

Rapee, R. M., Kennedy, S., Ingram, M., Edwards, S., & Sweeney, L. (2005). Prevention and early intervention of anxiety disorders in inhibited preschool children. *Journal of Consulting and Clinical Psychology, 73,* 488–497.

Rapee, R. M., Spence, S., Cobham, V., & Wignall, A. (2000). *Helping your anxious child: A step-by-step guide for parents.* Oakland, CA: New Harbinger.

Rapee, R. M., Wignall, A., Hudson, J. L., & Schniering, C. A. (2000). *Treating anxious children and adolescents: An evidence-based approach.* Oakland, CA: New Harbinger.

Rathvon, N. (2008). *Effective school interventions: Evidence-based strategies for improving student outcomes* (2nd ed.). New York: Guilford Press.

Reid, R. (1996). Research in self-monitoring with students with learning disabilities: The present, the prospects, the pitfalls. *Journal of Learning Disabilities, 29,* 317–331.

Reid, R., Gonzalez, J., Nordness, P. D., Trout, A., & Epstein, M. H. (2004). A meta-analysis of the academic status of students with emotional/behavioral disturbances. *Journal of Special Education, 38,* 130–143.

Resetar, J. L., Noell, G. H., & Pellegrin, A. L. (2006). Teaching parents to use research-supported systematic strategies to tutor their children in reading. *School Psychology Quarterly, 21,* 241–261.

Reyes, M., Buitelaar, J., Toren, P., Augustyns, I., & Eerdekens, M. (2006). A randomized, double-blind, placebo-controlled study of risperidone maintenance treatment in children and adolescents with disruptive behavior disorders. *American Journal of Psychiatry, 163,* 402–410.

Reynolds, C. R., & Kamphaus, R. W. (2004). *Behavior Assessment System for Children* (2nd ed.). Circle Pines, MN: American Guidance Service.

Reynolds, W. M. (1989). *Reynolds Child Depression Scale. Professional manual.* Lutz, FL: Psychological Assessment Resources.

Reynolds, W. M. (2002). *Reynolds Adolescent Depression Scale (2nd ed.): Professional manual.* Lutz, FL: Psychological Assessment Resources.

Rhoades, M. M., & Kratochwill, T. R. (1998). Parent training and consultation: An analysis of a homework intervention program. *School Psychology Quarterly, 13,* 241–264.

Rhymer, K., Henington, C., Skinner, C., & Looby, E. (1999). The effects of explicit timing on mathematics performance in second-grade Caucasian and African American students. *School Psychology Quarterly, 14,* 397–407.

Rhymer, K., Skinner, C., Jackson, S., McNeill, S., Smith, T., & Jackson, B. (2002). The 1-minute explicit timing intervention: The influence of mathematics problem difficulty. *Journal of Instructional Psychology, 29,* 305–311.

Rones, M., & Hoagwood, K. (2000). School-based mental health services: A research review. *Clinical Child and Family Psychology Review, 3,* 223–241.

Sanders, M. R. (1999). Triple P—Positive Parenting Program: Towards an empirically validated multilevel parenting and family support strategy for the prevention of behavior and emotional problems in children. *Clinical Child and Family Psychology Review, 2,* 71–90.

Sanders, M. R. (2007). The Triple P—Positive Parenting Program: A public health approach to parenting support. In J. M. Briesmeister & C. E. Schaefer (Eds.), *Handbook of parent training: Helping parents prevent and solve problem behaviors* (3rd ed., pp. 203–233). New York: Wiley.

Sanders, M. R., Markie-Dadds, C., Tully, L. A., & Bor, W. (2000). The Triple P—Positive Parenting Program: A comparison of enhanced, standard, and self-directed behavioral family intervention for parents of children with early onset conduct problems. *Journal of Consulting and Clinical Psychology, 68,* 624–640.

Schuhmann, E. M., Foote, R. C., Eyberg, S. M., Boggs, S. R., & Algina, J. (1998). Efficacy of parent–child interaction therapy: Interim report of a randomized trial with short-term maintenance. *Journal of Clinical Child Psychology, 27,* 34–45.

Senechal, M., & LeFevre, J.-A. (2002). Parental involvement in the development of children's reading skill: A five-year longitudinal study. *Child Development, 73,* 445–460.

Serketich, W. J., & Dumas, J. E. (1996). The effectiveness of behavioral parent training to modify antisocial behavior in children: A meta-analysis. *Behavior Therapy, 27,* 171–186.

Shaver, A. V., & Walls, R. T. (1998). Effect of Title I parent involvement on student reading and mathematics achievement. *Journal of Research and Development in Education, 31,* 90–97.

Shaw, D. S., Dishion, T. J., Supplee, L., Gardner, F., & Arnds, K. (2006). Randomized trial of a family centered approach to the prevention of early conduct problems: 2-year effects of the family check-up in early childhood. *Journal of Consulting and Clinical Psychology, 74,* 1–9.

Sheridan, S. M., Clarke, B. L., Marti, D. C., Burt, J. D., & Rohlk, A. M. (2005). *Conjoint behavioral consultation: A model to facilitate meaningful partnerships for families and schools.*

Cambridge, MA: Harvard Family Research Project. Retrieved January 22, 2008, from *www. hfrp.org/publications-resources/browse-our-publications/conjoint-behavioral-consultation-a-model-to-facilitate-meaningful-partnerships-for-families-and-schools*.

Sheridan, S. M., Eagle, J. W., Cowan, R. J., & Mickelson, W. (2001). The effects of conjoint behavioral consultation results of a 4-year investigation. *Journal of School Psychology, 39*, 361–385.

Sheridan, S. M., & Kratochwill, T. R. (2008). *Conjoint behavioral consultation: Promoting family-school connections and interventions* (2nd ed.). New York: Springer.

Shinn, M. R. (2002). Best practices in using curriculum-based measurement in a problem-solving model. In A. Thomas & J. Grimes (Eds.), *Best practices in school psychology–IV* (pp. 671–697). Bethesda, MD: National Association of School Psychologists.

Short, E. J., & Ryan, E. B. (1984). Metacognitive differences between skilled and less skilled readers: Remediating deficits through story grammar and attribution training. *Journal of Educational Psychology, 76*, 225–235.

Skinner, C., Cooper, L., & Cole, C. (1997). The effects of oral presentation previewing rats on reading performance. *Journal of Applied Behavior Analysis, 30*, 331–333.

Skinner, C., McLaughlin, T., & Logan, P. (1997). Cover, copy, and compare: A self-managed academic intervention effective across skills, students, and settings. *Journal of Behavioral Education, 7*, 295–306.

Skinner, C. H., & Smith, E. S. (1992). Issues surrounding the use of self-management interventions for increasing academic performance. *School Psychology Review, 21*, 202–210.

Snyder, R., Turgay, A., Aman, M., Binder, C., Fisman, S., & Carroll, A. (2002). Effects of risperidone on conduct and disruptive behavior disorders in children with subaverage IQs. *Journal of the American Academy of Child and Adolescent Psychiatry, 41*, 1026–1036.

Southam-Gerow, M. A., Kendall, P. C., & Weersing, V. R. (2001). Examining outcome variability: Correlates of treatment response in a child and adolescent anxiety clinic. *Journal of Clinical Child Psychology, 30*, 422–436.

Sparrow, S. S., Cicchetti, D. V., & Balla, D. A. (1995). *Vineland Adaptive Behavior Scales, Second edition*. Circle Pines, MN: American Guidance Service.

Spring, B. (2007). Evidence-based practice in clinical psychology: What it is, why it matters; what you need to know. *Journal of Clinical Psychology, 63*, 611–631.

Stage, S. A., & Quiroz, D. R. (1997). Meta-analysis of interventions to decrease disruptive classroom behavior in public education settings. *School Psychology Review, 26*, 333–368.

Stanger, C., MacDonald, V., McConaughy, S., & Achenbach, T. (1996). Predictors of cross-informant syndromes among children and youths referred for mental health services. *Journal of Abnormal Child Psychology, 24*, 597–614.

Stark, K. D. (1990). *Childhood depression: School-based intervention*. New York: Guilford Press.

Stark, K. D., Hargrave, J., Hersh, B., Greenberg, M., Herron, J., & Fisher, M. (2008). Treatment of childhood depression: The ACTION treatment program. In J. R. A. Abela & B. L. Hankin (Eds.), *Handbook of depression in children and adolescents* (pp. 224–249). New York: Guilford Press.

Stark, K. D., Hargrave, J., Sander, J., Custer, G., Schnoebelen, S., Simpson, J., et al. (2006). Treatment of childhood depression: The ACTION treatment program. In P. C. Kendall (Ed.), *Child and adolescent therapy: Cognitive-behavioral procedures* (3rd ed., pp. 169–216). New York: Guilford Press.

Steege, M. W., & Watson, T. S. (2009). *Conducting school-based functional behavioral assessments: A practitioner's guide* (2nd ed.). New York: Guilford Press.

Stone, B. P., Kratochwill, T. R., Sladezcek, I., & Serlin, R. C. (2002). Treatment of selective mutism: A best-evidence synthesis. *School Psychology Quarterly, 17,* 168–190.

TADS Team. (2004). Fluoxetine, cognitive-behavioral therapy, and their combination for adolescents with depression: Treatment for Adolescents with Depression Study (TADS) randomized controlled trial. *Journal of the American Medical Association, 292,* 807–820.

TADS Team. (2007). The Treatment for Adolescents with Depression Study (TADS): Long-term effectiveness and safety outcomes. *Archives of General Psychiatry, 64,* 1132–1144.

Taylor, L. K., Alber, S. R., & Walker, D. W. (2002). The comparative effects of a modified self-questioning strategy and story mapping on the reading comprehension of elementary students with learning disabilities. *Journal of Behavioral Education, 11,* 69–87.

Tiano, J. D., & McNeil, C. B. (2005). The inclusion of fathers in behavioral parent training: A critical evaluation. *Child and Family Behavior Therapy, 27*(4), 1–28.

Tilly, W. D. (2002). Best practices in school psychology as a problem-solving enterprise. In A. Thomas & J. Grimes (Eds.), *Best practices in school psychology–IV* (pp. 21–36). Bethesda, MD: National Association of School Psychologists.

Toney, L.P., Kelley, M. L., & Lanclos, N. F. (2003). Self-parental monitoring of homework in adolescents: Comparative effects on parents' perceptions of homework behavior problems. *Child and Family Behavior Therapy, 25*(1), 35–51.

Troia, G. A., & Graham, S. (2003). Effective writing instruction across the grades: What every educational consultant should know. *Journal of Educational and Psychological Consultation, 14*(1), 75–89.

Trowell, J., Joffe, I., Campbell, J., Clemente, C., Almqvist, F., Soininen, M., et al. (2007). Childhood depression: A place for psychotherapy: An outcome study comparing individual psychodynamic psychotherapy and family therapy. *European Child and Adolescent Psychiatry, 16,* 157–167.

Turner, K. M. T., & Sanders, M. R. (2006). Help when it's needed first: A controlled evaluation of brief, preventative behavioral family intervention in a primary care setting. *Behavior Therapy, 37,* 131–142.

U.S. Department of Education, Office of Special Education and Rehabilitative Services, Office of Special Education Programs. (2009). *28th annual report to Congress on the implementation of the Individuals with Disabilities Education Act.* Washington, DC: Author. Retrieved June 28, 2007, from *www.ed.gov/about/reports/annual/osep/2006/parts-b-c/28th–vol–1.pdf.*

U.S. Department of Health and Human Services. (1999). *Mental health: A report of the surgeon general.* Rockville, MD: U.S. Department of Health and Human Services, Substance Abuse and Mental Health Services Administration, Center for Mental Health Services, National Institutes of Health, National Institute of Mental Health. Retrieved May 9, 2007, from *www.surgeongeneral.gov/library/mentalhealth/home.html#preface.*

U.S. Department of Health and Human Services. (2009). *Summary health statistics for U.S. children: National Health Interview Survey, 2007.* Hyattsville, MD: U.S. Department of Health and Human Services, Center for Disease Control and Prevention, National Center for Health Statistics. Retrieved April 26, 2009, from *www.cdc.gov/nchs/data/series/sr_10/sr10_239.pdf.*

Valleley, R. J., & Shriver, M. D. (2003). An examination of the effects of repeated readings with secondary students. *Journal of Behavioral Education, 12,* 55–76.

Van Houten, R., & Thompson, C. (1976). The effects of explicit timing on math performance. *Journal of Applied Behavior Analysis, 9,* 227–230.

Visser, J., van der Ende, J., Koot, H., & Verhulst, F. (1999). Continuity of psychopathology in youths referred to mental health services. *Journal of the American Academy of Child and Adolescent Psychiatry, 38,* 1560–1568.

Wagner, R. K., Torgesen, J. K., & Rashotte, C. A. (1999). *The comprehensive test of phonological processing*. Austin, TX: PRO-ED.

Walkup, J. T., Albano, A. M., Piacentini, J., Birmaher, B., Compton, S. N., Sherrill, J. T., et al. (2008). Cognitive behavioral therapy, sertraline, or a combination in childhood anxiety. *New England Journal of Medicine, 359*, 2753–2766.

Webster-Stratton, C. (1985). The effects of father involvement in parent training for conduct problem children. *Journal of Child Psychology and Psychiatry, 26*, 801–810.

Webster-Stratton, C. (1998). Preventing conduct problems in Head Start children: Strengthening parenting competencies. *Journal of Consulting and Clinical Psychology, 66*, 715–730.

Webster-Stratton, C., & Hammond, M. (1997). Treating children with early-onset conduct problems: A comparison of child and parent training interventions. *Journal of Consulting and Clinical Psychology, 65*, 93–109.

Webster-Stratton, C., & Reid, M. J. (2003a). The Incredible Years parents, teachers, and children training series: A multifaceted treatment approach for young children with conduct problems. In A. E. Kazdin & J. R. Weisz (Eds.), *Evidence-based psychotherapies for children and adolescents* (pp. 224–240). New York: Guilford Press.

Webster-Stratton, C., & Reid, M. J. (2003b). Treating conduct problems and strengthening social and emotional competence in young children: The Dina Dinosaur treatment program. *Journal of Emotional and Behavioral Disorders, 11*, 130–143.

Webster-Stratton, C., Reid, M. J., & Hammond, M. (2004). Treating children with early-onset conduct problems: Intervention outcomes for parent, child, and teacher training. *Journal of Child Clinical and Adolescent Psychology, 33*, 105–124.

Wechsler, D. (2001). *Wechsler Individual Achievement Test—Second edition*. San Antonio, TX: Psychological Corporation.

Weinberger, J. (1996). A longitudinal study of children's early literacy experiences at home and later literacy development at home and school. *Journal of Research in Reading, 19*, 14–24.

Weisz, J. R., Hawley, K. M., & Doss, A. J. (2004). Empirically tested psychotherapies for youth internalizing and externalizing problems and disorders. *Child and Adolescent Psychiatric Clinics of North America, 13*, 729–815.

Wells, K. C., & Albano, A. M. (2005). Parent involvement in CBT treatment of adolescent depression: Experiences in the Treatment for Adolescents with Depression Study (TADS). *Cognitive and Behavioral Practice, 12*, 209–220.

Witt, J. C., Daly, E. M., & Noell, G. (2000). *Functional assessments: A step-by-step guide to solving academic and behavioral problems*. Longmont, CO: Sopris-West.

Woodcock, R. W., McGrew, K. S., & Mather, N. (2001). *Woodcock–Johnson III–Tests of Achievement*. Itasca, IL: Riverside.

Index

"*f*" following a page number indicates a figure; "*t*" following a page number indicates a table.